What Do We Know About Early Childhood Education?

Research
Based
Practice

Join us on the Web at

EarlyChildEd.delmar.com

What Do We Know About Early Childhood Education?

Research Based Practice

Sandra Crosser, Ph.D.

THOMSON

DELMAR LEARNING   Australia   Canada   Mexico   Singapore   Spain   United Kingdom   United States

THOMSON

DELMAR LEARNING

What Do We Know About Early Childhood Education?
Research Based Practice
Sandra Crosser

Vice President, Career Education SBU:
Dawn Gerrain

Director of Editorial:
Sherry Gomoll

Acquisitions Editor:
Erin O'Connor

Editorial Assistant:
Ivy Ip

Director of Production:
Wendy A. Troeger

Production Editor:
Joy Kocsis

Director of Marketing:
Wendy E. Mapstone

Channel Manager:
Donna J. Lewis

Cover Design:
Andrew Wright

Composition:
Larry O'Brien

Any additional questions about permissions can be submitted by email to thomsonrights@thomson.com

Library of Congress Cataloging-in-Publication Data

Crosser, Sandra.
  What do we know about early childhood education? : research based practice / Sandra Crosser.
    p. cm.
  Includes bibliographical references and index.
  ISBN 1-4018-5061-8
  1. Early childhood education--United States. 2. Early childhood education--Research--United States. 3. Action research in education--United States. I. Title.
  LB1139.225.C76 2005
  372.21--dc22

                        2004008352

NOTICE TO THE READER

Contents

PART II   What Does Research Tell Us about The Issues?

PART III   Connecting Research to Practice

Preface

Feeling a bit tired and sluggish, Alison made an appointment with the new doctor in town who quickly diagnosed her condition as a humor imbalance. It seems one of Alison's bodily juices was out of proportion, affecting her temperament. Not to worry. She would be feeling fine in no time. Taking a jar from the shelf, the doctor extracted two squirming leeches. Two would be sufficient to suck the bad humors from her blood. "Let's put them on your neck right here," he suggested.

The public expects doctors to conform to professional standards of practice that are based in solid medical research. Medieval superstition, hunches, and treatments will not do. Teachers, too, must know and apply best practice in their profession.

The No Child Left Behind Act made it clear that the federal government expects no less from teachers. The catch phrase "scientifically based research" was referenced 110 times in the body of the law. It is clear that Congress intended for scientifically based research to undergird educational practice if federal dollars are to be forthcoming.

Therefore, teachers certainly need to know the current research supporting best practice and gain experience thinking about how research findings can be translated into practice. However, because the knowledge base is constantly changing and growing, teachers also need to know how to access and evaluate research reports now and in the future.

What Do We Know About Early Childhood Education? Research Based Practice was written to

- introduce students to early childhood research resources.

- explore general guidelines for evaluating and interpreting research reports.

- present summarized findings of research concerning vital issues in early childhood education.

- challenge students to apply research findings to educational practice.

This text is appropriate for students preparing to teach children ages 3 through 8 in public school and other early childhood settings. It is also an excellent resource for exploration of early childhood issues at the graduate level. It may be used as a stand-alone text or as a supplement to add depth and practical applications of research to the introductory or survey course.

CONCEPTUAL APPROACH

Given government mandates, increased standards, and new accreditation requirements, teacher preparation programs need to reevaluate textbooks. New textbooks need to focus on what teachers need to know in order to base day-to-day practice on a strong knowledge base.

Although many questions about what is best for young children remain unanswered, we do have a significant knowledge base on which to build. That knowledge base needs to be made clear, concise, and accessible to undergraduate students preparing to be teachers and to practicing teachers engaged in professional development activities.

TEXT ORGANIZATION

What Do We Know About Early Childhood Education? Research Based Practice is written in three parts. In Part I the focus is on reading and interpreting research as a necessary background for the major section of the text. The case is made for the importance of a research base including professional and real political considerations one must keep in mind as a wise consumer of research.

Readers are provided with a wealth of resources to assist them in locating information and finding reliable answers to educational questions. Part I includes an entry-level introduction to government resources, educational organizations, professional journals, and Internet resources.

The author and Thomson Delmar Learning make every effort to ensure that all Internet resources are accurate at the time of printing. However, due to the fluid, time-sensitive nature of the Internet, we cannot guarantee that all URLs and Web site addresses will remain current for the duration of this edition.

Part II presents important early childhood issues and summarizes related background research. Readers are led to explore questions they will be expected to address professionally with parents, other education personnel, and the general public. The text addresses issues such as full-day versus part-day kindergarten; looping; academic redshirting; grade retention; school and class size; time-out; curriculum delivery models; assessment; readiness; kindergarten screening; and more.

Part III builds on earlier sections by inviting and intriguing students to apply their knowledge of research from Part I and their knowledge of the issues presented in Part II. Real-life scenarios, or vignettes, are written to draw out concepts from Part I and Part II. Scenarios are particularly suited to small group discussion and critical analysis. Each scenario is followed by questions to stimulate synthesis and evaluation. The scenarios presented in chapter 14 are geared for working and thinking with others. Activities provided in chapter 15 are excellent projects for individual work. Some of the activities can be completed quickly; others are longer-term projects. Suggested activities are varied, purposeful, and divergent; stimulate reflection; and can be great fun. Effort has been made to challenge, intrigue, and foster professional growth.

FEATURES

Several pedagogical features have been applied to the text in an effort to assist the student with comprehension.

SQ3R

The format of the textbook is a conversation. It is based on the SQ3R study method developed by Francis Robinson. Each letter stands for a step in the study strategy. Most people find that following the SQ3R study method is efficient and effective. Study time is reduced and comprehension is increased. These are the steps:

Step 1: Survey

Survey the chapter. Go to the end of the chapter and read the chapter summary. This gets you thinking about the topic and focuses on the main ideas. Then go through the chapter skimming headings. Look over any graphic aids and pictures. This familiarizes you with the content.

Step 2: Question

The second step is to raise questions about the content you are going to read. As you look through the text, notice that the chapter titles are in the form of questions. As you leaf through the book, notice italicized questions interspersed within the text. The conversational format is designed to help the reader raise questions, which assists with comprehension.

Step 3: Read

Next, read through the chapter. As you read, look for answers to the questions. When you locate an answer, underline it or make a note.

Step 4: Recite

Now talk to yourself. Ask yourself questions. Can you remember? If not, look at the text again.

Step 5: Review

The final R in SQ3R stands for review. Make certain that you understand the answers to the questions. Reread the summary at the end of the chapter, or meet up with a classmate to quiz one another on the content.

Chapter Summary

Each chapter ends with a short summary of the main ideas. It is useful to read a summary both prior to and after reading the chapter. The summary provides a quick overview, quick review, and check on understanding.

Using What You Know

Each chapter concludes with several suggestions for applying the information from the chapter to real life. These are extension activities designed to provide deeper understanding of the chapter concepts. Many of the activities involve professional observation or interviews, which would be well suited to a field experience course component.

Online Companion™

An Online Companion™ is available to accompany *What Do We Know About Early Childhood Education? Research Based Practice*. The Online Companion™ was designed to assist the reader explore research in early childhood education. For example, related links can be accessed to learn more about specific studies described in the reading. Critical thinking activities offer suggestions to spur analysis and reflection, challenging the reader to apply what is known to new situations. The Online Companion™ also contains related PowerPoint presentations, transparencies, and case studies to ponder and discuss. The Take Action section gives suggested activities for the reader who chooses to express professionalism by becoming more involved in the emerging early childhood knowledge base.

The Online Companion™ icon appears at the end of each chapter to prompt you to go on-line and take advantage of the many features provided. Please take a moment to check out the resources available at the Online Companion™ at http://www.earlychildhood.delmar.com.

ACKNOWLEDGMENTS

The author would like to thank the following reviewers, enlisted by Thomson Delmar Learning, for their helpful suggestions and constructive criticism:

Jennifer Aldrich, EdD
Central Missouri State University
Warrensburg, MO

Linda Aulgur, PhD
Westminster College
Fulton, MO

Nancy Baptiste, EdD
New Mexico State University
Las Cruces, NM

Jennifer Berke, PhD
Mercyhurst College—North East
North East, PA

Karen Danbom, PhD
Minnesota State University—Moorhead
Moorhead, MN

Pamela Davis, PhD
Henderson State University
Arkadelphia, AR

Sandra Wanner, PhD
University of Mary Hardin-Baylor
Belton, TX

Part One

Using Educational Research

Part I of this text is a toolbox. The tools it contains allow the reader to construct a solid understanding of the research base surrounding important issues in early childhood education as presented in Part II. Chapter 1 argues the case for basing day-to-day educational decisions on what we know from scientific research about teaching and learning. The reader is then challenged to consider the real-life practical and political constraints that sometimes interfere with implementing what we know about best practices.

In Chapter 2 the reader learns how to use the tools necessary for making sense of sometimes complicated and technical research reports. Tips are provided for detecting bias and for analyzing strengths and weaknesses of common research designs. Chapter 3 invites the reader to use an array of practical resources that have proven to be useful tools for locating particular types of educational research. Tools in hand, the reader is ready to encounter specific studies and evaluate reported findings described in Part II.

Chapter 1
Using Research to Inform Practice

Principal Walters sat down, face red and heart racing. His impassioned plea, he knew, would not make a difference in the end. The school board had heard his words but would most likely listen with its pocketbook. The school district was moderately well-off and was able to meet the needs of the daily operations, but salaries and benefits sliced off a hefty 85 percent of the annual funds. What was left had to stretch. But Principal Walters was not asking for money. He wanted permission.

Fueled by a desire to do what is best for children, Mr. Walters and his teaching staff came to the conclusion that the children in their K–2 neighborhood school would benefit academically if they were offered a full day of kindergarten, rather than the current half-day program. Together they had envisioned a way to creatively redeploy the current teaching staff so that they could provide full-day kindergarten for all children without hiring additional personnel. They took the proposal to the superintendent.

Reluctant to approve the plan, the superintendent explained that the district could not provide services unevenly. With four K–2 buildings in the district, it would be politically necessary to offer full-day kindergarten to all of the children or none of the children. Mr. Walters was, however, given time to plead his case at the next school board meeting.

"Mr. Walters, how do you know that a full-day kindergarten will be educationally better for the children?" asked the president of the school board.

Mr. Walters was stumped. Doesn't everyone realize that more is better? "It just takes common sense to know that a teacher can accomplish more with children in twice the time. In my opinion children would be better prepared for first grade if they spent more time in readiness activities during kindergarten."

(continued)

"Principal Walters, before we consider spending scarce funds on additional teachers and classroom space, we need to know what results to expect. What is your proof? Not your opinion, sir, but proof. This board is accountable!"

How do we know what results to expect? The principal is a professional. Shouldn't his opinion be valuable?

research base—body of professional knowledge supported by rigorous research evidence and the basis for making educational decisions

THE IMPORTANCE OF A RESEARCH BASE

In the past, Mr. Walters' professional opinion might have been enough for the school board. In the twenty-first century, the board wants the facts. Because elected officials must account to the public for increased spending on education programs, policy makers have rediscovered the importance of a sound **research base** to use in making decisions.

What is the research evidence that informs decision-making? If education is a profession, then there must be a professional knowledge base to inform. There must be a body of knowledge supported in research that indicates what is best practice. Decisions in classrooms and board rooms need to be based on that body of knowledge rather than on simple opinion, gut feelings, and common sense.

Do we have a sufficient body of educational research?

Professional Considerations

Though the professional knowledge base is far from complete, there does exist a substantial body of evidence that can be used to enlighten decision-making. Part of being a professional is being familiar with the evidence surrounding best practices and knowing the implications of the knowledge base for making decisions that affect the lives of children and their families. In that way teachers and other education professionals can evaluate the new information and make informed judgments.

Another part of that professional responsibility is knowing how to locate and evaluate current reports of educational research. Becoming a knowledgeable consumer of educational research is a vital part of becoming a teacher.

Just as a physician must know the most appropriate medical treatment for an individual medical condition, so the teacher must know the most appropriate educational course of action for an individual educational condition. Professional ethics requires that practitioners remain current in the field of study, relying on a strong and rigorous research base to inform practice.

The education profession has gained a dubious reputation for jumping on bandwagons rather than basing decisions on a reliable knowledge base. As a profession, we need to avoid the bandwagon mentality while we exercise caution and become more deliberate in determining where we are going and how we plan to get there.

This book is designed to help you, a future professional, to

■ become an informed consumer of research.

■ locate reliable sources for educational research.

■ be aware of current research findings concerning common issues in early childhood education.

■ apply research to classroom practice.

Part I of this book focuses on evaluating and locating educational research. Part II looks at current research about hot issues in early childhood education. Part III contains case studies and suggestions for individual projects and investigations that allow you to apply research to classroom practice in a practical way.

Political Considerations

Thinking back to this chapter's opening vignette, Principal Walters needed to be aware of the research implications for his bid to increase the length of the school day for his kindergartners. However, knowing the relevant research was not the only barrier he faced. Principal Walters encountered two political obstacles, as well.

First, while the principal was looking at the issue as it affected his own pupils and teachers, the superintendent was forced to look at the bigger picture. The superintendent recognized that he would have difficulty defending any decision that would provide educational resources to some but not all of the families in the district. In most instances, the superintendent is employed by the school board, which is either an elected or appointed body. Politically, the superintendent needs to keep both the public and the board members happy. In that reality, some decisions about educational issues may be made based on political considerations rather than solely on the merits of best practices.

The second political obstacle faced by Principal Walters was the board president's concern with **accountability**. Accountability became a buzzword during the 1990s and continues to echo loudly into the current century. Simply put, tax dollars cannot be continuously poured into the schools without some evidence that the dollars make an educational difference. There must be a return. The national love affair between policy makers and achievement tests came about as a result of the accountability movement. Due to the belief that results of dollars spent can be measured by proficiency and other achievement tests, we now spend millions of education dollars on testing.

Because Principal Walters did not know the research evidence well enough to address the issue of accountability and because the superintendent anticipated public displeasure with unequal opportunities, Principal Walters lost his case for full-day kindergarten. But the accountability movement has political implications at all levels, not just in the local arena.

> **But what happened to Principal Walters?**

accountability—assurance that resources spent on programs result in comparable learning outcomes

> **How does it happen that politicians are making decisions about the schools? Shouldn't education professionals be making those decisions?**

In order to understand how politics is related to public education, it might be helpful to take a side trip and look briefly at the organization of schools in American society. Then we can also see how the politics of education may influence educational research.

THE ORGANIZATION OF AMERICAN PUBLIC EDUCATION

As the founding fathers were deliberating on the best way to organize their experiment in democracy, they outlined in the Constitution the specific areas of authority and responsibility that were federal, or national-level government concerns. Education is not mentioned in the Constitution.

> **That was quite an oversight. A system of education must not have been important at the time.**

The framers of the Constitution recognized that when a government has control over education, it has the ultimate control—the potential to control

Organization of Public Education in the United States

U.S. Constitution

10th Amendment

Governor → State Legislature

State Board of Education

State Superintendent of Instruction

Local School Board

Local Superintendent of Schools

Principal   Principal   Principal   Principal

Teachers   Teachers   Teachers   Teachers

Citizens

Authority over education lies in the hands of the people.

minds. In the fledgling democracy, education was considered so important that any system of public education needed to be in the hands of the people. The Tenth Amendment to the U.S. Constitution specifies that any power not specifically given to the federal government or forbidden to the states automatically becomes a right reserved for the state level, a level much closer to the people. One of the residual, or reserved, rights was the right to establish a system of public education. Each state has the option to provide a system of public education. Therefore, the authority and responsibility for education resides at the state level.

It has been common practice for the states to delegate some of the authority for running the schools to the local school district level. The district school board is purposefully composed of ordinary citizens rather than education professionals. True to democratic principles, the people in the local community then become the watchdogs over education. But the state still retains the ultimate responsibility for the system of public education. Local school boards must operate within the rules and regulations of both the state department of education and the state school board. Local schools must also comply with the school-related laws enacted by the state legislature. The state superintendent and school board are responsible to the state legislature and/or governor.

> **Then what is the role of the local school board?**

Because governors and legislators are politicians, education has become a political enterprise. Various groups and organizations lobby for their special interests in hopes of swaying politicians. Party platforms include positions on education-related issues that are regularly debated. The political party in power can have a great effect on what happens educationally within each state. Typically about half of local school district funds come from the state level, and those funds are dependent on compliance with all state-level school laws and rules. So we find that major decisions about schools tend to come from politicians through political processes.

The federal government has an interest in influencing schooling but has little power to make anything happen. The only real power the federal government has in education is the power of the bribe. That is, the federal government has the capacity to <u>sway educational practice by offering dollars for programs.</u> Historically the federal government has used this carrot approach for social, economic, and defense purposes. Dollars have been offered for states to implement poverty intervention programs, foreign language instruction, drug education, and a host of other special interest programs to promote one political agenda or another. Just as the donkey is motivated by the carrot dangling just out of reach, so too the schools are motivated by promises of dollars for programs.

> **If education is constitutionally a responsibility of the states, how did the federal government become involved?**

Because school districts typically spend most of their operating funds on salaries and benefits, little discretionary money is left after paying the bills. Therefore, though federal funds represent only a small percentage of total income, those dollars become important dollars to the schools. Because schools are willing to comply with most requests in order to secure more money, the federal government has the capacity to sway practices.

Nationally, politicians have influenced practices by calling for schools to be accountable for the educational outcomes of dollars spent. Questions

The carrot approach

of accountability abound wherever dollars for educational purposes are dispensed. School district and individual school report cards supposedly provide evidence that education dollars are purchasing intended outcomes. In turn, districts and states stand on their heads and perform any number of contortions to satisfy federal accountability requirements.

Another way that politicians have influence over educational practices is through special issues advocacy. If a president has an interest in promoting a particular education program or policy, several channels are available because of the prominence of the presidency. A president can speak throughout the country about the issue. A president can appoint a like-minded secretary of the Department of Education and give instructions to promote certain issues. A president can influence legislation, party platforms, and federal budget proposals to advance favorite initiatives. On a smaller scale, governors have the same kinds of influence at the state level.

NATIONAL POLITICS AND RESEARCH

Political power can be used, as well, to influence the national research agenda. If a president is fond of a particular initiative, people in appointed positions can be expected to support that agenda. If, for example, school vouchers are in favor, look for research on school vouchers to be supported and publicized.

The No Child Left Behind Act provides a prime example of how a president can influence educational research. The act came about as part of the traditional reauthorization of the Elementary and Secondary Education Act, which restarts the cash flow to schools from the federal government after the previous reauthorization has expired. The act was set for renewal in 2002, which gave President George W. Bush the opportunity to advocate for a pet initiative.

Bush included several initiatives in the act, but one is particularly related to the topic of educational research. The act requires that school practices be grounded in **scientifically based research (SBR)**.

The term "scientifically based research" was used over 100 times in the final draft of that law. As a result, school districts must provide states with evidence that what they are doing is based in scientific research. In turn, the states must now offer proof to reassure the federal government that practices within the state are backed by SBR or funds will not be forthcoming.

Political influence on the national research agenda may come from other sources, as well. Debra Viadero (2002) reported in Education Week on the influence of advocacy-based think-tank studies. Citing potential bias and hidden agendas, some critics have accused conservative groups of using the media to publicize reports that have not been subject to review by experts. According to critics, those biased studies are then dramatized in the popular press and used as research evidence to lobby for certain projects or policy initiatives.

Whether or not such accusations are true, it would seem the course of wisdom for the professional educator to be watchful, to question, to be informed. As an advocate for children, one must put into practice only the best educational initiatives. That requires significant personal effort to maintain professional currency and insight into the interplay between schooling and politics.

scientifically based research— generally interpreted as results of rigorous research that has been statistically analyzed

SUMMARY

It has become both professionally and politically important for educators to apply evidence from sound educational research when making decisions about teaching and learning. Being a professional requires knowledge of best practice in the field of expertise. Therefore, the professional educator has a responsibility to know how to locate, evaluate, and apply evidence from the education knowledge base.

Because of the particular organizational structure of the American system of schooling, politics has the potential to impact the research focus and agenda of public education. It is vital, then, for educators to assume responsibility to remain professionally current, think critically, and be aware of political implications for educational practice. This professional awareness enables an individual to become a better informed decision maker and more effective advocate for children.

Key Terms

accountability
research base
scientifically based research

Using What You Know

1. Follow a newspaper's education coverage for a week. Do you detect any political influence or bias in the articles you read?

2. Go to your state department of education Web site. Is there any indication that your state is promoting scientifically based research?

3. Attend a school board meeting. What observations can you relate to the concepts discussed in this chapter?

For additional information on research-based practice, visit our Web site at http://www.earlychilded.delmar.com.

Chapter 2
Being a Wise Consumer of Research

The implication of the research was shocking: Children born in the summer should wait an additional year before attending kindergarten because the extra year would make them less likely to commit suicide (Uphoff & Gilmore, 1984; Uphoff & Gilmore, 1986). Maternal instincts and adrenaline rising, I found myself mumbling about my own two summer-born children as I flipped through the pages to find out more about this potential death threat to my babies.

"You can bet your booties my children aren't going to kindergarten when they turn five," I vowed.

As it turned out, the researchers did study summer-born individuals who had attempted suicide. However, there were very few subjects (suicides age 25 and younger during a 1½ year period from one county in one state). I had been misled by the summarized report of rather poor research.

READING AND INTERPRETING RESEARCH

How can I avoid being misled by research reports?

There is a difference between being a consumer of research and being a wise consumer of research. When reading research reports, it is important to ask two key questions. First, are there any potential sources of bias that could have been at work? Second, was the research designed and conducted rigorously?

Bias in Research

How can I detect bias?

Look at who conducted the research. Is the researcher affiliated with any interest group? Who would stand to gain from the results of the study? For example, would you expect a teachers' union to be in favor of school voucher programs, merit pay, or reducing class size? Which of those issues would a union publicize positively? What does the union stand to gain or lose?

Look at the publication itself. Is the publisher unbiased? Would an organization be likely to publish reports of research that run counter to its mission? If the report is a government publication, does it reflect pet projects of the political party in power? If a group or task force is reporting, find out how members were appointed and why the supporting agencies exist. Does the group have an ax to grind or a cause to promote?

Is the research self-published? Authors can pay to have their work published and distributed in a book format, eliminating critical review by editors and expert reviewers. Though the reported research could be a valuable addition to the knowledge base, it could also represent an inferior product, perhaps rejected by mainline publishers. It is often difficult to distinguish a self-published book. Look for a recognizable publishing house.

Is the publisher a newspaper or popular magazine? If so, be aware that results are probably condensed and may be pitched to increase readership. Findings may be exaggerated or distorted in headlines.

If the study is reported in a refereed professional journal, that is one possible indication of quality. A refereed publication does not print a manuscript until it has met the approval of an editor and several expert reviewers. However, most professional journals are aimed at a limited readership and are not as accessible as popular press newspapers and magazines. Most professional journals are not typically available at small public libraries, but large public libraries and university libraries usually do provide access. It is worth the effort to locate the original research report in order to examine the details of how the study was conducted and how conclusions were drawn.

Research Methods

I would rather eat nails! Those research studies are confusing. How can I understand what they mean?

There are some common methods used to study children and schools. It is helpful to become familiar with those methods in order to make sense of the reports and be a critical consumer of research. Entire courses and texts have been written on the subject of educational research, but for our purposes, we review some of the most common designs and highlight major strengths and weaknesses.

Systematic Observation

systematic observation—organized plan for observing subjects and recording observations in an orderly manner

Systematic observation allows the researcher to watch children and record their behavior. For example, if we were interested in children's fears and coping strategies, we might carefully observe children when they are frightened. We could record what they feared and how they responded. If we observed children during their natural, daily activities, we would be engaged in **naturalistic observation**. We could hire observers to shadow children and record fear-inducing events.

naturalistic observation—observations occur as subjects go about their activities in a real-world setting

If the event is not likely to occur naturally, the researcher might set up or structure a situation in which the event is likely to occur. In that case, the researcher would be using **structured observation** rather than naturalistic observation.

The child may not encounter anything he fears while the observer is watching. The process could take forever.

That method would give some interesting information, but there are ethical guidelines that researchers must follow. It certainly would not be ethical to purposefully frighten children. Researchers sometimes need to be creative in designing alternatives to structured observation. When structured observation is applied to situations that can do no harm to children, the method can be very useful.

So the researcher could frighten children and record what they did?

structured observation—occurs in a laboratory setting or other pre-arranged environment

Naturalistic observation occurs as children go about their daily activities.

Ainsworth (1978) used structured observation in her classic study of children's attachment. On a prearranged schedule, mothers brought their infants to a playroom filled with interesting toys. Mothers left and then returned to the room time and again. Observers recorded the responses of the child each time the parent left and returned. Known as the Strange Situation, Ainsworth's work provided important insights into the concept of attachment.

Is it possible that the observers could interpret what they see in different ways?

Yes, for example, a crying child's emotion could be interpreted in different ways by different observers. That is why it is important for the observers to be trained. Rigorous studies provide for such training and give evidence of **inter-rater reliability**. After training, observers should be very close in their decisions about recording behavior.

Observers may influence research in other ways, as well. The very presence of an observer has the potential to change a subject's behavior. Observers can also bias the results of a study by recording what they might like to see rather than what they do see. It could be difficult for a researcher to be totally objective. For that reason it is important for observers to be outsiders, unaware of the purpose of the study.

inter-rater reliability—observers are trained in recording observations to eliminate differences in interpretation

Self-Reports

self-report—research design using subjects who tell about themselves

Interviews, surveys, and questionnaires are all **self-report** measures. Subjects describe their actions, beliefs, values, thoughts, feelings, experiences, perceptions, or abilities. Because ethical considerations sometimes do not allow experimental research, self-reports have been used by researchers who study topics such as drug and alcohol use, sexual behavior, or fears. When studying fears, some researchers have asked children to name their fears. Other researchers asked parents to name their children's fears. Still others asked children to indicate on a fear thermometer what level of fear they felt as the researcher named possible fear inducers such as storms or monsters.

How does the researcher know whether people are telling the truth?

One must certainly use caution in interpreting the results of self-reports. It is possible that subjects' memories could be inaccurate. It is also possible that subjects might deny or exaggerate in order to create a false impression or to avoid embarrassment. For example, when four-year-old Taylor was asked about his fears, he put his hands on his hips, stuck out his chest, and boasted, "I'm not afraid of nothin'." In the same way an adolescent might underreport behavior to avoid punishment or overreport behavior to look good in the eyes of peers.

Are there ways to make it more likely that people will be truthful?

Researchers sometimes reassure subjects that their responses will remain anonymous in hopes of securing accurate responses. Assigning numbers rather than names to surveys and questionnaires is one method of maintaining anonymity. Another method is to have the subject respond to the questions on a private computer. Although self-reports are convenient and are focused on the topic of interest, they must be interpreted with caution.

Be cautious when interpreting self-reports.

Case Studies

Genie was isolated in a small room where she was often harnessed for hours to a potty chair (Rymer, 1994). Although basic needs of food, clothing, and shelter were met, Genie was denied human interaction, including language. Discovered when she was 13 years old, Genie provided a perfect subject for a **case study**.

Was it possible for a child like Genie to learn language? Whereas it would be unethical to isolate a child as an experiment, Genie's condition provided an opportunity to explore an important question.

A case study gathers information and describes events related to a single individual, program, school, or other entity. This in-depth study often provides information that could not be ethically gathered through experimental research. Although the case study format has the potential to provide insights, findings should not be generalized to other individuals or groups.

case study—research design to study in depth an experience or individual circumstance

Correlational Research

Correlational research is used to study the relationship between variables. The relationship may be positive: As one variable increases, so does the other. Or the relationship may be negative: As one variable increases, the other decreases.

correlational research—research design that investigates the patterns of how variables move

In research reports, correlations are generally expressed as a co-efficient, abbreviated r. The magnitude of a correlation ranges from r of -1 to $+1$. A zero correlation indicates that the variables are not related. A correlation of $+1$ indicates a positive correlation and a correlation of -1 indicates a negative correlation. The closer to 1, the stronger the correlation. By plotting how frequently variables occur, the researcher can statistically describe the relationship between variables.

If we know how two variables are related, couldn't we use that information to make predictions about what will happen?

Yes, if a strong correlation exists, we see a pattern emerge. Movement in the frequency of one variable allows us to predict an accompanying change in the second variable. For example, there is a positive correlation between height and intelligence.

Does that mean increased height causes increased intelligence?

There is a positive correlation between the number of drownings and air-conditioner sales. Does that mean that we could decrease drownings if we stopped selling air conditioners? It is quite possible that a third factor is the impetus for the correlation. For example, better nutrition and health care could account for both increased height and intelligence.

And the season of the year could account for increases in both drownings and air-conditioner sales?

Exactly. A correlation is simply a description of how variables move in relation to one another. A correlation does not indicate a cause or effect relationship between those variables. Nevertheless, it is a common error to assume that correlational relationships indicate causation. In evaluating educational research, one should not assume cause or effect when interpreting the results of correlational studies.

Can research be designed to uncover cause-and-effect relationships?

Experimental Research

Experimental research is appropriate when investigating causes and effects. In experimental research, the variables are manipulated. A treatment occurs. The researcher compares the results of the treatment to results without the treatment. Therefore, an **experimental group** receives the treatment, and the **control group** does not receive the treatment. Results of the groups are compared so that any differences attributable to the experimental treatment can be measured.

The factor that is manipulated, or changed, is called the **independent variable**. It can be changed independently. The variable that is not changed is called the **dependent variable**.

For example, a researcher might investigate the effects of preschool attendance on reading achievement in second grade. The experimental group would attend preschool, but the control group would not. Scores on achievement tests would be compared for experimental and control groups. In this case, the independent variable is preschool attendance, and the dependent variable is reading achievement. Statistical analysis of scores for each group gives an indication of the likelihood that there are real differences in group achievement.

experimental research—research design in which variables are manipulated and comparisons are made between groups

experimental group—the group receiving a treatment in experimental research

control group—in experimental research, the group receiving no treatment

independent variable—in experimental research, the variable that is manipulated

dependent variable—in experimental research, the variable that is not manipulated

Interpreting Correlations

There is a positive correlation between bathing suit sales and number of drownings. As one increases, so does the other.

A correlation may mean

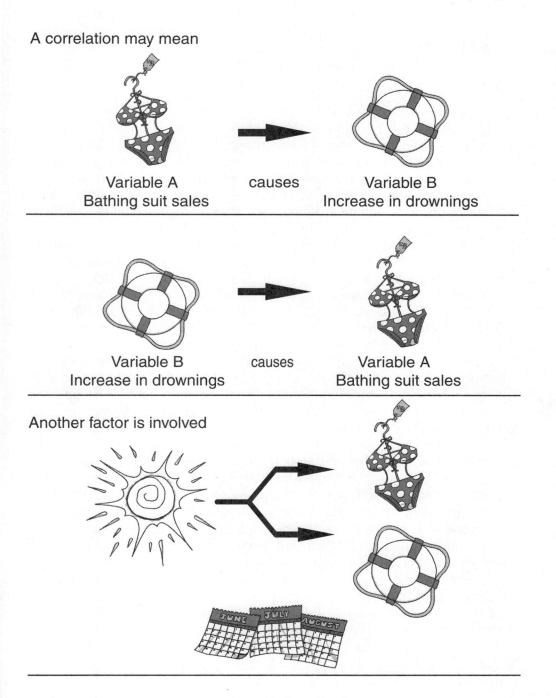

Variable A	causes	Variable B
Bathing suit sales		Increase in drownings

Variable B	causes	Variable A
Increase in drownings		Bathing suit sales

Another factor is involved

Correlations may not represent cause-and-effect relationships.

random selection—subjects for studies are selected in a random manner such that all potential subjects have the same opportunity to be selected

Experimental research involves effects of variables on subjects. In rigorous studies, the subjects are randomly selected. **Random selection** means that each individual has the same chance of being included in the group. Selection might be made by drawing names from a hat, by lottery, or using a list of random numbers. Whatever the method, it is important to include a representative sample in the list of potential subjects. If the subjects are only five-year-olds, or only male, or only from California, or only from the telephone book, then results of the experiment can only be generalized to the same population.

Designs

longitudinal design—the same subjects are followed over a period of time

cross-sectional design—subjects are assessed at only one point in time

In designing both correlational and experimental studies, the researcher determines whether it would be better to use a longitudinal or a cross-sectional design. In a **longitudinal design**, one group of subjects is followed over time and is assessed at numerous points. Time may be a matter of months or years. In a **cross-sectional design**, subject groups of different ages are assessed at the same time. A cross-sectional study is like a group snapshot at one point in time, whereas a longitudinal study is more like a chronological collection of pictures in a photo album.

Longitudinal studies help researchers look at single individuals over an extended time. Terman did just that when he followed a group of intellectually gifted individuals over their lifetimes (Terman & Oden, 1959). The study began in 1921 with 1,428 12-year-olds with IQ scores over 140. The study will continue until 2020 in order to cover the entire life spans of the subjects. Subjects have been evaluated on criteria such as professional success, marital status, health, and socioeconomic status at various points in their lives. From Terman's study, researchers have been able to identify typical characteristics of gifted people. The longitudinal design allows researchers to look at individual characteristics on a developmental continuum and provides the opportunity for the researcher to identify common patterns that might emerge.

A longitudinal study could also look at the effects of an intervention such as Head Start. The researcher would be looking for short-term and long-term effects on children who had experienced the treatment. For example, a study could look at achievement scores for graduates of Head Start compared to a similar group of children who qualified but did not attend Head Start. Are there achievement differences when subjects are in first grade, second grade, and third grade? Are there differences in these individuals when they become adolescents or adults?

The U.S. Department of Education has been conducting a major longitudinal study of 22,000 children who entered kindergarten in the 1998–1999 school year (NCES, 2002). The same group of children was tracked and assessed at six various points between kindergarten and fifth grade. The longitudinal design allows researchers to look at long-term effects of variables and determine whether or not patterns between earlier and later events emerge.

Wouldn't most researchers hesitate to commit themselves to long studies like these?

There are some drawbacks to the longitudinal design, and researcher time is a major consideration. In fact, Terman died before his study was completed, but others have continued his work.

Another drawback to the longitudinal design is the cost of continuing a study over a number of years. In addition, it may take years for data to be collected and become available for analysis. Subjects may move away or drop out of the study, leaving a group of subjects that may differ from the normal population in important ways.

The influence of history and the events occurring to the lives of the subject group may influence the findings as well, making results applicable to only a particular place or time or cohort group. For example, people who grew up during the economic depression of the 1930s may have particular personality traits as a result of being raised in those difficult times. They may be careful about spending habits, value savings, be suspicious of banking institutions, save leftovers, or keep a stash of cash at home where it is always accessible. Those traits might not be generalizable to other groups who were influenced by different times. This shortcoming of the longitudinal design is known as the **cross-generational problem**.

Because subjects in longitudinal studies are assessed repeatedly, they may become familiar with the questions or tasks. If subjects become test-wise, these practice effects may influence the results of the study. So, although longitudinal studies have great potential to expand our understanding, caution needs to be used when interpreting any results.

cross-generational problem—subjects who grew up during different periods of history may be different from one another in ways that might influence study results

Compared to the longitudinal design, the cross-sectional design is a more convenient way to investigate changes over time. Rather than follow the same subjects over an extended time, the cross-sectional design examines groups of subjects of different ages at the same point in time. For example, a researcher could assess the achievement of children who had attended Head Start by testing a group of first-graders, a group of second-graders, and a group of third-graders all at one time. A great deal of data can be collected over a short time. Although cross-sectional studies do not yield information about individuals, these studies can provide insight into what is typical of an age group. However, if there is a wide span of ages, one must be aware of a possible cross-generational problem—that the cohort groups might be different due to unique experiences during the period of time in which they lived.

The **sequential design** combines the best aspects of the cross-sectional and longitudinal designs. Separate cohort groups are identified as in cross-sectional research, but those groups are assessed repeatedly over time, rather than just once. For example, one might identify three separate age groups and assess them annually over a period of several years. The sequential design is less expensive and takes less time than the typical longitudinal study, and is regarded as a relatively strong design because it allows for both longitudinal and cross-sectional comparisons over a short period of time.

> Are there alternatives to the longitudinal design?

sequential design—combines aspects of longitudinal and cross-sectional designs by studying separate groups over time

EVALUATING EDUCATIONAL RESEARCH

Being aware of some of the strengths and weaknesses of research methods commonly used to examine education-related phenomena helps the reader of research to critically evaluate published claims of findings. But one of the

> Now I understand a bit about how educational research is conducted, but I do not feel confident that I will be able to evaluate what I read. How can I improve?

best ways to gain confidence is to practice. Read about and critique research reports in the news. Be alert to possible bias. Ask questions as you read. Here are some questions to think about as you read.

- How were the data collected?

- How was the study designed?

- Given the limitations of the methods, did the researcher draw appropriate conclusions?

- Were the subjects randomly selected? How?

- Is there a reasonable number of subjects?

- Is the sample representative of the general population?

- If the research is experimental, is there a control group?

- If the study is correlational, is there an alternate explanation for the findings?

- Does the researcher indicate possible limitations or shortcomings of the research?

- Who paid for the research?

- Who stands to benefit from the results?

- Have other researchers come to similar conclusions?

- Have the results been reviewed by other experts in the field and published in a reputable journal?

SUMMARY

Being a wise consumer of research means being alert to potential bias and being aware of the strengths and weaknesses of research methods and designs. Bias may be identified by asking who paid for the research and who stands to benefit from the results.

Systematic observation, a way to measure behaviors, may occur in a naturalistic setting or in a structured laboratory situation. Observers may influence the behavior of subjects, and there is also the potential that observers may bias data collection.

Self-reports as used in interviews, surveys, and questionnaires and are subject to falsification and therefore need to be interpreted with care. Providing assurances of anonymity are important in self-report research.

Case studies are valuable particularly when the subject presents a unique opportunity to study a phenomenon, setting, school, or event. Case studies describe an individual or situation and cannot be used in making broad generalizations about other individuals or situations.

Correlational research describes how variables move in relation to one another. Results are reported as correlation coefficients and do not indicate that there is necessarily a cause-and-effect relationship between variables.

In experimental research, the independent variable is manipulated, and the effects of that manipulation on the dependent variable are assessed statistically. In evaluating experimental research, it is important to consider the sample composition and how the sample was established. A control group is necessary for experimental research.

Studies may be designed as longitudinal, cross-sectional, or sequential. Longitudinal studies assess the same subjects repeatedly over time, whereas cross-sectional studies assess different subjects at one point in time. Sequential design combines some positive aspects of both the longitudinal and cross-sectional designs.

Knowledge of common research methods and designs is helpful in critically evaluating educational research. Original research reports provide important details that are helpful in determining the strength of any findings.

Key Terms

case study
control group
cross-generational problem
cross-sectional design
correlational research
dependent variable
experimental group
experimental research
independent variable

inter-rater reliability
longitudinal design
naturalistic observation
random selection
self-report
sequential design
structured observation
systematic observation

Using What You Know

1. Go to http://www.cpc.unc.edu for a description of Terman's study of gifted individuals. Search the term "Terman" and then click on "The Lewis Terman Study at Stanford University." Using what you know about research methods, what would you change to make the research design stronger? What cautions would one need to exercise in interpreting the results of Terman's study?

2. Access the National School Boards Association Web site at http://nsba.org and identify political issues and activities of this organization. How could the organization benefit from any of the issues you have identified?

3. Locate an original research report in a professional journal. Evaluate the research by answering the questions listed at the end of this chapter (see page 20).

For additional information on research-based practice, visit our Web site at http://www.earlychilded.delmar.com.

Chapter 3
Accessing Sources of Research in Early Childhood Education

Screening made her think of picking strawberries. Strawberries need to be screened. Too big and they are pithy inside; too little and there is nothing left once the stem is gone; not enough red and the taste turns sour; too ripe and they will not last until tomorrow. You have to screen strawberries.

Christine was on the screening committee—kindergarten screening, that is. "Do children need to be screened?" she wondered. "They aren't at all like strawberries."

But Christine's task was to gather research about kindergarten screening and make her report at the next committee meeting. She needed evidence, scientific evidence about screening kindergarteners.

"Focus!" Christine told herself as she walked into the library. "Stop thinking about strawberries and focus. Where will I look for screening research?"

Finding good sources in a library can be frustrating. Could Christine just check out some books or look for something on-line?

STRATEGIES FOR LOCATING INFORMATION

Although both of those approaches would likely turn up a number of results, there are more efficient strategies to target the most current and relevant information. There are excellent resources available to quickly and easily locate reliable education information. If Christine becomes familiar with the strategies, her search will more than likely turn up valuable resources in little time.

Books

Books are fine sources of information, including general topic overviews and background. Textbooks and other scholarly books may be found by initiating a library search. If the library does not own specific books, see the librarian about inter-library loan.

Most libraries have a reference section for volumes such as encyclopedias and handbooks that must be used at the library and cannot be checked out. Encyclopedias and handbooks are a good place to begin because they can provide comprehensive overviews that are helpful when first looking into a topic.

Sources that might be particularly useful in the field of early childhood education include the following:

- *Encyclopedia of Educational Research* (2001)

- *Encyclopedia of Special Education, Vol. 3* (1999)

- *Handbook of Early Literacy Research* (2001)

- *Handbook of Reading Research* (2000)

- *Handbook of Research on Teaching* (2001)

- *International Handbook of Curriculum Research* (2003)

- *Review of Research in Education* (annual)

- *The Educator's Desk Reference: A Sourcebook of Educational Information and Research* (2002)

- *The Handbook on Educational Research in the Asia-Pacific Region* (2003)

Although encyclopedias, handbooks, and other scholarly books may provide important information and comprehensive topic reviews, the time lapse between writing and publication makes them somewhat dated. Therefore, the most current information must be found elsewhere.

Where should Christine look for current sources?

Internet

The Internet is one way to quickly access a number of current sources, including government agencies, organizations, professional journals, and hundreds of other individuals and groups with something to say. It appears that many individuals and groups have a lot to say about education. Because anyone can have his own Web site and promote one cause or another, the reader must look for evidence that content is not biased and is firmly grounded in a strong research base. If the text offers only opinion or tries to sell a particular program, demand to see the evidence behind the claims.

Evidence is reported in both primary and secondary sources. The **primary source** is the original research report or article that contains the details of how a study was conducted and how conclusions were reached. Primary sources contain the information necessary for the reader to make critical decisions about the rigorousness of the study and evaluate the likelihood that the conclusions are logical. **Secondary sources** discuss the research, but in far less detail than primary sources. It may be difficult to critically evaluate the research findings from the limited information generally contained in secondary sources. Nevertheless, secondary sources such as newspaper articles can serve as a resource for locating the original research report.

Where can Christine find the evidence?

primary source—the original research report

secondary source—reports on or discusses aspects of the original research

Professional Journals

Primary sources for educational research are usually found in refereed professional journals. Manuscripts submitted for publication must meet high research standards and must be reviewed by several experts before being accepted for publication. Journals are in magazine format and are usually published monthly, bimonthly, or quarterly.

Recent journals are usually located in a section of the library labeled current periodicals. Back issues of professional journals are bound in volumes and arranged alphabetically by title in the periodical section of a library.

Some journals are available electronically and can be located by doing a library search or by checking with a reference librarian. There are also some journals available on line. Search by the title of the journal or the publisher. Access to on-line journals is frequently limited to members of whichever professional organization publishes the journal.

Where can I find professional journals?

Databases

Christine's most efficient strategy would be to search a **database**. As a collection of resources relating to a specific professional or intellectual discipline, a database serves as a lens to focus a search and can be accessed on line or through a library Web page. By searching a database, Christine will generate a list of bibliographic references she can then use to locate articles in the library's periodicals or in electronic journals.

Because Christine is in the library, let's assume that she goes to a computer with the library's Web page showing. She finds a link to databases. Because education is considered a social science, the most appropriate search would be in a social science database. Once Christine selects a database, she can usually search in three different ways.

She could search by keyword. A keyword is usually a concept like Christine's topic, kindergarten screening. The search can be limited by searching for references between specified years. As Christine locates and reads the articles generated by the search, she might come across references to other important articles. She can then use those references to search by author name or by the title of the article.

How will Christine know which journal has the information she needs about kindergarten screening?

database—collection of subject-related bibliographic references

Which databases are related to education?

Presented here are a number of databases, which can be particularly useful when accessing education-related articles. The most commonly used are described in more detail.

- Education Abstracts (400 periodicals in education published since 1985)

- ERIC (education-related research, documents, and articles since 1966)

- Professional Development Collection (index, abstracts, and full text for educators)

- Social Sciences Citation Index (index, abstracts, and cited references for social sciences articles)

- PsycINFO 1967–present (journals, dissertations, and book chapters in psychology)

- PsycINFO Historical 1887–1966 (journals, dissertations, and book chapters in psychology)

- Sociological Abstracts (Abstracts to articles on all aspects of sociology)

- What Works Clearinghouse (reviews of interventions and practices, evaluation studies, and test instruments for scientific research in education)

Which databases would be most likely to have usable information for Christine?

The Educational Resources Information Center (commonly known as ERIC), What Works Clearinghouse (WWC), and PsycINFO are important databases particularly related to issues in education. These resources can make the process of locating needed information much more efficient.

ERIC Resources

ERIC (Educational Resources Information Center) is a federally funded database specifically for education. ERIC can be accessed through most library home pages or by doing a search on the Internet. ERIC is an excellent place to start an investigation because it is current, comprehensive, and geared particularly toward education. The database contains bibliographic references, reports, conference papers, and **abstracts** of journal articles including both primary and secondary sources. Abstracts are short summaries of articles and are helpful in deciding whether or not it would be useful to locate the entire article. There are over 800,000 abstracts in the database, and others are added regularly as abstracts are updated monthly.

In addition to serving as a database, ERIC offers other helpful services. ERIC Digests are usually two-page summaries of research on special topics or current issues. Authors selected for their expertise write digests. There are hundreds of digests on line, and each digest lists references that can be used to locate additional sources. All digests can be accessed in

abstract—summarized report

their entirety directly on the ERIC Web site. Christine would be wise to look for her topic among the ERIC digests.

Though ERIC users must be discriminating, thinking critically about what they read, it may provide some level of reassurance to know that ERIC documents must be reviewed and must meet some criteria for scholarship before being included in the database.

What Works Clearinghouse

In line with the call for scientifically based research in the No Child Left Behind Act, Congress replaced the Office of Educational Research and Improvement (OERI) with the Institute of Education Sciences (IES). According to one political watchdog (Lewis, 2003), the IES mandate is to define and set the national standard for acceptability of educational research. That standard appears to be very rigid and limited.

IES established the What Works Clearinghouse in 2002 to provide an on-line database of high-quality research evidences for reference by educators, policy makers, and the general public. Although the goal sounds lofty, critics have expressed concern that IES will set discriminatory standards, favoring experimental studies using random assignment and control groups while excluding all other research designs (Lewis, 2003). The reader needs to be aware of that criticism when using What Works Clearinghouse. It would be wise, perhaps, to access more than one database when conducting a search.

PsycINFO

The PsycINFO database references psychology-related sources and emphasizes human development, learning, motivation, teaching, and related areas of study. It is available on line at most universities and can be individually accessed with an Internet connection. PsycINFO contains nearly 2 million sources dating from the 1800s to the present. References range from journal articles, to books, book chapters, technical reports, and dissertations.

Educational Organizations

Are there other reliable resources on line?

The major educational organizations maintain Web sites and publish a number of documents that can be useful resources. Some documents are available on line, and others must be purchased through the organization. If the organization publishes any journals, the articles from the most current issues can frequently be accessed on line. In some cases it is possible to search archives of past issues, as well.

The Education Resource Organizations Directory (EROD), part of the U.S. Department of Education Web site, lists over 3,800 state, regional, and national education organizations. Organizations that may be particularly useful when examining early childhood issues include:

■ American Educational Research Association (AERA)

■ Association for Childhood Education International (ACEI)

■ Association for Supervision and Curriculum Development (ASCD)

■ International Reading Association (IRA)

■ National Association for the Education of Young Children (NAEYC)

■ National Association of Elementary School Principals (NAESP)

■ National Council of Teachers of Mathematics (NCTM)

■ National Council for the Social Studies (NCSS)

■ National Science Teachers Association (NSTA)

■ Phi Delta Kappa (PDK)

■ World Organization for Early Childhood Education (OMEP)

Other Sources

The U.S. Department of Education (ED) and all state departments of education produce and publish reports and statistics for public consumption. The state departments of education focus on regional concerns, whereas ED covers a broader spectrum. The Web site for ED is a rich resource that provides links to "Educational Research and Practice: Reports and Studies." The *Digest of Education Statistics* is also available from ED and is downloadable. Another important downloadable file, *Early Childhood Longitudinal Study Kindergarten Class of 1998–99*, may be of particular interest to early childhood professionals.

The newspaper *Education Week* is a highly respected publication geared to reporting issues and events in K–12 education. The paper maintains an on-line archive of articles and links for up-to-date information on a national level. The newspaper publishes two large-scale reports each year: *Quality Counts* and *Technology Counts*. State-by-state comparisons and evaluations are part of *Quality Counts*. The 2003 *Quality Counts* spotlighted quality issues in early childhood education.

SUMMARY

There are numerous strategies for accessing research efficiently and effectively. Thinking critically and being aware of sources of potential bias are crucial to evaluating the quality of information. Books, handbooks, and encyclopedias provide background but may not contain the most current information available on the topic.

Reports are classified as primary or secondary. A primary source is the original report in detail. A secondary source is a more general discussion of the primary report and may contain little information about how the research was conducted.

Up-to-date information is usually located in journal articles, which can be accessed using databases. Education organizations also publish reports, studies, and research and post much of that information on the Web site.

The U.S. Department of Education and state-level departments of education are often fruitful sources for statistics and research reports.

Key Terms

abstract

primary source

database

secondary source

Using What You Know

1. Go to the U.S. Department of Education Web site and become familiar with the resources available.

2. Conduct an ERIC search for Christine.

3. Obtain a professional journal and read an article of interest.

4. Read an issue of *Education Week*.

For additional information on research-based practice, visit our Web site at http://www.earlychilded.delmar.com.

Part Two

What Does Research Tell Us About the Issues?

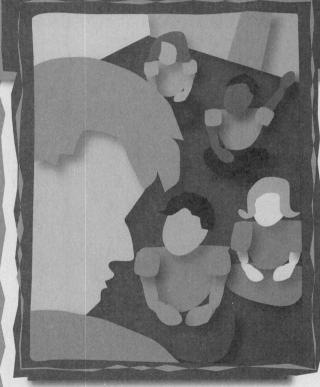

If teachers and administrators are to make wise decisions based on scientific research, they must study the research base. Part II attempts to present the current state of understanding about some of the most commonly questioned issues in the early childhood arena. Although every attempt has been made in Part II to describe the current state of knowledge, educators must be aware that what we say we know today may be viewed as a misconception tomorrow. The knowledge base is ever changing. Therefore, it is important that educators not only understand and implement the best of what is currently known, but also realize their professional obligation to continuously seek out, evaluate, and be open to new research findings.

Part II begins by asking the big question: Does early education make a difference? Smaller, but vitally important questions follow: Who is coming to school, and how are the demographics changing? Is there a best age to start school? How much time should children spend in school? Questions are asked about specific practices, such as holding children out of kindergarten, retaining children in grade, putting children in time-out, implementing a specific curriculum delivery model, or instituting transition kindergarten classes. Assessment issues, family involvement issues, and issues surrounding discipline are explored as Part II focuses on research findings. After digesting the findings of specific studies in Part II, the reader is invited to apply what has been learned by completing the suggested activities in Part III.

Chapter 4
Does Early Education Make a Difference?

The car needs new tires, the refrigerator is making strange noises, and the insurance is due. Kelly and Kris are young parents living on a budget and raising a three-year-old daughter, Jordan. They would like to send Jordan to preschool because they want her to have a strong start to her education, but Kris, a teacher himself, wonders where he can come up with an extra $100 a month for even a part-time program. Is it really necessary to send Jordan to preschool? Will she need to attend preschool in order to start kindergarten on an even footing with other children? Will Jordan be ready for kindergarten if she does not attend preschool?

That is a tough decision. Is there any evidence that preschool makes a difference?

PRESCHOOL

There is a substantial body of research concerned with educational outcomes of preschool experiences. However, most of that research has been focused on early intervention programs for children living in poverty or for disadvantaged children. Kelly and Kris do not live in poverty, so their child would be considered advantaged.

Warash (1991) studied the effects of preschool experience on advantaged children. The experimental group attended preschool prior to kindergarten. The control group did not attend preschool, but some members of the control group did attend child care prior to kindergarten. The two

Children who attend high-quality preschools achieve at higher levels.

groups were compared in first, second, and third grade. Children who had the prekindergarten experience outperformed children without prekindergarten in both mathematics and reading scores in first grade and third grade. In addition, children who had attended preschool had higher mean scores on academic self-esteem when they were in second and third grades. It is important to note that the effects were long term, evident years after the preschool experience itself. Children who were given a preschool experience achieved at higher levels over an extended time and expressed more confidence in their capabilities.

It looks like Kris needs to find a night job so he can send Jordan to preschool.

Making educational decisions based on a single study can be a risky proposition. There could have been other variables that caused Warash to find academic differences between the preschool and nonpreschool groups. For example, all children had some type of kindergarten, first-, and second-grade experiences that could have influenced the findings. It is always wise to look for multiple sources of evidence when interpreting research findings.

Have other studies examined effects of preschool on advantaged children?

Another longitudinal study followed 733 children from ages 4 to 8 (Peisner-Feinberg et al., 2001). The subjects had attended 160 community child care centers in four different regions of the United States, from California to Connecticut. The researchers were looking particularly for any long-term effects of child care quality on children's cognitive and social skills. The statistical analysis accounted for influence of experiences in kindergarten through second grade. The results indicated that children who attended high-quality preschools benefited in the long term. For example, children who were placed in higher-quality centers compared to those placed in lower-quality centers were better at understanding spoken language, had better math skills, demonstrated fewer behavior problems, were more sociable, and had better cognitive and attention skills when they were in second grade.

The researchers separated achievement results according to the mothers' levels of education. It is common practice to use mother's level of education as an indication of socioeconomic status. The analysis indicated that quality of preschool experience was particularly important for children whose mothers were less well educated. Therefore, the children who were most at risk also had the most to gain from increased quality of child care. The researchers pointed out that the long-term advantages were equivalent in years to about half of the children's lived lives.

Exactly! Different programs may have different effects on different populations. Quality of programs seems to be a defining factor. A number of studies have found positive effects for high-quality early childhood programs. Conversely, poor-quality programs also seem to have specific effects. For example, Howes (1990) studied children who had been in low-quality early childhood programs for an extended time. Those children demonstrated distractibility and low task-oriented behavior.

One indicator of quality that has been used in several studies is the nature of the interaction between the teacher and the children. When teachers are supportive of children, engaged with children and their activities, and interact positively with children, the emotional climate of the classroom includes more smiling and laughing than in classrooms where teachers ignore or interact minimally with children (Hestenes, Kontos, & Bryan, 1993). The closeness of the teacher-child relationship in preschool was reported to be a strong predictor of later social skills (Peisner-Feinberg et al., 2001). The researchers proposed that when children have positive, early relationships with alternate caregivers, they may be learning a pattern of behavior that serves them well as they establish later relationships with other authority figures.

Child care quality may also be influenced by the nature of the state regulations governing centers. Each state sets its own rules and regulations governing licensure, and those standards vary across the country. The nature of those rules and regulations may impact children's development as evidenced when Florida made its regulations more stringent. Children's cognitive and social competencies were measured prior to and after Florida's regulations concerning teacher qualifications and child-to-adult ratio were strengthened (Howes, Smith, & Galinsky, 1995). Under the more rigorous Florida standards, children's skills in language, behavior, cognitive development, and social competence improved. Nevertheless, it would seem important to determine which regulations related to a specific skill or behavior. If we knew, for instance, that language skills were enhanced by a certain space allocation per child, then regulations could be adjusted accordingly. There is a need for more research regarding the relationship of standards to outcomes, but we do have substantial evidence supporting the link between the quality of a program and the effects on children.

> So children who attend preschool may be affected differently depending on the quality of the program?

A positive emotional climate includes more smiling and laughing.

Do most child care centers provide high-quality environments?

Studies of quality indicate an overwhelming challenge to do better. The *Cost, Quality, and Child Outcomes in Child Care Centers* study evaluated community child care centers in four states (Helburn et al., 1995). This large-scale study ranked quality measures of programs and determined that most child care fell into the poor to mediocre range. Programs for three- and four-year-olds were generally poor, but programs for infants and toddlers were ranked even worse. Ten percent of preschools and 40 percent of infant toddler programs were ranked less than minimal. Only 24 percent of preschools and 8 percent of infant toddler programs were ranked as excellent. Conversely, 90 percent of parents considered the centers their own children attended as very good quality.

How could there be such difference in judgment?

There may be several possible explanations. Perhaps the study rankings of quality were inaccurate. Perhaps the parent rankings were incorrect. If parents are unable to spend time at their child's center observing the daily activities and interactions on a regular basis, it may be difficult for them to make accurate judgments of quality. It could also be that in a particular area there is no one program that stands above the rest, acting as a model for discriminating quality. If parents have never seen excellent programs in action, they may not know what quality programs should look like. A beat-up jalopy might look like a dream machine to someone riding a bicycle with a flat tire.

Early Intervention Programs

A number of early childhood programs have targeted children deemed to be at academic risk because they live in poverty. The oldest of these initiatives is Head Start, a federally funded program for children of families living below the poverty level. Begun in 1965 as an effort to boost the skills of children at risk of school failure, Head Start attempted to close the educational gap between advantaged and disadvantaged children in the hopes of breaking the cycle of poverty.

The author was one of those first Head Start teachers the summer of 1965. Because the program was initially designed as an eight-week summer experience, teachers scoured the local neighborhoods recruiting children, then brought their charges together for a few weeks of living and working in a simulated kindergarten setting.

Since that time Head Start has grown substantially, currently serving over 900,000 three- and four-year-olds in nearly 19,000 centers nationwide (Head Start Bureau, 2002). About 70 percent of the children served by the program are minorities at an average annual cost of approximately $7,000 per child (Head Start Bureau, 2002). Services to children and their families are comprehensive and locally administered by school systems and community-based nonprofit organizations. Related programs now serve children and families from birth through primary school ages, but there are not enough centers to serve many of the children living in poverty who qualify for the program. There have been numerous calls to expand funding so that all disadvantaged children can be served.

Early studies of Head Start's effects on children were both disappointing and controversial. There were some initial findings that IQ scores improved and academic achievement was raised for children who attended Head Start programs. Hopes for Head Start were dashed when research reports indicated that the limited initial academic advantages typically washed out by second or third grade (Lazar & Darlington, 1982).

One possible explanation is that children who live in poverty are likely to attend poor-quality schools, so the initial advantage is deteriorated by poor educational experiences in kindergarten through third grade. One must also consider that all the disadvantages associated with poverty continue to impact the child just as all the advantages of living above the poverty level continue to impact other children. The gap widens.

Although the initial feedback about the effectiveness of Head Start was less than positive, later studies have looked at factors in addition to achievement scores in the early grades and are reporting long-term positive effects for children who have attended Head Start preschool.

In a large-scale study of 622 subjects, Oden, Schweinhart, and Weikart (2000) looked at characteristics of Head Start graduates when they were 22 years old and compared them to subjects who would have qualified for Head Start but did not attend. At age 22, 95 percent of Head Start girls had either graduated from high school or had obtained the GED compared to 81 percent of subjects who had not attended Head Start. In addition, 10 percent more of the nonparticipants had been arrested for a crime.

What programs are available to children who live lives in disadvantaged circumstances?

That is a lot of money to spend on a program. Before we spend more, shouldn't we know whether Head Start works? What results do those tax dollars buy?

Why would those academic advantages disappear?

What long-term effects have been associated with Head Start?

When Latino Head Start participants were compared to their brothers and sisters who did not attend Head Start, significant differences were uncovered. Fewer Head Start participants were retained in any grade, and they scored higher than their nonparticipating siblings on vocabulary and mathematics tests (Currie & Thomas, 1999).

The High Scope/Perry Preschool study involved an original group of 58 African American three- and four-year-olds from low-income homes (Schweinhart, Barnes, & Weikart, 1993). The project was developed by the Division of Special Services of the Ypsilanti School District, Michigan, between 1962 and 1967. Children who took part in the program lived in poverty and demonstrated low IQ scores, creating a risk for school failure. Subjects were randomly assigned to experimental and control groups. Children in the experimental group attended preschool half days for five days a week for two years. The High/Scope Educational Research Foundation conducted follow-up studies of participants from both the experimental and control groups at ages 15, 19, and 27. In this longitudinal study an unusually large 95 percent of the participants were retained, strengthening the follow-up findings.

At age 27, compared to the control group males, Perry preschool males had higher monthly earnings, were twice as likely to own their own homes, and were less likely to have received social services in their adult years. Court records indicated that male Perry graduates had a lower mean number of arrests (3.8) compared to the control group (6.1). In addition, 12 percent of male Perry graduates had been arrested five or more times compared to 49 percent of the control group males (Schweinhart, Barnes, & Weikart, 1993).

The picture for female Perry graduates at age 27 was positive as well. Compared to control group females, graduates had fuller employment, higher earnings, fewer children out of wedlock, and were more likely to be married. Mean number of arrests for Perry females was 0.4 compared to 2.3 for the control group. Sixteen percent of the control group females, but none of the experimental group females had been arrested five or more times (Schweinhart, Barnes, & Weikart, 1993).

For males and females combined, findings significant at the .05 level indicated advantages in IQ scores on the Stanford-Binet, higher achievement scores on the California Achievement Tests, higher earnings, higher incidence of home ownership, higher incidence of owning a second automobile, higher educational attainment, less use of social services during adulthood, fewer arrests, and fewer drug arrests (Schweinhart, Barnes, & Weikart, 1993).

A study by the Administration for Children, Youth, and Families compared an Early Head Start experimental and control group of 3,000 low-income infants and toddlers. Compared to the control group, the Early Head Start participants did significantly better on cognitive, language, and social-emotional indicators (Schweinhart, 2001). Results are in only through age 2, but the study is ongoing.

FACES, a longitudinal, quasi-experimental study of Head Start participants begun in 1997, has been examining improvements in children's skills as they move through the Head Start program. There was no control group in this design. Researchers reported better than expected growth in vocabulary, language, and social skills as well as better skills in literacy and mathematics during the kindergarten year for children who had attended Head Start (Schweinhart, 2001).

Given the reduction in social services provided to Head Start graduates, it has been calculated that investment in Head Start actually saves dollars. If this intervention does decrease crime and reliance on welfare and if participants do have higher incomes and property wealth, it has been estimated that taxpayers are provided with a return of $7.16 for each dollar spent on the program (Schweinhart, Barnes, Weikart, Barnett, & Epstein, 1993).

If we are to truly determine the effects of Head Start, it would seem prudent to study children in typical settings. Because some of the research frequently quoted in support of Head Start has been conducted at model programs, there has been an interest in expanding the research base to look at what is happening in a more representative sampling of centers. Therefore, in response to Congress, the National Head Start Impact Study is being conducted. The study has two primary goals: First, compare the school readiness levels and impacts on families of children enrolled in Head Start to children not enrolled in the program; second, determine factors that could affect the results of Head Start programs. The study will use experimental designs and random assignment. Data will be collected between 2002 and 2006 and will follow children through first grade (Schweinhart, 2001).

> According to these studies, Head Start has great results and is a sound investment of tax dollars.

The Child-Parent Center Program

> Is Head Start the only large early intervention program?

The Chicago Child-Parent Center (CPC) program is nearly as old as Head Start. Begun in 1967, CPC is a federally funded, center-based program offering educational and social services to families living in some of the poorest areas of Chicago. Unlike Head Start, the programs are operated by the public schools and focus on academics. Children enter the program at age three and exit at age nine. Children in this extended intervention program receive services longer than they would in Head Start.

> Do children do better in school when intervention lasts longer?

The Chicago Longitudinal Study has been tracking 1,539 low-income, 93 percent Black CPC graduates at various points in their educational careers for 15 years (Reynolds, Temple, Robertson, & Mann, 2001). Results from this major study of compensatory education respond to the criticism that many of the Head Start research findings have been based on small demonstration programs. It would be important to compare results of the two sets of research findings. We should look at CPC research to determine whether or not it is consistent with the Head Start findings.

A comparison group that had attended a variety of alternate preschool and elementary school programs was used as the control. Interesting effects were seen when comparisons were made when subjects were in the seventh grade (Reynolds & Temple, 1998). CPC participants had higher reading achievement scores than their counterparts, had experienced fewer grade retentions, and had been placed in special education settings less frequently.

At age 20, CPC participants appeared to be advantaged both educationally and socially over the comparison group subjects (Reynolds et al., 2001). Those who participated in CPC preschool for one or two years had higher high school graduation rates, fewer special education placements, higher levels of education, lower arrest rates, fewer arrests for violent crimes, and lower dropout rates. The effects were particularly strong for males.

Children who participated in the preschool/extended program through second or third grade consistently outperformed the comparison group, but not at a level of statistical significance. However, they were less likely to be retained in a grade or placed in special education. The authors of the research report indicate that there may be limitations to the long-term benefits of the extended program (Reynolds et al., 2001).

> Is it safe to conclude that it is most effective to provide intervention programs when children are three- or four-years old?

Considering that the Chicago CPC was a rigorous, large-scale study providing longitudinal information, the reported results are important to consider. Nevertheless, it would be wise to remember that decisions should be based on the results of more than one study. The CPC population was urban, and the intervention program was specific to a particular timing, duration, and program delivery model. Studies of other extended interventions could give us insight by either reinforcing or calling into question the effects of extended, school-age intervention. Let's look at a different large-scale and rigorous study of early intervention for children born to impoverished families in a moderately small, southern college town.

The Abecedarian Project

The Carolina Abecedarian Project is an early intervention with a twist. Whereas the Chicago CPC program extended intervention through the early elementary school years, the Carolina Abecedarian Project extended intervention into infancy, as well. Perhaps it should be called early, early intervention because subjects entered the program as three-week- to three-month-old infants. Children were randomly assigned to experimental and control groups. The experimental group participated in specific center-based care with teachers trained to promote cognitive, social, and language development. Child care services were provided full time, year round from infancy through age five. Both control and experimental groups received nutrition and health services. Differences became evident early on. By age 12 months, differences in intelligence measures began to emerge. Children in the intervention group showed a definite advantage over the control group in IQ from age two onward (Campbell & Ramey, 1995; Ramey, Campbell, & Blair, 1998).

A second segment of the study began at kindergarten entrance when the control and experimental groups were both split and subjects were randomly assigned to school-age intervention or no intervention status. In this manner it was possible to study effects of school-age intervention for children who had attended the prekindergarten as well as children who had not attended the prekindergarten program.

School-age intervention was provided by a resource teacher who worked with children at school, provided supplemental materials, and made home visits. The school-age intervention lasted for three years.

Subjects were followed through age 21. Long-term advantages were associated with the subjects who participated in the prekindergarten program. Compared to nonparticipants, participants had higher achievement scores, were more likely to be enrolled in college or other form of advanced schooling, and were a year older when the first child was born (Campbell & Pungello, 2000).

Whereas the school-age intervention showed important effects on achievement in reading, math, and written language, the achievement scores improved with increased years of intervention. The most impact was observed for children who had been part of the five-year child care/prekindergarten intervention. The early intervention seems to have counteracted some of the negative impact on learning that has been associated with poverty. The highest levels of reading and mathematics achievement were associated with the group having preschool and school intervention, followed by preschool intervention only. Children who had intervention only when they were school-age scored higher than the control group, but lower than the groups that had experienced preschool intervention (Ramey, Campbell, & Blair, 1998).

The design of the study did not allow for an analysis of which factors were related to achievement gains. Was it the timing, duration, or delivery model? Though there remain questions to be answered, it seems fairly certain that early intervention has a greater impact than school-age intervention alone.

Kindergarten

Although a number of studies have been undertaken to examine effects of prekindergarten programs, there has been little research into the effects of kindergarten. Howard (1986) compared achievement of 367 children with public kindergarten, private kindergarten, and no kindergarten experience. The children were not poor or otherwise at risk. Through third grade, achievement test scores were higher on 81 percent of the subtests for the children who had attended kindergarten. There were no statistical differences between scores of children who had been in public kindergarten and those who had been in private kindergarten.

The same subjects were studied years later by other researchers to see whether differences in academic achievement observed at third grade had continued through high school. Using school records, researchers examined grade point averages, ACT scores, graduation rates, and special education placements (Prince, Hare, & Howard, 2001). Compared to the control group with no kindergarten experience, children who attended either public or private kindergarten appeared to have an academic advantage as they had statistically significant higher grade point averages and higher English, mathematics, science, and composite scores on the ACT. There were no differences among the groups in special education placements or graduation rates.

> So if prekindergarten interventions are effective and school-age interventions are less effective, what is the effect of kindergarten?

Other studies of kindergarten children have relied on reports of parents and teachers (Zill, 1995). As in self-report research, one must be cautious when interpreting results. Did the parents and teachers remember accurately? Did they report accurately? A direct assessment of children's skills before and after kindergarten attendance would provide a more objective way to compare growth. In response to that need, the U.S. Department of Education initiated a giant project, the Early Childhood Longitudinal Study, Kindergarten Class of 1998–99 (ECLS-K).

Initiated in 1998, the ECLS-K was designed to follow 22,000 children from kindergarten through fifth grade (West, Denton, & Germino-Hausken, 2000). Skills were assessed in the fall and spring of the kindergarten year. As a group, children's reading and mathematics scores increased substantially over the kindergarten year (West, Denton, & Reaney, 2002). Differences were not apparent in the type of kindergarten program or school attended. Nor were there differences when characteristics of children and their families were considered.

That is surprising. Children who are at risk because of poverty or other causes fall behind other children before kindergarten. Doesn't poverty make a difference in achievement once children enter kindergarten?

Generally, children were learning and were making progress regardless of risk factors. However, the differences were in what was being learned rather than how much was being learned. Children with at least one risk factor tended to be learning more basic reading and mathematics skills. Conversely, children without risk factors were learning more sophisticated reading and mathematics skills. Those who were advantaged at the start continued to be advantaged. Even though children considered to be at risk made substantial progress during the kindergarten year, they did not catch up (West, Denton, & Reaney, 2002).

SUMMARY

Does early education make a difference in the lives of children? The earliest research into effects of early education focused on short-term academic gains that faded during the elementary school years. Later studies have pointed out the personal and social gains associated with early educational experiences. In general, preschool and kindergarten benefit all children, but those benefits may be different for different children.

Intervention programs for at-risk children tend to boost long-term success, but do not in themselves provide an antidote to the venom of poverty. Children appear to benefit most when interventions are timed prior to kindergarten rather than during the primary school years.

Because the evidence in support of early education is so strong, it would make sense today to ask how, when, and for whom early education is able to make a difference. Regardless of timing, delivery system, or duration of the early schooling experiences, evidence from research indicates that the quality of preschool programs is key to maximizing the positive effects of early education.

Using What You Know

1. In the opening segment of this chapter, you read a vignette about a young couple deciding whether or not to spend limited family income for their daughter to attend preschool. Now that you have read the chapter, how would you advise Kris and Kelly?

2. Would your advice be the same if Jordan were from a family living in poverty?

For additional information on research-based practice, visit our Web site at http://www.earlychilded.delmar.com.

Chapter 5
Who Is Coming to School?

Line up all the children starting kindergarten this fall and they would stretch from Washington, DC to Chicago. There are 4 million children entering U.S. kindergartens annually.

Who are these children? What do they look like as a group?

DEMOGRAPHICS

First-time kindergartners generally are in good health, weigh about 46 pounds, and are about 45 inches tall (West, Denton, & Germino-Hausken, 2000). Only 32 percent of the children live in two-parent homes, and those who do are likely to be White (NCES, 2003).

According to their parents and teachers, kindergartners typically are prosocial, make friends, join in play activities, and offer comfort to one another (West, Denton, & Germino-Hausken, 2000). Teachers report that two thirds to three quarters of entering kindergartners pay attention, seem eager to learn, and persist at tasks, though girls are perceived as better than boys at sticking with a task (West, Denton, & Germino-Hasken, 2000). Parent ratings of their children's creativity, ability to keep on task, and eagerness to learn are higher than ratings given by teachers. It is important to note that parent and teacher ratings should be interpreted cautiously because opinion is subjective.

Race/Ethnicity Percentage of U.S. Public School Students: 2000-01

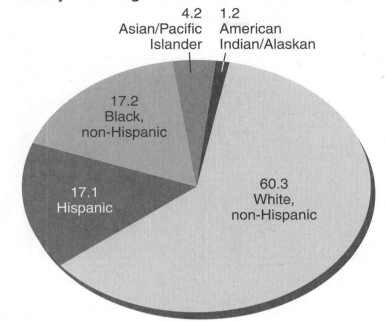

Race/ethnicity percentages of U.S. public school students: 2000–01. Data from the National Center for Education Statistics.

If kindergartners are like other public school children, the majority is Caucasian (60.3 percent). The minorities are Hispanic (17.1 percent); Black, non-Hispanic (17.2 percent); Asian/Pacific Islander (4.2 percent); and American Indian/Alaska Native (1.2 percent) (Young, 2003).

Classroom composition varies greatly across the country. For instance, Maine, New Hampshire, Vermont, and West Virginia are 90 percent White, non-Hispanic, whereas New Mexico is 51 percent Hispanic. The District of Columbia and Mississippi both have over 50 percent Black, non-Hispanic K–12 students (Young, 2003).

Demographers predict that all states except Arkansas and Mississippi will experience an increase in minority students before 2015 (Olson, 2000b). The largest growth group will be Hispanic, with a projected increase of about 60 percent. That means that by the year 2025 close to one fourth of school-age children will be Hispanic (Olson, 2000b).

However, the largest minority populations will be found in just a few states. New York, Florida, California, and Texas will be likely to continue to be leaders in multiracial, multicultural school populations (Olson, 2000b).

By 2040 the percentage of non-Hispanic White school-age children will drop below 50 percent, turning the majority into the minority (Olson, 2000b). In six states and the District of Columbia, minorities have already become the majority as California, Hawaii, Louisiana, Mississippi, New Mexico, and Texas have school populations that are 50 percent or more non-White (Young, 2003).

Is this breakdown typical throughout the United States?

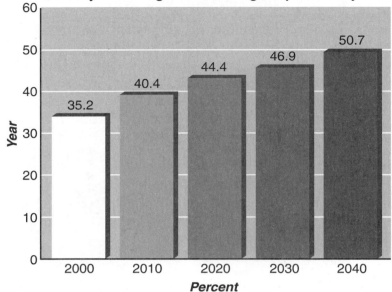

Minority percentages of school age population by year. Data from the National Center for Education Statistics.

Does this mean there will be more children from poor families coming to school?

Although the median income of families with children is $50,000 (Anne E. Casey Foundation, 2003), about 680,000 kindergartners live in poverty. About 7 percent of children live in extreme poverty, defined as below half of the established poverty income level (Anne E. Casey Foundation, 2003). The highest percentage of children living in poverty is minority status and in the age group under six years (Olson, 2000b). Therefore, as the percentage of minority children increases, one would expect a corresponding increase in the level of childhood poverty.

Will the children of poverty be found mostly in the urban, inner-city schools?

Children live in poverty in urban (40 percent), suburban (37 percent), and rural (23 percent) areas (Olson, 2000a). Although the poverty level is highest in urban areas, the suburbs are currently experiencing the fastest rate of poverty growth (Olson, 2000a). Childhood poverty can be found anywhere, and the effects of poverty on learning begin even as the child is developing in the womb.

Though individual children have been known to break through social and economic barriers, there are group characteristics that are correlated with achievement. Even as children first come to school, there are cognitive differences in what they know and can do related to socioeconomic status, race, and ethnicity (NCES, 2003). We also see clear differences in living conditions, home activities, and resources available to youngsters living in need. It is clear that children do not start school on a level playing field.

What is the best age to start school?

ENTRANCE AGE

Age has been the factor most often used to determine entrance to kindergarten, but there is little agreement about what that age should be. Across the country children start school at different ages. The youngest kindergartners may be 18 months younger than the oldest kindergartners. Surprisingly, that difference may exist not only between states and school districts, but within the very same classroom, as well.

The National Association for the Education of Young Children (NAEYC) (1995) has taken the position that age is the only logical requirement for entrance to school. The organization opposes holding children out of kindergarten and does not support efforts to change kindergarten entry dates. "Raising the legal entry age is a misdirected effort to impose a rigid schedule on children's growth in spite of normal differences" (NAEYC, 1995, 2). Though the key factor that has been used to determine kindergarten eligibility has been age, there is no clear evidence that one entrance age is better than another.

In the United States, the magic age has been five years, though internationally there is variation. Numerous cutoff dates by which the child must have reached his fifth birthday have been popular over the years as school districts and states have experimented with a variety of configurations. In the past, some states established the child's fifth birthday as the entry to kindergarten, ironically providing the youngest children with the least school experience before entering first grade.

> **What is the most common cutoff date?**

State entrance requirements are all over the calendar, but the most common kindergarten entry month is September. In some states, children must turn five by June 1. In other states the cutoff date may be July, August, September, October, December, or January. Five states leave the age decision up to local school districts (Saluja, Scott-Little, & Clifford, 2000). The most recent trend has been to back off the entrance date so that children will be older when they begin formal schooling. But regardless of whether the cutoff date is June or January, when the school year begins there will always be a younger and an older group of kindergarten children.

> **Is it helpful for children to be older when they enter kindergarten?**

That is a difficult question to answer because a successful kindergarten year will depend on what the child encounters in the kindergarten classroom. The goal is to have the curriculum and expectations match the child's developmental capabilities. However, there has been a trend for the kindergarten curriculum to become increasingly like the traditional first grade curriculum. Because the academic expectations for kindergarten then become higher, the phenomenon has been labeled the **trickle-down curriculum** (Shepard & Smith, 1989).

When the curriculum is a poor fit for five-year-olds, the older children in a class tend to be more academically successful simply because they are better able to meet the increased expectations. In effect, the school curriculum then puts normally developing children at risk of failure.

trickle-down curriculum— increased academic expectations have resulted in first grade curriculum taught in kindergarten

ACADEMIC REDSHIRTING

In order to provide their children with an academic buffer, or edge, some parents have opted to hold their children out of school an extra year making them among the oldest rather than the youngest in their kindergarten class.

First grade curriculum has trickled down to kindergarten making the atmosphere more academic and passive.

academic redshirting—purposefully delaying kindergarten entrance so that the child will be older and more competitive

Children are held back in hopes that they will be thrust ahead—a slingshot effect. Delaying kindergarten a year to give the child extra time to mature has been called **academic redshirting**. The term was borrowed from the athletic practice of delaying team participation for certain individuals while the athlete hones his skills and then becomes eligible to participate at an older and more competitive age.

In one large-scale, nationally representative study, researchers discovered that 9 percent of U.S. children had been held out of kindergarten (Zill, Spencer-Loomis, & West, 1997). That translates to 360,000 children delaying school entrance annually. This academic redshirting is most common for Caucasian boys born in the second half of the year and is usually an option chosen by affluent families (Zill, Spencer-Loomis, & West, 1997). Redshirting is a decision to purposefully delay starting school for children who are otherwise eligible to begin kindergarten.

If a child's birthday will make him one of the youngest in his class, would it be better for the child to delay kindergarten or should he start on time?

If we look at the literature on the topic, we find much opinion and little solid research. In addition, there are some difficulties interpreting the research that does exist. Some researchers report advantages to redshirting, and others do not. One of the reasons it is difficult to interpret and compare results of the studies is due to variation among the ages of the youngest and oldest groups. If the youngest group is born in the summer months and the youngest group in a different study is born in the fall, children could be as much as seven months different in ages. In some studies the youngest group is the same age as the oldest group in another study, complicating our understanding of what happens to children when they are redshirted.

Another problem with interpreting results of redshirting studies is how to measure any social or achievement differences. In some studies, achievement tests were administered. In other studies, teachers or parents were asked to recall a child's school experiences. Still other studies asked parents and teachers to rank children on various characteristics. Report cards, special education placements, and number of grade repetitions have been studied. Some studies were flawed by methodological errors. Few studies matched and compared children of similar intelligence.

Differences in school expectations is still another factor that comes into play when attempting to determine how to define and measure any advantage to delaying entrance. If the curriculum is a paper and pencil, direct instruction model children will achieve different skills from children placed in a discovery model, or constructivist classroom. Because the goals and academic emphasis of programs differ, children's achievement outcomes will necessarily differ, as well. Therefore, when comparing the results of studies, it becomes difficult to determine whether achievement differences are related to children's age or to the curriculum they have experienced.

Nevertheless, we find that redshirting is commonly practiced, and educators continue to recommend that parents hold children out of kindergarten even though the practice is not supported by research. A position paper issued by the National Association of Early Childhood Specialists in State Departments of Education (NAECS/SDE) (NAECS/SDE, 2000) questions the legality of school personnel recommending that children delay entrance. The argument is when schools practice redshirting the child is deprived of the right to educational services. NAECS equates redshirting with "simply subtle forms of retention" and calls for an end to the practice (NAECS/SDE, 2000, 2).

Let's look at some of the research. Springer (1997) asked parents and teachers to rate their second graders' social skills. Those ratings were then compared to the ages of the children when they entered kindergarten. In that study, kindergarten entrance age was not correlated with later social skills. If parent and teacher opinions were accurate, there is no long-term social benefit to redshirting.

> Do the youngest children in a group exhibit poor social skills? Do they have problems adjusting?

In another study (Spitzer, Cupp, & Ross, 1995), social-emotional adjustment was assessed using multiple measures including information from interviews of children during kindergarten and first grade, teacher ratings, report cards, and self-reports. The children reported no age-related differences in their own feelings of loneliness, competence, adjustment, or social acceptance. When children ranked each other, there were no age-related differences in social acceptance.

During interviews, teachers said they believed that older children had better social skills, but when the same teachers marked the social skills section on report cards, there were no age differences in markings. Report cards showed no correlation between age and social development (Spitzer, Cupp, & Ross, 1995).

The same researchers looked at other areas of the report cards and found that report cards did not reflect age-related differences in physical skills, language, or math achievement. It was concluded that being among the youngest in a class was not a disadvantage and was not related to being socially rejected or neglected (Spitzer, Cupp, & Ross, 1995).

DiPrima, Zigmond, and Strayhorn (1991) also used report card conduct checklists to look at social skills. Their analysis revealed no behavior differences between youngest and oldest groups of children. So if there were behavior differences, they were not identified by the teachers on report cards.

However, Byrd, Weitzman, and Auinger (1997) did find conduct differences. Rather than examining report cards, these researchers asked parents to describe their adolescent children using a standardized behavior problem index. Scores on this instrument rise with the number of behavior problems. Results indicated that adolescents who had been held back from kindergarten demonstrated more behavior problems than did adolescents who had entered kindergarten on time. Twelve percent of held-back children scored above the 90th percentile on the behavior index compared to only 7 percent of children who had entered kindergarten on time. But these findings held true for only one group of children—Caucasian males, which is also the group most often held out of kindergarten.

Social adjustment was assessed in the Early Childhood Longitudinal Study (NCES, 2003) by asking parents to recall any negative comments made by teachers over a period of two to three years. Children were first and second graders at the time of the study. Parents reported their recollections about negative teacher comments. Parents reported that children who had been held out of kindergarten had received fewer negative comments from teachers than did children who had entered kindergarten on time.

The researcher was counting on parents having good memories about teacher comments. How do we know the memories were reported accurately?

That is always a problem with self-reports. Memories can fail, and motivation can affect responses. Studies using direct measures or observations of social interactions would be more objective, but difficult and time-consuming to conduct. Before drawing conclusions, it would be important to look at results of additional research.

DeMeis and Stearns (1992) took a different approach. Assuming that children who have social problems would be more likely to be referred for psychological help, researchers looked at records of referrals for psychological services and compared them to children's entrance ages. DeMeis and Stearns found no differences related to age.

So most research indicates that young children do not have social problems when they start school on time. Do they have academic problems?

DiPrima, Zigmond, and Strayhorn (1991) conducted a longitudinal study with a large urban sample. The longitudinal design gave the opportunity to examine any academic differences that might show up or disappear over time. At the end of first grade the children were tested, and scores of older kindergarten entrants were compared to scores of younger entrants. The older entrants had higher math scores. When researchers retested the same subjects four years later, there were no longer any achievement differences between the groups. The short-term advantage faded out. Researchers concluded that, compared to entrance age, the child's socioeconomic status was a more powerful predictor of academic achievement.

Poverty impacts educational opportunity.

That plan would give useful information, but would be difficult to implement. However, school records can be used to locate similar data. Achievement test scores of fourth and fifth graders were compared for children who were on-time and held-back kindergartners (Crosser, 1991). In addition, children were matched in order to compare boys with boys and girls with girls. The pairs were then matched for similar intelligence test scores. Each pair consisted of two summer birth date children: one held out and one who entered on time. Would there be differences in achievement? Composite, or overall, test scores were higher for the children who had been held back from kindergarten entrance. The older boys also scored significantly higher than younger boys did in reading.

> **Has anyone held back a group of children and compared them to a group of children who entered school on time?**

If we look at the results from only one study, we may be misled. If a study has been replicated or expanded upon and if the results are similar, then we can have more confidence in the findings. A strong research base is built up by multiple studies. However, in the current research base, we have conflicting results about the issue of academic achievement and kindergarten entrance age. We need to examine other related studies before drawing conclusions. Each study approaches the issue from a slightly different perspective.

Cameron and Wilson (1990) used the Iowa Test of Basic Skills to compare achievement for redshirts and on-time entrants. This study also controlled for IQ. Children who had been redshirted did not show any academic advantage as a result of being held out.

> **That seems to be clear-cut. Should boys wait until they are six years old to start kindergarten?**

Thinking that children with academic problems would most likely be referred for special programs more frequently than children without academic problems, DeMeis and Stearns (1992) compared referrals for special programs. No differences in number of later school referrals for special academic help were found between young and old groups of kindergarten entrants. The younger entrants also qualified for gifted programs at the same rate as the older children.

Preschool attendance may be an important consideration to consider in the entrance age issue. The number of years a child has attended preschool may mediate the effects of age on achievement. The evidence is not strong, so further study is needed. Gullo and Burton (1992) found that younger and older kindergartners that had experienced two years of preschool showed no achievement score differences at the end of kindergarten. But, if children had only one year of preschool, older children scored higher than younger children did. More research is needed before reasonable conclusions can be drawn.

Others compared achievement test scores for reading and math (Morrison, Griffith, & Alberts, 1997). Subjects were old kindergartners, young first graders, and older first graders. At the end of first grade all groups had made the same amount of progress. There were achievement differences, but all groups progressed at similar rates. Therefore, the researchers concluded that entrance age was not a good predictor of achievement.

If there were differences in what the children achieved, why did the researchers conclude that age was not involved?

The differences in achievement were starting age differences. Think about it in terms of travel time. Let's assume that three people start traveling westward at the same time from three different cities—New York, Cleveland, and Chicago. They all travel at the same speed for the same number of days. All three will travel the same distance even though they will not reach the same end destinations. Those who started ahead will remain ahead.

Have researchers compared report card grades for on-time and held-out kindergartners?

Grades for language and mathematics were the subject of a study by Spitzer, Cupp, and Ross (1995). Using information recorded by teachers on kindergarten report cards, authors of the study found that neither language nor math grades were related to children's kindergarten entry ages.

What role does a child's intelligence play? Are smarter children going to succeed regardless of how old they are when they start school?

Grenninger (1997) looked at entry age and achievement for Head Start graduates. Standardized achievement test scores and ratings by teachers were used to compare young and old entrants. Grenninger concluded that intelligence was more important than entry age. Intelligence scores, not entry age, could be used to predict both achievement test scores and teacher ratings of children's achievement.

Isn't holding-out a better decision than sending a young child to school and taking a chance he will fail kindergarten?

Children who had delayed entry to kindergarten were compared with retained children (Kundert, May, & Brent, 1995). The school district entrance cutoff date was December 1. The average rate for retaining children in grades K–5 (12.8 percent) was compared to the rate for children who delayed kindergarten (6 percent). The difference was not statistically significant, though the researchers wondered if parents and teachers were perhaps reluctant to retain children who were already old for their grade in school. The authors of the study point out that we do not know the reasons parents decided to delay kindergarten entrance, though the high rate of later special education placements for the delayed group may give some indication. If delaying entry masked the need for special services, children were poorly served by the delay. The authors of the study concluded that delaying school entry is not an appropriate strategy.

Results from the Early Childhood Longitudinal Study (NCES, 2003) also indicate that children who delayed kindergarten were less likely to have been later retained in a grade. Nevertheless, children who delayed kindergarten performed as well as children who had started when they were age-eligible. It was concluded that delaying kindergarten entrance neither helps nor harms later school performance.

It is important to remember that there are going to be normal developmental differences among children even when they are the same age. When we expand the age range, those differences become even more pronounced. We must keep starting age differences in mind when making any achievement comparisons.

As reported in *America's Kindergartners* (2000) during the first part of the Early Childhood Longitudinal study, researchers conducted one-on-one assessments, interviewed parents, and surveyed teachers with a questionnaire. When children entered kindergarten, there were age differences in achievement. So, before any formal schooling took place, there were age differences with older children outperforming younger children who were born between September and December.

Yes, we would expect differences, particularly at this young age simply because each year represents such a large portion of the child's life span. It would be more important to look at any differences at the end of the kindergarten year.

> **Wouldn't you expect younger children to know less than children a year older?**

At the end of the kindergarten year both groups had made a year's growth. Children were learning at about the same rate, but they were learning different things. The younger children were learning more basic concepts; the older children were learning more sophisticated or advanced concepts (West, Denton, & Reaney, 2002).

> **Were there differences at the end of kindergarten?**

Narahara (1998) conducted a review of the entrance age literature, with the goal of determining overall what the research evidence would indicate. Narahara drew the conclusion that school age does not affect academic achievement. Nevertheless, the research has been a bit hit-and-miss. Younger and older groups are not the same ages in all of the studies. There also may be some concern in accepting self-report evidence. Some studies controlled for intelligence, but others did not. Another concern is the subjective nature of much of the evidence. For example, teacher ratings of behavior on report cards, referrals for special services, and frequency of grade retention can vary across settings—even among classrooms in the same school.

As is the case in many education-related questions, we need more definitive research. However, until that research is forthcoming, it is

> **The overwhelming indication seems to be that holding children out of kindergarten will not help them or harm them, but some of the evidence still raises questions. How do parents make the right decision?**

important for educators to be knowledgeable about the state of current research and base recommendations on what is known rather than what is supposed. Professionalism requires that recommendations be grounded in a sound knowledge base. Given the state of knowledge, blanket recommendations to delay kindergarten entry for certain groups of children would be unprofessional.

If parents continue to hold out children from kindergarten, what are the implications for those children?

Personal Implications

The personal implications will vary with the individual, but all will have feelings about being off time. Those feelings may be positive or negative. Children who are held out will experience life events at different times from those experienced by their classmates. Growth spurts, loss of a tooth, eligibility for sports teams, driving age, onset of puberty, and numerous other age-related events will be different. Age at graduation, college entrance, loss of one year of adult earnings may be more or less important for any given individual. But there are other implications, as well. Consider the implications for both the curriculum and social policy.

Curricular Implications

Because parents have been holding out 360,000 children each year, the composition of the kindergarten classroom has changed. Although delaying entrance has been an effort to homogenize the classroom, it has the potential to do just the opposite. Rather than making children in a group more alike, we see the age range expand from 12 to 24 months with the oldest children 30 percent older than the youngest in the class (Meisels, 1992).

That age difference is significant. When some children enter on time and others do not, the younger children may appear immature and academically inferior. Curriculum changes to meet the capabilities of the older children, and the younger children then appear deficient, not "ready" for kindergarten. Parents and teachers decide that young children should be given a year to get ready, and the average age of kindergartners rises. The term, graying of the kindergarten (Bracey, 1989), describes the phenomenon.

Redshirting accelerates the curriculum and may be a force toward making the kindergarten more academic because the class is loaded with older children (Meisels, 1992). There is some indication that kindergarten teacher expectations are inappropriate for the developmental skill level of five-year-olds (NCEDL, 1998). Young children who enter on time, therefore, may be considered candidates for grade retention or alternative programs, failing when they have barely begun.

Social Policy Implications

Children who are held out of kindergarten are mostly White, male, and from affluent homes (Zill, Spencer-Loomis, & West, 1997). They are economically advantaged and tend to enjoy the experiences and environment associated with that advantage. If they are held out of school for a year, they are likely to enjoy social and intellectual stimulation such as preschool or trips and other educational experiences. When they do enter school, it is most likely that the school will be in an advantaged area.

On the other hand, parents of children who are living in poverty may not have the option to delay kindergarten entrance. Kindergarten is free. A year of child care is expensive. Therefore, the child who lives in poverty is likely to start school when she is age-eligible, even if she will be one of the youngest in her class. She may be forced to compete with classmates a full year older and may face a curriculum that is developmentally inappropriate.

If we compare the held-back child from an advantaged circumstance with the on-time but young entrant from a disadvantaged background, differences in achievement may not be related to age at all. Any differences in achievement may be related to socioeconomic and family factors rather than entrance age (DiPrima, Zigmond, & Strayhorn, 1991). The practice of holding children out so that they can get ahead has the potential impact of widening the already unacceptable educational gap between the affluent and the poor.

If 9 percent of eligible children are delaying entrance, then the system is not working for 360,000 children. And if parents feel they must protect their children by excluding them from school, we should probably take a look at what we are doing in those schools. We need to look at the expectations, curriculum, grouping patterns, and alternative ways to organize groups of children so that they can individually make continuous progress. When readiness becomes an evaluation criterion applied to schools rather than to individual children, there will be neither need nor question about delay.

> **What can be done to change this practice?**

Long ago and far away there was a magical garden where caterpillars stretched in the tall, tall grass and climbed over sticks and played hide-and-seek in the wildflowers that grew at the edge of the woods. And in that magical caterpillar garden no one was hurried. All of the caterpillars munched on mulberry leaves and learned important things as they grew fat.

Then, in due time, each caterpillar wrapped himself in silk and grew wondrous wings. Each butterfly emerged when ready, basked in the sunshine until its wings were strong and dry, then fluttered off to ride the breezes.

The caterpillar garden was a wonderful place, until one day the king decided that the caterpillars were really taking too much time stretching in the grass and climbing on sticks and playing hide-and-seek in the wildflowers. The king decided that caterpillars needed to learn important things . . . basic skills like how to fly. So the king made a proclamation that all caterpillars who entered the garden must be ready to fly.

All caterpillars were screened before they could be admitted to the caterpillar garden. Only caterpillars who were able to fly could stay.

From near and far caterpillars came to be screened. They held their breath and puffed out their chests and jumped into the air. But not one of those caterpillars flew.

The king was perplexed. He called together all the wise men and asked them what was wrong with the caterpillars. Why didn't they fly? The wise men scratched their heads and called for a commission to study the problem. The commission met for days and days, then issued their report.

The report condemned just about everything: It condemned the system of financing the garden; it condemned the parents of the caterpillars for their children's failure to grow wings; it condemned the gardener for using the wrong gardening methods.

Nevertheless, the report declared that the situation could be changed. There should be transition gardens where caterpillars who did not pass the screening test could go to practice waving their legs and jumping from high places so that they, too, could learn the basic flying skills. There should be readiness gardens for caterpillars who could not fly because they were developmentally delayed. There would be flight instructors to give special intervention.

The king read the report and provided funds for the programs targeting the at-risk caterpillars. But the king had an even better idea. All caterpillars who could not fly should simply wait outside the garden until they were older and had become butterflies. Then they could come to live in the garden because then they would be "ready." Then they would be acceptable.

So now there are no caterpillars in the caterpillar garden. Instead, butterflies demonstrate their skills at takeoffs, landings, gliding, and fluttering in place. And the caterpillars? Why, some of them have special classes and special teachers to help them learn basic flying skills. Some of them have been labeled "developmentally delayed" and "at risk." Some simply wait and others begin to pupate. The garden has changed. No one stretches in the tall, tall grass or eats mulberry leaves, or plays hide-and-seek in the wildflowers. The once magical place has become a butterfly garden, just fine for fluttering and drinking nectar, but certainly not a place for a caterpillar.

SUMMARY

The composition of the kindergarten classroom is becoming increasingly diverse with minority populations taking on majority status. Projections indicate that the trend will continue but will be uneven across the country with the largest minority populations occurring in a few states.

Poverty can be found in all settings including urban, suburban, and rural schools. The highest rate of growth is in suburban areas. Young children are the largest group living in poverty.

The face of the kindergarten has become wrinkled as children are older and many are being held out to give an extra year to become "ready" to meet the increasing challenges of school. Entrance age requirements vary across the country with no optimum entrance age.

The research base does not uphold efforts to change cutoff dates or restrict entry to school based on any criteria other than age. Redshirting has not been demonstrated as an effective strategy for either social or academic purposes.

Key Terms

academic redshirting
trickle-down curriculum

Using What You Know

1. Find the demographic information for school-age children in the state or states where you might teach. What are the projected enrollments by race and ethnicity?

2. Interview a kindergarten teacher about school entrance age policies and beliefs. Does the research base uphold the policies and beliefs?

3. Find the kindergarten entrance age regulations for the state in which you will teach. (Start with your state department of education Web page or go to the library and find your state's school laws.)

4. Find the age ranges in several area kindergarten classes. How do they compare? If there are differences, can you determine why those differences exist?

5. Visit a kindergarten classroom. Through observation, write the names of the four children you believe are oldest and four children you believe are youngest. Check your predictions with the teacher.

For additional information on research-based practice, visit our Web site at http://www.earlychilded.delmar.com.

Chapter 6

How Much Time Should Young Children Spend in School?

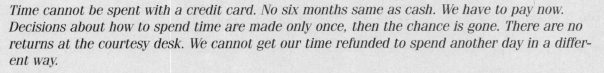

Time cannot be spent with a credit card. No six months same as cash. We have to pay now. Decisions about how to spend time are made only once, then the chance is gone. There are no returns at the courtesy desk. We cannot get our time refunded to spend another day in a different way.

Children have few choices about how to spend their time because adults and institutions see fit to make a number of significant time choices for them. One of the major choices made for children is where they will spend the days of their growing up years. Increasingly, that time is being spent in out-of-home alternate care. How does time in child care affect children's development? Is there an optimum age or critical number of hours beyond which effects are harmful?

As children reach school age, the issue of time emerges again as adults determine how much time children should spend in kindergarten. Are half days too little? Are whole days too much? In this chapter, we explore some of what the research has to say about time in the lives of children.

HOW DO PRESCHOOLERS SPEND THEIR TIME?

According to the National Center for Education Statistics (2002), more than half (56 percent) of all children ages three through five are enrolled in some form of child care, including Head Start, nursery school, and prekindergarten. Over a 10-year period, total enrollment has increased about three

Who is Taking Care of the Children?

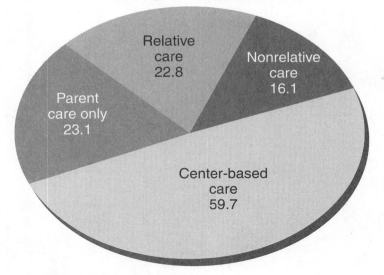

Who is taking care of the children?

percent for three-year-olds, six percent for four-year-olds, and nine percent for five-year-olds not yet in kindergarten. Older children are more likely than younger children to participate in alternate care, and Black children are most likely to be enrolled in child care regardless of family income. Participation increases as mother's employment status and level of education increase. Children are also more likely to be enrolled if their family income is above poverty level.

The decade of the 1990s saw a substantial reduction in the number of children who were cared for by parents. In 1991, 31 percent of children received parental care only. By 1999 that figure decreased to 23 percent.

Early studies looked mainly at the effects of child care on the **attachment** between parent and child. Findings indicated that there were neither positive nor negative consequences for the relationship. Child care did not interfere with attachment. Those findings were later questioned because the studies were conducted in settings such as university child care facilities where the quality of care was generally higher than in typical settings. When Belsky (1988) studied the attachment patterns of children in more typical child care settings, he concluded that babies were at risk of developing insecure attachments with parents if the infants spent more than 20 hours weekly in child care during the first year of their lives.

Belsky's work was criticized by others because of the methodology he used. There are both opponents and proponents for infant child care, but the question is not fully resolved. More research in needed.

The question of how child care affects children is complicated by the fact that there is such variation in the quality of child care programs. Differences in quality could make differences in outcomes for children. Therefore, more current research has focused on the effects of the quality of child care.

Is it harmful for children to grow up in child care?

attachment—nature of the love relationship between parent and child

More and more children are spending their days away from home in alternate care.

The age of the child and quality of care seem to be related (Howes, 1990). Children who experienced low-quality child care as one- and two-year-olds were evaluated when they were kindergartners. Subjects were compared to children who either had been enrolled in low-quality child care at an older age or had not experienced low-quality care at all. As kindergartners, the subjects who had experienced low-quality care early in their lives had more difficulty staying on task, were more distractible, and demonstrated less compassion toward others.

However, children who spent more time in high-quality child care were rated high in leadership, attractiveness, popularity, and assertiveness when they entered school (Field, 1991). Effects of the quality of child care were even more pronounced in a Swedish study by Andersson (1992). Children who had begun high-quality child care before their first birthday were compared to children who had started child care at an older age.

Family relationships, sensitivity, and care are more important than time in child care.

Between the ages of 8 and 13, achievement was higher for the group who had entered child care before their first birthday.

Perhaps the most comprehensive study of the effects of child care is the National Institute of Child Health and Human Development's longitudinal study, begun in 1991. Data continues to be collected for 1,364 mothers and children from 12 U.S. cities (NICHD 1997; NICHD, 2002). Indications are that the warm, caring, sensitive parent is more important than child care experiences for the healthy emotional development of the child. The media picked up on one aspect of the research relating quantity of child care to child aggression. That relationship could be due to the difficulty in measuring social competencies. Because the instruments used to measure social competencies are not as well developed as those for measuring cognitive competencies, the researchers utilized several social measures to compensate for the deficiencies. These methodology problems may have been responsible for the research results related to child aggression. Additional study is necessary.

Nationally, it is true that upper-class families access the highest-quality child care. Middle-class children receive the lowest quality of care, and lower-class children are in care that is the most variable (Phillips, Voran, Kisker, Howes, & Whitebook, 1994). Because much of the care for poverty-level families is provided by governmental agencies, there is nearly always a quality control mechanism written into the program. However, a relative or neighbor may provide nonmaternal care with no licensing or other quality requirements. Middle-class families are left to what they find available and affordable.

> The effects of child care seem to depend on the quality of the program. Is access to quality child care related to the family's wealth?

The effect of child care is not a question of time, but rather a question of program quality.

The effect of child care is not a question of time, but rather a question of program quality. High-quality programs appear not to harm development. However, the family relationships, particularly the sensitivity and caring levels, are more important to the child's healthy development than the amount of time spent in child care.

HOW DO KINDERGARTNERS SPEND THEIR TIME?

Nearly 4,000,000 children spend part or all of their day in kindergarten. Half-day programs (55 percent) are slightly more popular than full-day programs (45 percent), but a number of state legislatures have been considering the move to full-day programs (Galley, 2002).

Kindergarten attendance policies vary from state to state. Districts are required to offer kindergarten, but children are not required to attend in Alabama, Arizona, California, Connecticut, Florida, Georgia, Hawaii, Illinois, Indiana, Iowa, Kansas, Maine, Massachusetts, Minnesota, Mississippi, Missouri, Montana, Nebraska, Nevada, North Carolina, Oregon, South Dakota, Utah, Vermont, Washington, Wisconsin, and Wyoming. In 33 states, districts are required to offer half-day kindergarten; full-day is mandated in 8 states and Washington, DC. Oklahoma has also mandated full-day kindergarten, but at this writing the mandate is not in effect because it is unfunded. Nine states do not require school districts to offer kindergarten at all. Those states are generally considered to be high in local control of school policy initiatives, so the decision about whether and how much kindergarten to offer is left to the discretion of local school districts (Galley, 2002).

HALF-DAY OR FULL-DAY KINDERGARTEN

A good way to know which schedule would result in higher cognitive and social-emotional growth would be to conduct a large-scale longitudinal study. Assign randomly selected subjects to half-day and full-day kindergarten classrooms with similar teachers and programs, being certain that subjects were representative of children across the country. Assess children as they enter kindergarten in the fall and again in the spring when they exit kindergarten. Comparing results for both groups should give some indication of short-term outcomes from half-day and full-day programs. Continue to assess children on a regular time line as they move through school in order to determine whether or not there are any long-term effects related to schedule.

In an ideal world, a study design would have all these elements. However, in the real world, a research project may be limited by both financial considerations and access to children. Whereas the expense of conducting a research study may be limiting, researchers may also see the need to compromise when working in the real world of the schools. Because educational research is often carried out within the public school system with its accompanying regulations and restraints, the ideal study design may not be possible. Researchers seldom have the liberty to design and implement the perfect study.

As a consequence, kindergarten schedule studies typically contain only some of the desired elements identified earlier, complicating the process of trying to make sense out of the research results and leaving holes in the knowledge base. As an example, Hildebrand (2001) reported on a comparison of half-day, full-day, and alternate-day schedules. Pretests and posttests were administered for math, reading, and writing. Children were assessed on academic behaviors as well. Teachers rated the academic achievement of their own pupils. Of the five teachers, the half-day teacher rated her group highest. That comparison should be weighed in light of the subjective nature of self-reports.

> **Should kindergarten be half day or full day?**

The impact of teachers could certainly influence comparisons among treatment groups. Because the same teacher taught both half-day groups and because teachers rated the children, it is particularly important to evaluate the results of the study with care.

Other cautions are also in order. Subjects were placed in classes by the principal based on perceptions of the individual needs of the children. Therefore, subjects were not randomly assigned to treatment groups. In addition, the subjects were not representative of the larger population, as they all attended one school district in Nebraska. Although the curriculum in all classrooms was reported to be the same, the author of the study made the point that the teachers had different philosophical dispositions about how to implement the curriculum. In addition, the researcher reported that teachers varied in the degree to which they implemented

> **If there was just one teacher for the half-day children, could differences in achievement be related to the teacher rather than the amount of time the children were in school?**

developmentally appropriate practices in their classrooms. There were also differences in the consistency with which developmentally appropriate practices were applied.

In this study there were only five teachers for all three schedule types: two full-day teachers; one half-day teacher who taught two sections of kindergarten; and two teachers who team-taught in an alternate-day program. Observations revealed that the teachers were different. Each teacher had a particular philosophical orientation, and each teacher differed in the use of developmentally appropriate practices. For example, the half-day kindergarten teacher was skills oriented and was least likely to use developmentally appropriate practices.

Given the many differences among the classrooms, it is possible that factors other than the program schedule could be responsible for any achievement or social-emotional differences that might have been found.

Did the researcher find any academic differences for these groups?

There were no significant differences among the groups in math or writing achievement. However, in the area of reading, the full-day group did score higher than either the half-day or alternate-day groups. But we cannot be certain that any differences were related to how many hours the children were in school. There is the possibility that the difference in reading achievement could be related to the difference in teaching. For example, if a test measures specific skills, then children who have been taught reading from a separate skills approach would be likely to score higher than children who have been taught to read using a more wholistic approach with emphasis on comprehension.

Although the full-day group may have had an academic advantage, the half-day group had significantly higher scores in behaviors related to achievement. Ratings for originality, independent learning, involvement, productivity with peers, and approach to teacher were highest for half-day children and lowest for children who attended an alternate-day program. The half-day children also demonstrated the least amount of inattentive behavior, the least failure anxiety, and the least intellectual dependency.

Did the children develop these qualities because they were in a half-day kindergarten rather than a full-day program?

Although the evidence does indicate that the children were different at the conclusion of the study, it would be interesting to determine whether the children were different when they entered kindergarten, or whether the differences emerged as the children traveled through the kindergarten year. Teachers rated their pupils only in the spring of the year, so there is no way to assess any change in behavior that might be related to whether the child attended kindergarten half days, full days, or alternate days.

Superintendents and principals need to make policy decisions even though the studies may not be perfect. Based on what the current research evidence indicates, is full-day kindergarten better than half-day kindergarten?

There have been no indications that attending school all day is harmful to children. Research does indicate that full-day kindergarten may be beneficial for one group of children in particular. Because a number of studies have indicated that children living in poverty have higher achievement when they attend all-day kindergarten, we find that children of low-income families are more likely than others to be provided with whole-day kindergarten programs (Finn, 2003; daCosta & Bell, 2000; Nielsen & Cooper-Martin, 2002; Stofflet, 1998; Weiss & Offenberg, 2002). The Anchorage School District conducted a longitudinal study of the effects of full-day kindergarten and found that there were no important long-term effects that could be related to part- or full-day kindergarten attendance except for children who attended schools in poverty areas (Stofflet, 1998). Though studies have shown some mixed results, the research demonstrates rather consistently that full-day kindergarten is related to academic achievement, at least for some groups of children (NCES, 2003; Zakaluk & Straw, 2002; Gullo, 2000; Elicker & Mathur, 1997; Welsh, 2002; Cryan, Sheehan, Wiechel, & Bandy-Hedden, 1992; Hough & Bryde, 1996; Fusaro, 1997).

There are conflicting findings. Behaviors that facilitate achievement may improve with attendance in full-day kindergarten. Compared to half-day kindergartners, children who attended full day were more independent learners, were more productive and involved, were more reflective, and were able to approach the teacher without shyness, anger, withdrawal, or blaming behavior that was more common among the half-day children (Cryan et al., 1992). But that is the finding of only one study. Hildebrand (2001) studied the same characteristics and came up with opposite results. Hildebrand found that children in half-day programs exhibited the same characteristics Cryan found in children who attended full days. We need stronger evidence.

There may be a social advantage to spending more time in school. Children who attended full day were observed to have more social interactions (Hough & Bryde, 1996), which could simply be the result of having more time together. Elicker and Mathur (1997) also found a social skills advantage for children who attended all day. Nevertheless, there are conflicting findings. Analysis of the data from the Early Childhood Longitudinal Study revealed that children attending full-day kindergarten were more likely than those in half-day programs to have problems making the adjustment to school (Hausken & Rathbun, 2002).

Early studies indicated that any gains were short-term with little evidence that benefits extend beyond first grade (Finn, 2003). However, more current research has found longer-term gains. For example, Gullo (2000) examined nearly 1,000 second graders' achievement on the Iowa Test of Basic Skills and found that in reading and mathematics, children who had attended full-day kindergarten outscored children who had attended half-day kindergarten. Full-day children were also less likely to have been retained in a grade (Gullo, 2000). Similar achievement and grade retention advantages emerged for the full-day cohort in a large-scale study of 8,290 kindergarteners in 27 school districts (Cryan et al. (1992).

> **Are children better prepared for first grade when they attend kindergarten for a full day?**

When teachers were surveyed about their program preferences, those who taught in all-day programs preferred the extended program to half-day sessions. They stated that they had more time to know the children and their families (Elicker & Mathur, 1997). Teachers also reported that they preferred the all-day program because it provided flexibility and extra time for individual instruction (Greer-Smith, 1990; Housden & Kam, 1992; Elicker & Mathur, 1997).

Some school districts have gone to a program variation in which children attend kindergarten all day, but only on alternate days. A child might attend all day Monday, Wednesday, and Friday of one week and Tuesday,

> **How do teachers feel about full-day kindergarten?**

Teachers preferred the all-day program because of extra time and flexibility.

Thursday of the next week. There are other variations on this theme as well. Begun in the 1970s during an oil shortage, the full-day, alternate-day bussing schedule was viewed as a way to save dollars by eliminating the need for the midday bus run and noontime crossing guards.

The alternate day format continues today. Superintendents who were interviewed about the reasons for the decision to provide alternate-day kindergarten cited cost savings and transportation problems as factors contributing to their decision (Legislative Office of Education Oversight, 1997). It is interesting to note that the decision did not revolve around the needs of children or the curriculum.

Good (1996) was interested in teachers' perceptions of the alternate-day program, so she surveyed a group of 37 teachers at the end of the first year after they had made the change from half-days to alternate days. Teachers reported a variety of concerns including fatigue, irritability, and aggression among children; more difficulty making the initial separation adjustment; lunch room problems; increased stress levels among children; and lower achievement. Teachers reported increased fatigue and stress themselves. It was perceived that there were problems scheduling planning time and special activities. Teachers found communication with parents more difficult, but believed the parents liked the alternate-day program even though they sometimes found it confusing.

Teachers found that the alternate-day program impacted curriculum. Although there was increased time for projects and self-directed play, the lack of continuity caused teachers to eliminate calendar activities and increase time for review. Teachers reported that curriculum units and theme studies "disintegrated" (Good, 1996) because children were not in school every day.

What happens when children are in school is probably the most important question to consider when debating the half-day versus full-day issue. Educational accountability and responsibility would require that if a district implements full-day kindergarten, there must be value added, rather than simply added time. Sadly, that is not always the case. In an Ohio study, the Legislative Office of Education Oversight (1997) reported that in some Ohio districts children were experiencing full-day kindergarten by simply doubling-up. The program did not become more individualized or child-centered. Instead, children were required to repeat the exact half-day morning activities again in the afternoon or, just as astonishing, replay an entire day's classroom experiences the following school day.

Though such reports bring shame to the profession, there is some evidence that teachers do behave differently in half-day and full-day programs. Teachers adjust their structuring of time, activities, and the nature of their interaction with pupils.

Compared to part-day programs, all-day programs are more likely to have individualized instruction, more small group instruction, and offer more small group activities (Hough & Bryde, 1996; Morrow, Strickland, & Woo, 1998). Children in the whole-day programs are more likely to have opportunities to engage in self-selected activities, free play, gross motor skills, and learning centers. Researchers believe those types of activities may reduce the stress associated with less developmentally appropriate classroom situations (Elicker & Mathur, 1997).

Nevertheless, in several studies, children in both half-day and whole-day kindergartens spent hours of their time in large group, teacher-directed instruction (Elicker & Mathur, 1997; Morrow et al., 1998). This circumstance is in direct contradiction to the generally accepted guidelines for developmentally appropriate practice (NAEYC, 1997). In one study, children in half-day programs spent half of their time in whole group, teacher directed lessons, whereas children in all-day programs spent one third of their time the same way (Elicker & Mathur, 1997). Whatever the reason behind the inappropriate expectations, educators need to become advocates for vibrant classrooms where the system values curiosity more than compliance, promotes investigation rather than memorization, and replaces tedium with intrigue. We see, then, that what truly matters is not how many hours children spend in kindergarten, but what experiences those hours buy.

> Is the full-day program like the half-day program, or is the curriculum different?

TIME AND LEARNING

Time in school does not necessarily equal learning time. After all, we need to use the bathroom, get drinks, sharpen pencils, collect lunch money, put headings on papers, listen to announcements, solve social problems, hand out supplies, collect permission slips, walk to the library, pick up the spilled crayons, and a million other tasks unrelated to academics. Given the nature of the schools, the multiple purposes they serve, the needs of children, absences, classroom management, and demands of institutions, it has been estimated that schools could consider themselves fairly efficient if children are engaged in active learning half of the time school is in session (Karweit, 1988).

Doesn't that estimate come from a mighty old reference?

During the 1980s, several important national reports criticized the state of U.S. education, bringing schools to task for ineffective and inefficient practices. It was proposed that poor public schools were putting the country at risk because children were not being prepared to live as productive citizens. An educational reform movement was born out of that criticism. Time became a favorite topic of the school reformers. There were studies of student time-on-task that equated instructional time with achievement. Proponents suggested longer school days, year-round schools, and other plans to increase student time in school with the goal of improvement in achievement. The shorter American academic year was blamed for poor academic standings internationally. Increased time-on-task was touted as the cure-all for educational woes, and the public was regularly shocked by media descriptions of wasted time in schools.

Prisoners of Time, a 1994 document produced by the National Education Commission on Time and Learning, called for maximizing the use of time in schools and reconceptualizing the academic calendar. But time was considered a single concept. All time was the same.

More recently, time has been studied as a multifaceted concept with each facet related to learning in a different way (Marzano, 2000).

allocated time—time scheduled for school to be in session

instructional time—the part of the school day allocated to academics

engaged time—the part of instructional time when students are cognitively engaged and on task

academic learning time—part of engaged time when tasks are successfully completed because students understand

■ **Allocated time**—the number of school days and hours in the school calendar

■ **Instructional time**—actual time devoted to teaching and learning

■ **Engaged time**—time students are attending and behavior is on task

■ **Academic learning time**—part of engaged time when students are learning successfully

Academic time is at the center of Figure 6.1 because it represents the heart of learning. Students are spending academic time when they are not making errors, are understanding, do not need remediation, and are successfully completing learning tasks. Though there is a positive correlation between achievement and allocated time, it is small. However, the correlation between time and achievement is much stronger during academic time. Allocated time is both abundant and general, where instructional, engaged, and academic time become increasingly scarce and specialized.

How will I know that my students are spending academic time?

It may be difficult to determine when and how much academic learning is taking place because to know requires either the technology or psychic ability to read minds. Typical studies of time-on-task have been criticized because "they don't get inside the students' heads. They rely on observation" (Bracey, 2001, 555).

According to Zimmerman (2001), allocated time is most abundant and easily measured, whereas academic time can only be born when task difficulty and learner capability is precisely aligned. It is somewhat like an eclipse and possibly as rare. Even then, only the learner may recognize the moment.

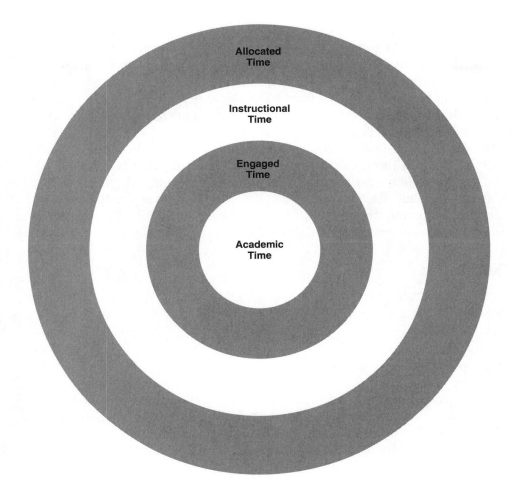

Figure 6-1 School time

SUMMARY

How preschool children spend their time seems to be more important than how much time is spent in preschool. Quality programs with warm, supportive, and sensitive caregivers may produce some positive outcomes. Low-quality care has been associated with negative outcomes. Regardless of program and time in alternate care, parents are still the most important factor in the child's development.

Across the nation there is great variation in kindergarten attendance policies. Slightly more than half of the kindergarten population attends half day programs. What children do during their kindergarten time appears to be more important than the number of hours spent in the classroom. However full-day kindergarten has gained in popularity and seems to be of particular benefit for children at academic risk due to effects of poverty.

The uses of time during the school day and year make it clear that learning and time in school are only slightly related. Different uses of school time have been identified. Allocated time is represented by the entire school calendar and is used for multiple purposes, including management, discipline, noneducational routines, and learning. Instructional time is allocated for teaching and learning, but students may not be attending and on-task. During engaged time, students are on-task and interacting with the material to be learned, but may be making errors, misunderstanding, and needing remediation. Academic time represents the smallest but most precious learning time in school, the time when there is alignment of content, task, and student capability allowing students to experience successful completion of the learning task.

Key Terms

academic learning time   engaged time
allocated time   instructional time
attachment

Using What You Know

1. Check your state department of education Web site to find out more about your state's kindergarten requirements. Are districts required to offer kindergarten? Are children required to attend? Are there minimal time requirements for the school day and school year?

2. Interview a kindergarten teacher or parent about the pros and cons of their kindergarten schedule.

3. Observe and record the uses of time in a primary classroom. Can you identify instructional, engaged, and academic times? What percent of allocated time is used for instruction?

4. After observing the use of time in a classroom, list four ways the teacher could use time for nonacademic purposes more efficiently.

For additional information on research-based practice, visit our Web site at http://www.earlychilded.delmar.com.

Chapter 7

How Do School Grouping Patterns Affect Children?

It's a gaggle of geese, a tower of giraffes, a bloat of hippos, a pride of lions, and a shiver of sharks. But how should children be grouped? Although a giggle of girls, a swagger of boys, a pride of pupils, or a flock of children might seem appropriate descriptors, they only happen outside of the schoolhouse doors. The American system of education groups children within political divisions, among schools, and across classrooms. There are first graders, second graders, primary and intermediate units, Mr. Taylor's class, and Miss Lipinski's school.

Grouping configurations have been determined for practical and financial reasons, to satisfy a particular political agenda, to match developmental needs, to address a social problem, to adapt to a specific curriculum design, and to meet enrollment demands. In this chapter, we look at the research on some of the most common grouping patterns.

GROUPING BY AGE

Grouping by age is the most common pattern in this country, though it was not always so. As the nation was being settled, schools sprung up where communities developed. In sparsely settled areas, children of all ages were grouped together. Instruction was in small groups with one teacher responsible for all levels. Deserted or converted one-room schoolhouses still stand today throughout parts of the Midwest where a section of each township was set aside for the education of resident children.

A section of each township was set aside for a local school with grassroots control.

As the school-age population increased, larger schools were built and more teachers were hired. School districts consolidated. At the time it was practical to group children by age, move them through an academic year as a cohort group with one teacher in a self-contained classroom, break for the summer to work on the farms, then begin a new year with a new teacher in the fall. This egg-carton-grouping pattern persists. We have first graders, second graders, third graders, each in their own classroom cell with a designated teacher. If we assume that children of a given age are fairly similar in their educational progress, the class would be a similar, or **homogeneous**, group of children, which would facilitate planning and instruction.

homogeneous grouping—children who are academically similar are grouped together for instruction

The self-contained classroom grouping pattern would work nicely if all children developed at the same rate and learned with equal ease. But because children come packaged in so many different ways, there have been innovators who have, from time to time, questioned, tweaked, fiddled with, adjusted, and sometimes totally reconceptualized our ways of grouping school children.

Why are most schools still organized into separate classes and grades?

Change can be difficult to implement. Old ways become comfortable. New ways may feel threatening. Inertia sets in. What was good enough for me should be good enough for my children. We have always done it that way. Why should my children be guinea pigs? I like things they way they are. How do we know the new plan will work better? I am too old to change. How much would the change cost? Will teachers need to be trained? There are a million reasons to keep doing what we are doing in the same ways. There should only be one major reason to change—to improve the education of children.

A Medical Parable

Suppose that a hundred and fifty years ago, at the dawn of modern medicine, there was just one doctor in every town so whatever illness you had, you went to that doctor.

It was the most natural thing in the world. Population was sparse, and travel difficult. Medicine itself was not well understood and all doctors, wherever they lived, had just about the same minimal knowledge and training.

Suppose that as time passed knowledge of medicine grew. Medical specialties developed as doctors received specific and advanced training. There were brain surgeons and pediatricians and dermatologists and so forth, each with their own interest and expertise.

Then suppose that the government passed a law which said the following: "Every patient must go to the doctor closest to his or her home!!"

And people thought this was the most natural thing in the world since they had been doing it that way for a hundred and fifty years. So brain surgeons treated children's diseases, pediatricians treated skin diseases, dermatologists performed complex brain surgery, so on and so on. True, doctors sometimes complained that their advanced training wasn't all that helpful on the job. They said they had learned the wrong things. They felt frustrated. The patients, too, sometimes complained about the quality of medicine in their neighborhood. Some even changed houses to get a different doctor. And everyone thought this was the most natural thing in the world.

Suppose lots of well-meaning people wanted to help. So they did a research study called, "How Effective is Healing?" They wanted to find out why some medical practices were more successful than others. They studied thousands of doctors and measured every conceivable variable associated with the practice of medicine—patient-doctor ratio, number of books in the medical library, etc., and etc. They also gathered data on doctors' own training—whether they had studied neurosurgery, anesthesiology, or whatever. And they did elaborate studies on doctors' fees, thinking that those who charged their patients more money would be better practitioners. But doctors continued treating patients based on their residence rather than their illness.

I suppose you know what the study found. Why, it was the most natural thing in the world. It found that the only variable consistently related to medical success was patients' general state of health to begin with. Generally healthy patients responded well to treatment; sick ones didn't. Doctors' fees, the size of their offices, types of advanced training and so forth didn't matter all that much.

Finally, suppose that some people stomped their feet and ranted and raved. "The medical profession is no better now than it was one hundred and fifty years ago." They said. "There's no point in paying doctors very well. All they need is a few basic skills and home remedies. The studies show conclusively that all this extra medical education and specialized training is worthless."

Now wouldn't that be the most natural thing in the world?

Introduction to School Finance by Jones, copyright 1985. Reprinted by permission of Pearson Education, Inc., Upper Saddle River, NJ

How do different grouping plans affect children and their learning?

To answer that question, let's look at some research evidence for grouping patterns within the traditional classroom setting. Then we can examine innovations in grouping that may be schoolwide such as looping, mixed-age grouping, and same-sex classrooms.

WITHIN-CLASS GROUPING

Whole group instruction is a plan of grouping that relies on uniformity. All students receive the same quality of instruction, and that instruction may be geared to specific student outcomes or standards. The teacher needs to make only one lesson plan and gather one set of materials. Typically the teacher explains, then children practice. However, whole class instruction does not provide for differentiated instruction, which is necessary to make the match between content and the learner's capabilities and current level of understanding. Even if children are the same ages, they will have achieved different conceptual levels, will learn at various rates, will have different background information on which to build new concepts, and will demonstrate differences in motivation.

What kind of grouping will account for those differences?

Small group instruction may be designed in several ways. Dyads, or pairs, may work together; children may be placed in groups by their preferences or interests; cooperative learning groups may be utilized; clusters of same ability students may be placed within one class; teachers may form groups based on student characteristics; peers may tutor one another; children may be grouped by ability. When children are grouped by similar ability, it is called homogeneous grouping. Instruction is expected to be effi-

Whole group instruction does not meet individual learning needs.

cient because group members will be learning at a similar speed. When group members are placed together by mixed ability levels, it is known as **heterogeneous grouping**.

The assumption in heterogeneous grouping is that low-ability children will learn from higher-ability group members and high-ability group members will gain deeper understanding of material from teaching others.

Many advantages of small groups have been proposed (Lou, 2000). Within-class small groups allow for remediation or extension and enrichment depending on the needs of the pupils. There is flexibility in pacing and instructional strategies used to match objectives to individual needs. In small groups there is freedom to debate, discuss, explain, and discover. Peers may tutor one another, strengthening understanding.

For over a century, educators have debated the help or harm derived from grouping children by ability. There have been several reviews of the research. Though reviewers find generally positive effects for within-class grouping, the size of the effects have varied and results for ability groups have been inconsistent (Lou, 2000). Until recently it has been difficult to sort out the results of that research because each study is slightly different, results have been contradictory, and few studies have contained all the elements of solid, scientifically based research.

The **meta-analysis** technique has permitted greater insight into the effects of grouping programs. A meta-analysis is a technique for synthesizing the results of a great number of quantitative studies involving a research problem. In a strong meta-analysis, there is a set of criteria used to include only the strongest studies for analysis. Those studies are identified, and the results are combined to draw conclusions. Statistics allow for more thorough analysis, which results in an **effect size**. The effect size is used to compare groups. Larger effect size indicates more practical significance, greater likelihood that the groups do differ.

In a meta-analysis of within-classroom grouping, 51 studies were analyzed (Lou, Abrami, & Spence, 2000). The studies varied by grade level, subjects, duration, and intensity of grouping patterns. The studies also varied in how achievement outcomes were measured; whether students in groups were equivalent; whether teachers were equivalent; whether there had been training, similar materials, similar schools, or use of rewards. The researchers looked for factors that accounted for the variance in within-class groups.

Overall, the meta-analysis revealed that small groups benefit all ability levels. Effect sizes were higher for children who were grouped with others of similar ability (homogeneous grouping). Within those homogeneous groups, the effect sizes were higher when cooperative learning methods were used, particularly in elementary school classrooms. Results were better when teachers had been trained in using small group instruction. It was concluded that small group instruction is maximized when teachers are trained, students are grouped by ability and cohesiveness, and cooperative learning strategies are used (Lou et al., 2000).

In an analysis of research on ability grouping, James Kulik (2001) also concluded that the success of a grouping arrangement depends on program features. For example, if children are grouped by ability but all groups learn the same content, part of the advantage associated with small groups is

heterogeneous grouping—children with mixed levels of ability are grouped together for instruction

meta-analysis—statistical analysis of numerous research studies focusing on the same problem

effect size—statistical treatment to aid in determining the practical significance of a research finding

lost. When content remains the same, children in both low- and average ability groups achieve the same amount as they do in a mixed-ability grouping, but the self-esteem of the children in the low group rises. When high-ability children were taught in a homogeneous group with no change in the content, their self-esteem dropped, but their achievement rose slightly compared to high achievers who were grouped heterogeneously. But, if the curriculum changes to match the ability levels of the children, all levels of homogeneously grouped children outperform control groups in mixed-ability classes.

What is the best size for a small group?

Lou, Abrami, and Spence (2000) found the most positive effects when groups had three to four members. But Rogers (1998) reported that children who demonstrate low ability do best if they are paired with a high-ability partner. There is a down side to these dyads, as they may not be as beneficial for the high-ability member of the pair. It has been suggested that gifted children drawn from the top 5 percent in the school should be grouped in clusters of three to six in a classroom (Rogers, 1998).

How does ability grouping affect children who are gifted?

When the level of instruction, pace, and content are differentiated and adjusted upward, children who are gifted appear to be advantaged by working in small, homogeneous groups (Balzer, 1991; Kulik, 2001). There may be other advantages as well.

The following is a task given to children who were classified as gifted (Sheppard & Kanevsky, 1999). There were two groups: one was homogeneously grouped; the other, heterogeneously grouped. Over several sessions, subjects in both groups were asked to create and discuss a machine analogy for their mind while solving a problem. Students were interviewed, created drawings, and produced written materials. Clear differences in the groups emerged.

The heterogeneous group members were less spontaneous, expressed fear of copying or being copied, produced shorter descriptions of their analogies, and were less willing to take risks. In contrast, the homogeneous group members were more fluent, more creative, gave longer and more sophisticated descriptions, produced more dynamic and abstract images, and were self-starters who were eager to bounce off of others' ideas. Homogeneously grouped children had the confidence to take risks, and their ideas were unique. Because the study was limited, it would not be appropriate to draw generalized conclusions, but perhaps future research will replicate or expand on the intriguing findings.

MULTIAGE GROUPING

multiage grouping—children of mixed ages are placed in the same classroom to facilitate interaction

There are numerous ways to implement **multiage grouping**. That may be part of the reason it is so difficult to ascertain any advantages or disadvantages. In a multiage classroom, children are grouped with a range in ages of at least one year. Children may be together for a year or perhaps for several years. They may remain with the same teacher for subsequent years, or change teachers each year. One plan has all children remaining in the same classroom for two years with the oldest segment of the group moving on at the end of the year. A new group of youngest children would then join the group. Whatever the multiage configuration, the goal is to provide opportunities for children of different ages to interact and work together. Therefore, any small group work would not be based on age.

Results of studies of multiage grouping have shown inconsistent findings. Half show no academic differences when compared to children grouped by traditional grade levels (Kinsey, 2001). In studies that did find academic differences, children in multiage classes scored higher than children in single age classes in language and mathematics. When results showed positive differences for multiage groupings, both high and low achieving students benefited, but results were best for boys, Blacks, children of low socioeconomic families, and children who had been under-achievers (Kinsey, 2001). One must keep in mind that the academic advantages did not appear in half of the studies, so more definitive research is needed.

For some specific groups of children, there may be academic advantages to being in classes with others who are older or younger (Holloway, 2001). For example, Lloyd (1999) found that high-ability third graders (I.Q. of 125 or higher) who had experienced three years in a multiage group demonstrated statistically significant increases in reading achievement. Lloyd (1999) reported consistently positive achievement advantages for children who were in classes where the age range spanned three years.

The number of years children spend in a multiage class might influence achievement findings. Whereas Lloyd looked at outcomes for children who had been in a multiage class for three years, Gorrell's (1998) subjects had been in a multiage class only one year. Gorrell compared one-year gains in scores on a standardized achievement test for fourth graders from both

Mixed-age grouping may benefit children who have poor social skills.

traditional and multiage classes. There were no significant differences in either reading or mathematics scores. Further research will be necessary if we are to untangle the relationships among grouping patterns and achievement.

Are there any other benefits of multiage grouping?

Research has consistently demonstrated social and emotional benefits related to multiage grouping. Long-term effects include higher self-esteem, more prosocial behaviors, less aggression, better attitude toward school, and increased leadership (Kinsey, 2001).

There is some indication that children behave differently in mixed-age and single-age groups (Evangelou, 1989). It seems that older children tend to behave in a more nurturing manner toward younger children than toward age-mates. Though children of similar ages make friends, they also exhibit more aggression. Therefore, it has been suggested that mixed-age grouping might benefit children who have poor social skills because they will naturally behave in more prosocial ways toward their classmates who are younger. More evidence is needed.

NONGRADED/UNGRADED GROUPING

nongraded/ungraded grouping— mixed ages are grouped together to make groups homogeneous

Nongraded/ungraded groupings also put together children across grade levels, but the purposes are different. Multiage grouping places children of different ages together in order to facilitate interactions and helping behaviors. The goal is to have children instruct and learn from one another. The purpose of nongraded grouping is not to facilitate interaction. The purpose is to make the groups more alike so that instruction can be geared to each child's level. Mixed ages are flexibly regrouped for homogeneous instruction and children progress at their own rate (Slavin, 1993). Nongrading was popular in the 1950s and 1960s, nearly disappeared for the next two decades, but made a reappearance during the early 1990s. The earliest forms of nongrading relied heavily on individualized instruction with children moving through a series of skills at their own rate. Large, open classrooms and learning centers were popular, but not necessary to the implementation of nongrading. More recent plans have implemented a simpler form with children learning in groups in more traditional classroom settings. Slavin, Karweit, and Wasik (1993) report evidence of achievement benefits from the more recent nongraded format.

SAME-SEX GROUPING

same-sex grouping—children are grouped by gender to improve achievement

At various times there have been moves to group students by gender (**same-sex grouping**), with the hopes that achievement and academic attentiveness would both improve. There may be classrooms or entire schools for boys or girls. Some secondary schools have tried separating boys and girls for classes within the same building. California experimented with single-sex public education as former Governor Pete Wilson encouraged legislation allocating funds for initiating pilot programs. Six districts opened single-sex academies as a choice for families. Those academies faced major political and implementation problems that proved fatal (Datnow, Hubbard, & Woody, 2001).

There are currently a number of same-sex private schools, but single-gender plans have been battered on a number of legal fronts when implemented in the public school system. Title IX, the 30-year-old law that outlaws gender discrimination, has been invoked by opponents of single-sex schooling. The law requires that schools provide comparable services and facilities, which can mean increased expenditures.

A recent change in interpretation of Title IX was envisioned as a way to offer same-gender schooling as another choice for families. As an additional incentive, schools were invited to apply for $3 million in grant money available for implementing single-sex education initiatives. As a political football, same-sex schooling may find itself kicked around a bit more with changes in the national political scene (Fletcher, 2002; Associated Press, 2002; Raspberry, 2002).

Do boys and girls do better in schools where they are separated?

The academic tie has not been pulled tight in research, but there are some intriguing case studies. Western High School in Baltimore has been limited to girls for 160 years and has a strong academic tradition. Ninety-four percent of Western's graduates go on to college (Fletcher, 2002). The high academic achievement may be related to the fact that students attend a same-gender school, but it could also be related to other factors. To be accepted at Western, girls must meet rigorous criteria, which changes the population dramatically. We need more information before concluding that single-sex education produces academic gains.

In one study, adolescent girls achieved more in science when they were separated, but boys did the same (Spielhofer, O'Donnell, Benton, Schagen, & Schagen, 2002). The only differences were for pupils who started out as low achievers. The low achievers did better academically in single-sex schools.

LePore and Warren (1997) compared test scores and found no increase over students in coeducational settings. In a New Zealand research project, Harker and Nash (1997) found initial achievement differences, but after they controlled for socioeconomic status and ability, those differences disappeared. A Nigerian study did uncover differences in achievement, with girls in single-sex schools scoring higher in math than their coeducational counterparts (Lee & Lockheed, 1990). With so little research in such varied settings, it may be that another variable could be at work influencing achievement results. It could be important to look at factors like private versus public school, class size, expectations, socioeconomic levels, ability levels, and other possible influences on achievement.

Are there social or emotional advantages to single-sex schooling?

Some research has been focused on attitudes and behaviors rather than achievement. There have been reports of positive gains in leadership when males and females are separated (Haag, 2000). There are also indications that girls who attend separate schools hold less stereotypical ideas about gender roles and those ideas continue into the college years (Haag, 2000).

There are also some fascinating ties to girls and self-esteem. A small-scale study that took place in Ireland indicated that there may be a connection between single-sex schooling and girls' source of self-worth (Haag, 2000). Whereas that study reported positive results for attendance at same-gender schools, an Australian study (Mensinger, 2000) found indications that girls attending single-sex schools were more likely to be dissatisfied with their bodies and subsequently exhibit more eating disorder symptoms. Although the implications are interesting to consider, the jury is still out because there is not yet enough reliable evidence to determine a verdict.

LOOPING

looping—the teacher stays with the same group of children for more than one year, then loops back to pick up another group

Looping is a grouping pattern that keeps teacher and class together for two to three years. The class then moves on, and the teacher loops back to pick up a different group of children. The pupils may be of a single age or multiage. There are a number of descriptive studies and case study reports, but little quantitative evidence about the effects of looping. There are no reports of any adverse effects and some indication that looping may improve attendance, behavior, relationships with parents, and achievement. However, the evidence is spotty and inconclusive.

Looping has been popular in Europe and Asia, particularly in secondary schools. The Waldorf school movement started in Europe and was imported to the United States, where it took hold but never became a dominant influence. In Waldorf schools the teacher stays with a group of children from first through eighth grades.

Looping has also been used in Japanese high schools where students stay with a single teacher, for example in mathematics, for the course of the high school experience. There is also some looping in Japanese elementary schools. Some German schools also use the looping organizational pattern.

In this country, Project FAST (Families Are Students and Teachers) in East Cleveland, Ohio, has gained a reputation as a looping school. Positive achievement results and increased parental involvement have been reported (Hampton, Mumford, & Bond, 1997).

Looping has been mandated in first through eighth grade in Attleboro, Massachusetts, where improved attendance, higher test results, fewer special education referrals, less grade retention, and fewer disciplinary problems have been associated with looping (Gaustad, 1998). Positive impact on discipline among eighth graders was also reported in the Tolland, Connecticut looping pilot program (Lincoln, 1998).

There have been reports that participating students, parents, and teachers all have positive attitudes toward looping (Jacobson, 1997). Nichols and Nichols (2002) surveyed parents about their attitudes and perceptions of their children's looping experiences. Parents of looping children reported stronger attitudes toward school than parents of nonlooping children. It would seem important to consider that parents and teachers who volunteered to work within an innovative setting may be different from parents and teachers who did not volunteer, and that factor could have influenced responses to the survey. As in other grouping issues, the research base for looping is shaky, needing reinforcement before we will be able to decide with any certainty the value of the practice.

SUMMARY

James Thurber once said, "It is better to know some of the questions than all of the answers." Thurber would appreciate the abundance of questions and lack of answers we have about grouping students. We most often group children with others the same age, but we do that more out of habit than for educational reasons.

Small-group instruction benefits children of all ability levels and is best when teachers have been trained, groups are homogeneous, and when cooperative learning strategies are used. The effects of small-group work on achievement depend upon the quality of instruction including changed, adapted content and strategies to match student needs. Differentiated and adjusted content and pacing are important for small-group work with gifted children.

The purpose of multiage grouping is to take advantage of student interaction and peer teaching. Although there are a number of multiage configurations, the most important component is quality of what happens in the classroom. Grouping configuration does not ensure quality instruction or academic achievement. Social and emotional benefits have been found to be rather consistent with increased self-esteem and more prosocial behavior associated with multiage grouping.

Although there may be social and emotional as well as achievement advantages to nongraded, same-sex, and looping grouping patterns, research is limited and inconclusive.

Key Terms

effect size
heterogeneous grouping
homogeneous grouping
looping

meta-analysis
multiage grouping
nongraded/ungraded grouping
same-sex grouping

Using What You Know

1. Visit a school where children are grouped across ages for all or part of the day. What adaptations do the teachers make?

2. Observe a child who has been classified as gifted. Under what conditions does this child produce the most creative responses? What happens when the child is grouped in homogeneous or heterogeneous small groups? Compare your observations to the textbook.

For additional information on research-based practice, visit our Web site at http://www.earlychilded.delmar.com.

Chapter 8

What Are the Effects of Failure?

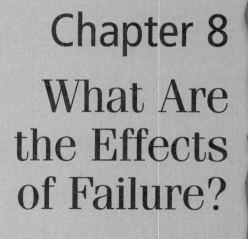

The researcher called it age-grade retardation, but Mom said he was being held back. The principal explained that he was being retained, his sister teased that he had failed, Grandma mentioned he would be a repeater, and the big kid next door said he had flunked. Whatever they called it, it did not feel good . . . even though he was only six years old.

If he is six years old, that must mean he failed kindergarten. Is that possible? Do children flunk kindergarten?

GRADE RETENTION

When children are not able to meet the expectations of the system, they may become candidates for being retained. That can and does happen even in kindergarten. Kindergarten has not escaped the trend for greater emphasis on mastery of academic skills, so as expectations increase, there are increased numbers of children who find it difficult to live up to those expectations. It has been reported that one fourth to one third of kindergartners are retained (Foster, 1993).

Is grade retention as frequent for older children?

Nationwide, 2.4 million students are held back a grade every year at an estimated annual cost of $14 billion (Anderson, Whipple, & Jimerson, 2002). Grade retention has increased a whopping 40 percent since the 1980s, most likely as a direct result of more stringent academic standards and high stakes testing (National Association of School Psychologists, 2002). Census

Minority children are the most likely to be retained.

data indicate that approximately one third of all children have been retained by the time they are ready to enter high school and minority males are the most likely candidates for retention (Thompson & Cunningham, 2000). By the time a child is nine years old, the effects of poverty have already increased the odds of retention for Black and Hispanic youth by 50 percent, with continued reliance on testing having the potential to result in even greater social disparities (Hauser, Pager, & Simmons, 2000).

Research demonstrates consistently that there is a positive relationship between being retained and dropping out of school. Being retained in any grade, including kindergarten, increases the chance that a child will drop out of school, and being retained twice nearly guarantees dropping out (Thompson & Cunningham, 2000). In Detroit, students who had been retained twice had a dropout rate of 90 percent (Meisels, 1995b). In Chicago, 30 percent of students who were retained twice by 8th grade dropped out even before entering 9th grade (Johnston, 2000).

Evidence from a longitudinal study in Baltimore sheds more light on the issue. Researchers found that 65 percent of students who were retained dropped out of school compared to an 18 percent dropout rate for those who were never retained. The dropout rate increased to 94 percent for those students who had been retained in both elementary and middle school (Viadero, 2000). Because minorities are more likely to be retained, minorities are also more likely to become school dropouts.

In their summary of the research on retention and social promotion, Thompson and Cunningham (2000) reported that transition years are high-frequency times for students to be retained. The retention rate tends to rise at the end of first grade after the transition into elementary school and at the end of the years immediately following the transitions to middle and high school.

> **What kind of social disparities could come from testing?**

> **Are students more likely to be retained at any particular grade?**

Does retaining children improve their academic achievement?

GRADE RETENTION AND ACHIEVEMENT

The wisdom of the 1990s called into question any efforts to retain children. Though a few experts pointed out discrepancies in research findings, most reports indicated that children who were retained in grade suffered negative consequences. Very strong statements were made condemning the practice. "Even though the professional literature definitively states the harmful effects of retention, the practice continues to be widely used" (Foster, 1993). Meisels (1995b) warned that "retention is virtually indefensible as a policy designed to improve the outcomes of young children."

But when critics began looking a little closer, they found there were some problems with the studies. Some were small, limited to only one school district. In other studies, there were small numbers of children or differences in children. Most of the groups studied were neither random samples nor nationally representative. Not all research used comparison groups, and when they were used, some comparison groups could have been exposed to different curricula. Whereas the most dependable research would have been experimental, randomly assigning students to repeat and promotion status, there were only three studies that had been conducted experimentally, and those were dated, having been done prior to 1942 (Karweit, 1999).

Those were all important considerations when evaluating the results of research. But an even more important difference became evident as researchers looked for reasons to explain the inconsistent findings. What they discovered was that the design of the study predictably determined the results. If the study was designed one way, it found in favor of grade retention. But if the study was designed a different way, results were exactly the opposite. Both designs represented responsible research efforts, but conclusions were different.

How could the design of a study affect the subjects' achievement?

Of course the research design did not change anything about the subjects' actual achievement. The studies made different comparisons, and it was those comparisons that affected the results. Some studies compared children who were retained to children the same age who had been promoted. Other studies compared children who had been retained to other children who were in the same grade, and therefore younger. Because the comparison groups were different, the results ended up to be different, too.

Retained children were at a disadvantage when compared to children their same age who had been promoted. It would be reasonable to assume that retained and promoted children were different just due to the fact that some were not promoted. The promoted children had the advantage even when the school term was starting.

Add to that advantage a year of exposure to the second grade curriculum. Let's imagine that Raul and Jacob both attended the same first grade. At the end of the year Raul went on to second grade and Jacob repeated first grade. During his second year in first grade, Jacob was taught first grade addition and subtraction again. That same year Raul reviewed addition and subtraction but then went on to learn multiplication. When both boys were tested, Raul was able to answer the multiplication problems, but Jacob could not answer correctly what he had not yet been taught. When children the same age are compared, the results indicate that children who are retained do not achieve as much as children who are promoted (Karweit, 1999).

If we change the design of the study so that we are comparing Jacob's test results to scores of other first-graders in his class, we are comparing a child who is seven years old to children who are six years old. Because he is older, Jacob's scores will look better. It would then be reasonable, but misguided on the face of the evidence, to conclude that retaining children is a good practice. It is important to remember that the design of the study determines the results. When children in the same grade are compared, the results favor retention. But when children the same age are compared, the results favor promotion (Karweit, 1999).

> **What happens when Jacob's scores are compared to the other children in his first grade class?**

Several meta-analyses and syntheses of research have been conducted. When a meta-analysis approach is used to look at effects of retention, the two designs tend to neutralize each other, resulting in the conclusion that there are no positive or negative effects of retaining children in grade (Karweit, 1999). It might be a better idea to make different comparisons. For example, we could compare Jacob's achievement scores before he was retained to the scores he earned after being retained. Karweit's (1999) analysis indicates that before-and-after comparisons typically indicate that children who are retained do make progress. It would be important to find out how we can predict which children will make the most progress. We need to know if there are any characteristics that would allow us to determine in advance whether or not a child would make sufficient progress to warrant a year of retention.

> **Would this be a good time to conduct a meta-analysis? A researcher could collect the relevant studies and analyze them statistically to determine overall the academic effects of failing children.**

Baltimore City Schools conducted an interesting design variation (Viadero, 2000). The gap in achievement between retained and promoted children was measured twice: once before and once after the retention year. Raul and Jacob would be compared before and after Jacob was retained. The achievement gap would serve as the comparison. Did the gap narrow after retention? For the subjects in the Baltimore study, the gap was reduced after retention. That does not mean that the gap was eliminated. The effect may be one similar to dieting. One can be overweight before the diet begins, lose weight, but still be overweight when the diet plan is finished. Do we call the diet a success? Do we call the retention a success?

Because the decision to retain a child has major long-term effects on a child's life, it is important for educators to keep abreast of current research. Next we look at several such projects that have been recently undertaken in an effort to learn more about the effects of retaining children.

School Performance of Children Who Repeat Kindergarten

The U.S. Department of Education published a report entitled *The Elementary School Performance and Adjustment of Children Who Enter Kindergarten Late or Repeat Kindergarten: Findings from National Surveys.* The project analyzed school failure data collected by telephone for the

National Household Education Survey. The resulting report (Zill & West, 1997) was compiled from parent interviews of 4,260 first and second graders. The large sample was nationally representative and randomly sampled. The total sample included cohort groups from 1993 and 1995.

Parents reported that 6 percent of the 1993 group and 5 percent of the 1995 group repeated kindergarten or entered a transitional class between kindergarten and first grade. For the 1995 group alone that figure represents 383,000 children. Compared to children who were not retained, there were more males and more children who were developmentally delayed in the retained group. Repeaters from the 1993 cohort were more likely to be from families living in poverty and parents were less likely to have been college educated, but that was not true for the 1995 cohort. Because results from the two groups were different, we need more evidence before drawing any conclusions.

The waters muddy even more when we look at the source of the information. Parents were asked to remember comments made by teachers and written on report cards about their child. This is a form of self-report and must be interpreted with caution. More objective sources of information would have been of value.

Parents reported that after two years in kindergarten, children who had repeated were not able to keep up with their classmates. School work was significantly worse in first and second grade. However, statistical analysis allowed researchers to determine that the differences were not due to retention. Instead, other factors accounted for the differences in achievement. One of those factors was related to the large number of children who were developmentally delayed, and the other factor was related to minority status.

In summarizing the findings from the study, the authors concluded that retaining children was not significantly related to either adjustment to or performance in school. In other words, they found no benefit to retaining children.

Chicago's *Children First Education Plan*

In Chicago, grades 3, 6, 8, and 9 have been designated as gateway points where children are required to pass an achievement test in order to be promoted to the next grade. Chicago public schools instituted the Children First Education Plan to help children meet the increased academic requirements. The plan provides for early identification, after-school help for children in need of assistance, and mandatory summer school for children who do not pass the test. If a child still cannot pass the test after interventions have been used, he is retained.

Do the children benefit from being retained?

The Chicago schools were interested in that question, so they conducted a study of the achievement of children who were retained. Children who ended up being retained did demonstrate gains as they worked through the interventions, but still did not pass the gateway test. The interventions were helpful to the children but did not boost achievement enough to pass the required tests, so the children were retained. Nevertheless, after an additional year of schooling, the investigators concluded that children who were retained were not helped by the second year at the same grade level.

Prospects Data Analysis

Congress mandated the collection of information known as *Prospects* in 1988 as part of the reauthorization of Chapter I. The data set was constructed from a longitudinal study of a large, national sample. However, the sample was not nationally representative because children who were poor and disadvantaged were overrepresented. Though the information was meant to be used in comparisons of children who had and had not been in Chapter I, the data was found to be useful in studying the grade retention question as well. Because it was a longitudinal study, data was collected over a four-year period, allowing researchers to track achievement before, during, and after a student had been retained. Information was obtained on 9,240 subjects who entered first grade in 1991 at 196 different schools. Information came from student achievement tests, student files, parents, teachers, principals, and school district level records.

Five percent of the children repeated kindergarten; 3 percent were placed in a transition class between kindergarten and first grade; and 6 percent repeated first grade. By third grade, 18.4 percent had repeated a grade, and most of the time children repeated only once. Although many retentions happened before and after the first grade, 51.8 percent of all retentions happened in first grade.

How many children were retained?

Retained children were most likely to be male (61 percent). Teachers reported that about 30 percent of children with health problems or disabilities were retained, raising the question of whether or not retention interferes with identification of severe problems (Karweit, 1999). Children who repeated a grade tended to come from large families with lower incomes and low occupational prestige. Their families were mobile with 10 percent of the families moving between the kindergarten and first grade year. Mothers had lower education levels than mothers of children who were promoted. More than twice as many promoted children attended preschool.

How were the retained children different from those who were not retained?

Children who were retained in kindergarten were different from those retained in first, second, or third grade. Children who were retained in kindergarten were mostly White, rural, from the West, and attended a medium poverty school. Children who were retained in first grade or later tended to be urban, Black, from the South, attended high poverty schools, and participated in Title I. The rate of retention in this study was highest in the South and lowest in the Midwest.

Karweit (1999) reported that both age and grade comparisons upheld the patterns observed in other studies. That is, when retained children were compared to their younger classmates, test results showed positive effects during the retention year but gains decreased in the following years. When retained children were compared to others their age who had been promoted, results did not show positive effects for retention.

Did repeating a grade improve the achievement of children in this large sample?

Using school records to do research provides a kind of backward crystal ball. Researchers using the *Prospects* data were able to look back at the school records, find all children who had been retained at any point, and examine their histories to see if any patterns would emerge.

When researchers examined achievement test scores for all children who had ever been retained, they found a pattern. In that pattern, they found initial differences when children started first grade. There was a beginning school gap. Those who failed first grade started out the year way behind compared to those who ended up being promoted to second grade. The children who were not promoted to second grade scored lower at the start of first grade on comprehension, vocabulary, and math. The children did not start school on even ground. By the end of the first grade year, that gap between groups had increased dramatically. Some children were retained in first grade, and some went on to second grade.

Children were tested again after repeating first grade, and the gap was compared once more. There was still a gap. The retained children did not catch up to the promoted children, but the gap narrowed. And that gap was smaller than the beginning school gap. Children had made progress. They were still not on a level playing field, but they were progressing.

Children were tested again at the end of second grade. The gap had started to widen again, although it was still not as big as the beginning school gap. The retained children had experienced a loss, but the achievement gap was still smaller than it had been when they first started elementary school.

Did the deterioration in scores continue through third grade?

The data end with second grade, so we do not know what happened in the following years. In some other studies, there have been positive effects of retention for three years, followed by a washout (Thompson & Cunningham, 2000). But the important difference in the *Prospects* data study was the discovery of a changing achievement gap.

The relationship between retention and achievement remains complex and illusive. However, there is more to the retention puzzle than academic achievement.

Children experience stress when they are retained.

EMOTIONAL IMPACT OF FAILING A GRADE

Children find being retained stressful. Byrnes (1989) interviewed children who had failed a grade. Whereas 6 percent expressed positive responses, 84 percent indicated that they would feel upset, sad, or bad if they were retained. It is striking that 27 percent of the children did not identify themselves when asked if they knew anyone who had been retained. In most research, children have indicated that failing a grade is a stigma, a punishment to be avoided (Foster, 1993).

In one study, children were asked to rate the stress of various life experiences. Failing a grade was ranked just under the possibility of going blind or the loss of a parent (Yamamoto, 1979).

It is important to look at differences in generations. That is why the Yamamoto study of 1979 was replicated in 2002. Sixth graders were asked to rate items in a list of 20 stressful life events. The rankings were somewhat different. Children reported that being retained was even more stressful than indicated in prior decades. Anderson, Wipple, and Jimerson (2002) reported that being retained was the most stressful life event of all—even more stressful than going blind or the loss of a parent.

First grade seems to be a particularly risky point for emotional adjustment, but it is a point where children are frequently held back. When children are retained in first grade, their academic and emotional adjustments are negatively affected (Thompson & Cunningham, 2000).

> Times have changed since those studies were conducted. Today's children could perceive retention differently. Is there current research?

Several possible explanations have been offered. Bracey (1999) suggested that both teachers and parents see only the short-term result during the second year. The child appears to be doing better and struggling less with the same content. If Colton was unable to spell weekly word lists last year but does a little better this year, teachers and parents are convinced that Colton would have been even worse off if he had been promoted.

Because we cannot practically conduct controlled experiments with randomly assigned subjects, teachers tend to rely on their intuition. It just makes intuitive sense that if a child struggles in second grade, she will have even more trouble if promoted to third grade.

Teachers are the major factor in retention decisions, but they seldom find researched-based policies or strong guidance about the topic at the school district level. The American Federation of Teachers (Lawton, 1997) looked at the grade retention policies of the country's 85 largest school districts and found them quite variable and frequently vague. Some districts restrict the number of times a student may be retained, as in Houston where it is permitted once in grades K–4 and once in grades 5–8. Other districts have written policies that are too general and lack standards for making decisions. The Clark County, Nevada, policy statement indicates that if a student is to be promoted, progress "should be continuous and student advancement through the curriculum should be according to the student's demonstrated ability" (Lawton, 1997). Two teachers could come to completely different decisions about the same child. Without specific guidance, teachers rely on their own attitudes, not the research base (Pouliot, 1999). Furthermore, teachers observe children repeating during the retention

> If there is so much evidence that retaining children is stressful and does not really work, why do teachers continue to do it?

year, ascertain that children are learning, then conclude that grade retention is good practice (Pouliot, 1999). The cycle continues.

Then what are teachers to do when children fall behind their classmates? Should they hold them back or send them to the next grade?

Each child must certainly be considered on an individual basis. There may be times that extended illness or other unusual circumstances may influence the promotion/retention decision. But overall, retaining children to repeat a grade simply does not achieve the goal of catching the child up to her peers. Failing children, even in kindergarten, has been described as "unintended consequences and good intentions gone wrong" (Meisels, 1995b).

Given the current climate of holding children accountable for a narrowing curriculum and higher academic demands, it is likely that more and more children will be repeating grades. It is a simplistic and perhaps cruel solution to remove a child from friends and peers in order to simply repeat an unsuccessful experience.

It is also poor practice to promote a child to the next grade if that child is unprepared to meet the requirements. This social promotion sets the child up for future failure. Neither grade repetition nor social promotion are good for children.

Are there options that are good for children?

If a child fell and injured herself while running with her friends, we would not think of standing on the sidelines and urging her to get up and run fast to catch up with the others. Neither would we send her back to the starting line to run the race again with a group of younger children. We would go to the child, assess her injuries, and provide first aid while offering emotional support. If the child were seriously injured we would secure proper medical care.

That is exactly what we need to do in education. We need to identify children who are falling behind academically early on (Lawton, 1997; Thompson & Cunningham, 2000; Karweit, 1999; Anderson et al., 2002). It is not acceptable to wait until the end of the year to determine whether or not the child will be promoted. During the interval, the child may bleed to death academically. Early identification needs to be followed by intensive, targeted instruction. Remediation must be individually determined according to the child's strengths and weaknesses. It is similar to first aid. Provide immediate care. If the child needs more help, refer for special services.

If the child is retained, she should not be a repeater. In other words, the second year should not be just a replay of the first year. Karweit (1999) found that the results of retention depended on what happened the second year. The results depended on whether or not the child received intensive, targeted instruction. Karweit (1999) explained that when children are retained because they have fallen behind, repeaters are actually repeating. They repeat by having very similar teachers, class size, grouping, instructional time, and the same content. The issue that affects the results of being retained is whether or not children are just being recycled through the old, or whether they received extra services specific to individual needs during the retention year (Karweit, 1999). Children who are falling behind academically need early identification and early, prescriptive remediation (Thompson & Cunningham, 2000).

TRANSITION CLASSES

Developmental kindergarten, prekindergarten, prefirst, readiness kindergarten, junior first grade, and kindergarten II are sometimes lumped together under the name of **transition classes**. These extra-year programs are viewed by some as a quick-fix alternative to retention (Ostrowski, 1994). They are attempts to provide for children who are age-eligible, but developmentally or academically not expected to succeed if they progress to the next grade.

Prefirst grade has been around for at least 50 years (Southard & May, 1996) with many school districts across the country expressing pride in offering transitional classes (Southard & May, 1996; Binkley, 1989; Horm-Wingerd, 1993; May & Kundert, 1993). One review indicated that from 50 to 80 percent of school districts offered transition classes (Matthews, May, & Kundert, 1999).

Despite the lack of evidence in support of transitional programs, Horm-Wingerd's (1993) survey of 78 first-grade teachers indicated that teachers supported transitional programs and believed them to be beneficial even though the practice is not upheld by research. Part of the problem in connecting teachers to research seems to be that there have been few longitudinal studies. Teachers see immediate improvement, but long-term results are invisible as children move on through the grades. Nevertheless, it is particularly important for teachers to be informed, because in most cases it is the teacher who recommends placements.

> Some schools offer special classes before and after kindergarten for children who are not ready to go on. What are the effects of those classes?

transition classes—extra-year classes before kindergarten or first grade

Transition classes do not equalize achievement.

What are the long-term results of transition classes?

Connell and Evans (1992) compared children who had participated in a transitional program after kindergarten to several other groups of children: those who had not been part of a transitional program; those who were recommended for the transitional program but did not participate; and retained students. When the children were in fourth grade, they took the Stanford Achievement Test and a self-concept test. Authors of the study reported no impact on achievement, but higher self-esteem for children who participated in the transitional first grade.

Although transition classes may be well-intentioned interventions to try to help children who lag behind academically, they do not equalize achievement levels (Karweit, 1999; Matthews, May, & Kundert, 1999). Transition classes have the same effect as grade retention (National Association of School Psychologists, 2002), they are expensive, and they delay a student's entry into the workforce.

If holding back does not work and promoting unprepared children does not work, what is a teacher to do with children who lag behind?

There is no magic dust to sprinkle over the heads of children who fall behind, but we might be wise to look at what the schools can do to accommodate and enable these children, rather than to blame and shame them. We have seen that early detection of trouble spots and immediate intervention targeted at specific problems is the course of action recommended by professionals. That solution is workable within the current structure of most schools.

There is also the option of changing the lockstep system of grades to better meet the needs of all children. There is really no need to maintain the egg-carton classrooms prevalent today. There is no need to perpetuate first, second, third grade classes for nine months, then succeed or fail to move on. Children's natural spurts and plateaus in all areas of development might be better accommodated if we were to move to grouping patterns that provided children with more time than one year to shape up or ship out. Looping, nongraded classes, multiyear primary units, and other innovative strategies better facilitate continuous progress for all children. But habits are hard to break—after all, we have always done it that way.

SUMMARY

The effects of retaining children vary with the comparisons made. When children the same age are compared, retention is not beneficial. When children in the same grade are compared, retention appears to be academically beneficial. But when we compare the gap in achievement between children who have and who have not been retained, we find that failing a grade reduces the gap for the short term, but not for the long term. Retention does not close the gap. Even after children are retained, they are still not generally performing adequately and do not catch up to their peers. There are social and emotional costs and stress associated with being retained at any level, including kindergarten. There are particularly strong correlations between being retained and dropping out of school.

Transition years are popular points for being retained. Holding children back is a policy that is frequently used nationwide. Better solutions to avoid the problem of promotion or retention include early detection and targeted intervention when children first begin to have academic problems. Multiage and multiyear variations in grouping children could provide alternatives to retention. However, transition classes and extra year programs appear to be as ineffective as grade retention if the goal is to equalize achievement.

Key Term

transition classes

Using What You Know

1. Visit a public school classroom or two and try to identify children who have been retained. Check your predictions with the teacher. What were the indications that influenced your answer? Have the retained children caught up? What is their academic standing with their peers?

2. During a field experience in the month of March, a college student was instructed by the teacher, "Ignore Mary and let her play with the things in her desk. She is going to fail, so it doesn't matter what she does the rest of the year. Spend your time with the other children." Using what you know, respond to that teacher.

For additional information on research-based practice, visit our Web site at http://www.earlychilded.delmar.com.

Chapter 9

How Does the Physical Environment Affect Young Children?

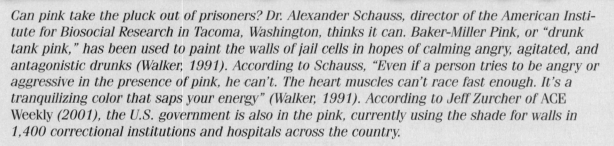

Can pink take the pluck out of prisoners? Dr. Alexander Schauss, director of the American Institute for Biosocial Research in Tacoma, Washington, thinks it can. Baker-Miller Pink, or "drunk tank pink," has been used to paint the walls of jail cells in hopes of calming angry, agitated, and antagonistic drunks (Walker, 1991). According to Schauss, "Even if a person tries to be angry or aggressive in the presence of pink, he can't. The heart muscles can't race fast enough. It's a tranquilizing color that saps your energy" (Walker, 1991). According to Jeff Zurcher of ACE Weekly (2001), the U.S. government is also in the pink, currently using the shade for walls in 1,400 correctional institutions and hospitals across the country.

Baker-Miller Pink, a color close to bubble gum, has also been used to paint the walls in football locker rooms—for the visiting team, that is. Whether or not pink takes the fight out of the adversary, assistant coach George Lumkin of the University of Hawaii complained when the visitor locker rooms at the University of Iowa and Colorado State University were painted pink. As a result, the Western Athletic Conference ruled that locker rooms may be painted any color, but it must be the same color for home team and visitor locker rooms (Zurcher, 2001).

Does pink really take the fight out of the warrior?

The claim is questionable, but it is a good example of how the environment might be used to manipulate behavior. Environmental psychology—the study of the interaction between environment and behavior—has something to say about how the environment might impact learning and behavior in schools as well as in jails and locker rooms.

THE INTERNAL SCHOOL ENVIRONMENT

Educators need to be aware of how color, temperature, ventilation, noise levels, lighting, and space affect learning. No one of these environmental elements will magically make all children gifted learners, but attention to the living conditions within the classroom promotes learning.

What are some of the classroom environmental features a teacher needs to be aware of in order to promote learning?

Color

When the principal invited the teachers to select new paint colors for classroom walls and bulletin boards, Miss Coville chose orange and pink. After two days of vibrating with the 24 children in her care, Miss Coville asked the principal for permission to repaint.

Color has been found to have varying effects on people. Several studies have indicated that cool colors such as blue and green tend to lower blood pressure and reduce behavior problems (Sydoriak, 1987; Pile, 1997). Soft, neutral colors are good for classrooms because they minimize glare, particularly when mild colors are also used on floors. Contrasts among areas of the room are then limited (Pile, 1997). On the other hand, stairs and hallways should be corridors of bright color in order to offer some stimulation while moving from one work area to another (Pile, 1997). Design experts suggest that preschool and kindergarten classrooms might be done in warm tones of stronger colors.

The classroom environment impacts learning.

Temperature, Humidity, and Ventilation

School room temperature, humidity, and ventilation are also key ingredients affecting learning and social behavior (Graetz & Goliber, 2002). Excessive heat has been shown to contribute to hostility (Graetz & Goliber, 2002), so thermostats should be set between 68 and 74 degrees Fahrenheit and humidity should be moderate (Schneider, 2002). Appropriate adjustments should be made when students are working in small groups or around a computer where temperatures could rise.

Good ventilation is particularly important because, in relation to body weight, children breathe a larger volume of air than do adults. That results in increased levels of carbon dioxide in the atmosphere, which can lead to headaches, drowsiness, and difficulty with concentration (Kennedy, 2001).

Noise

Noise pollution can be an additional environmental barrier to learning. External noise from sources such as lawnmowers, traffic, or barking dogs can interfere with achievement (Schneider, 2002). When there is excessive external noise, students become dissatisfied, feel stressed, and achieve less (Schneider, 2002).

Interior noise has also been associated with increased stress levels, which has the potential to interfere with teaching and learning. In a 1999 study of acoustics (Feth & Whitelaw, 1999), 32 classrooms were assessed for noise levels. Only two of the classrooms met the recommended standard set by the American Speech-Language-Hearing Association. Though classrooms must necessarily have some level of noise, high levels of noise have been found to interfere with achievement because noise interferes with concentration and attention. High levels of noise have also been related to increased behavior problems (Schneider, 2002).

Lighting

Consideration needs to be given to classroom lighting as an environmental factor that can influence learning. It has been argued that one type of artificial lighting is better than another, but the best lighting appears to be daylight (Schneider, 2002). Jago and Tanner (1999) recommend that 20 percent of classroom walls should be windows, with Tanner (2000) recommending that a basic classroom be built with a minimum of 72 square feet of windows to let in natural light. At a minimum there should be at least one window in each learning area.

There is some indication that fluorescent lighting could heighten physiological arousal, which may be problematic particularly for children who already have difficulty with impulse control (Graetz & Goliber, 2002). There is also some indication that fluorescent lighting might interfere with sociability (Kuller & Lindsten, 1992). Although lighting quality will not be the sole cause of one student's achievement and another's failure, both glare and dim lighting can cause discomfort, which could interfere with concentration and, as a result, impact achievement.

Daylight is the best light. There should be windows in learning areas.

Space

I have noticed that some classrooms are much smaller than others. Is there an optimum classroom size?

In the United States, each state sets standards for square footage requirements in its schools. As an advisory recommendation, the Council of Educational Facility Planners International (CEFPI) has made recommendations but cautions that curriculum, type of building, and geography should be taken into consideration when determining classroom size (Wohlers, 1995). There is great variation in sizes of classrooms across the country with smaller classrooms more common in the warmer, southern tier of states where it is easier to extend indoor spaces into the outdoors (Wohlers, 1995).

Tanner (2000) reasoned that adequate classroom size could be determined based on figures of personal social distance preferences (49 square feet per person in elementary school). The average classroom is

900 square feet. Therefore, if there are 20 or more children in an elementary classroom, the room is too small by 129 square feet. So, there should be no more than 17 children in the typical, 900 square foot classroom.

Whatever the classroom size, the defining factor of whether or not there is enough space has to do with density. How many people occupy the space? What kind of activity is expected in the space? Overcrowding has been related to stress, overstimulation, arousal, reduced privacy, loss of control, and aggression (Tanner, 2000). When too many people are in too little space, problems erupt.

Nevertheless, it is important to be aware that feelings of being crowded are culturally variable. The personal space required for feeling comfortable and preference for social distance may be different for individuals within the classroom, including the teacher. When that personal comfort zone is violated, individuals may feel stress. In turn, when others maintain more social distance than is preferred, the environment is also uncomfortable. This emotional discomfort leads to movement toward or away from the other individuals in the environment in an effort to restore comfortable distance (Graetz & Goliber, 2002).

Overcrowding has been related to aggression, stress, and loss of control.

OUTDOOR ENVIRONMENTAL FACTORS

Are there environmental factors that work to affect behavior in the schoolyard?

Many of the studies of school playgrounds and outdoor facilities take the form of anecdotal reports and qualitative accounts. There is a need for controlled studies of how outdoor school spaces relate to achievement and behavior. In a major study of outdoor space, the review of the literature found reports of impressions, but little empirical research evidence (Education Development Center, 2000).

We do find that traditional playgrounds are dangerous. Annually, school playgrounds are the sites of 17 fatalities and approximately 170,100 injuries serious enough to require an emergency room visit (Education Development Center, 2000).

Of the limited research base available, a study by Ledingham (1998) provided some possible insight into different uses of playground areas by subjects who were considered behavior problem children. Sometimes the subjects played on structures like slides and climbers. Other times they played in areas where there was no equipment. When children played on structures, they played alone. But when they played in areas with no equipment, they played with others.

Mood was also correlated with where children played. When children were playing in remote areas of the schoolyard, their moods were negative; but when they were playing on structures, they demonstrated more positive affect (Ledingham, 1998). It would be interesting to know whether mood affected choice of play area, or whether playing in an area brought on the feelings. Mood and play were also related to social skills. The children with strong social skills played in more areas than did the children who were either aggressive or withdrawn (Ledingham, 1998).

Our knowledge of how the outdoor environment interacts with children's learning and behavior is limited, indeed. With future rigorous, controlled studies, the knowledge base could be strengthened.

CLASS SIZE

Class size and **pupil/teacher ratio** are two different terms used to discuss relationships of professional staff to children. Class size refers to the number of children for each teacher in a classroom. It is simply a matter of counting children, teachers, and classrooms. However, it is important to note that the concept of class size is different from the concept of pupil/teacher ratio. When pupil/teacher ratio is computed, the school nurse, psychologist, librarian, and everyone else on the professional staff are counted as teachers. Therefore, a pupil/teacher ratio figure could lead one to believe that there are fewer children in a classroom than there actually are. It is important to keep that distinction in mind when looking at the class size research.

At this writing the National Center for Education Statistics reports an average of 21 students in each self-contained classroom at the elementary school level, excluding special education units where classes are quite small. Across the nation, state averages range from a low of 17 to a high of 24 students per classroom. Sparsely populated states tend to have

class size—ratio of children to teachers

pupil/teacher ratio—ratio of children to all professional school personnel

the smallest numbers. Maine, Montana, Nebraska, North Dakota, South Carolina, Wyoming, and Vermont average from 17 to 18 students per teacher. Arizona, Oregon, Utah, and Washington are highest at 24 students per classroom.

For some years the education community has been looking to pinpoint the optimum class size for gains in student achievement. The debate has become political with special interest groups such as teachers' unions supporting smaller classes and conservative groups such as the Heritage Foundation downplaying the need to reduce class size. The issue has even become partisan with Democrats pushing for funding to reduced class size and Republicans lukewarm to such measures. Nevertheless, federal legislation was passed allocating $1.2 billion in 1999 and $1.3 billion more in 2000 for hiring more teachers with the effect of reducing class sizes to 18 or fewer. Funds were targeted at high-poverty and high-enrollment districts. States have joined the effort as well, with 32 states implementing various class-size reduction programs and/or limiting class size by law (*Education Week,* 2003).

With all that money going toward making classes smaller, lawmakers must be confident that small classes work. Is there research to back up spending big dollars to reduce class sizes?

Some of the early studies were small, did not control for the influence of other variables, or involved just one school or district. It was difficult to draw meaningful conclusions from the data until the meta-analysis technique was introduced. Meta-analysis of earlier studies indicated that small classes of fewer than 20 students were related to short-term, small gains that were greatest in the early grades. Those gains were particularly helpful to children who were from disadvantaged backgrounds (Biddle & Berliner, 2002). But what was really needed was a large, rigorous, experimental study—a study that could show definitively the effects of smaller classes.

Then, in the mid-1980s the state of Tennessee took a highly unusual step. The State undertook a four-year study to find out whether small classes were really better after all. Tennessee's project STAR (Student/Teacher Achievement Ratio) has been touted as one of the best-designed studies in the history of educational research. The project studied children in three different classroom conditions: standard classroom with one teacher and 20 or more children; standard classroom plus the supplement of an untrained, full-time aide; and small class of about 15 children per teacher. Children under study entered kindergarten in 1985 and spent four years in the same class configuration. Children and teachers were randomly assigned. There were 79 schools, 328 classrooms, and 6,300 students, and all district types were included in the study (Finn & Achilles, 1990).

Did children in small classes learn more?

Children took a standardized achievement test. When scores of children in the standard classes were compared to those in standard classes supplemented with a teacher's aide, there were no differences in scores. But, children in the small classes of 15 made significant gains in achievement in all the areas tested. And those scores got better and better the longer students had been in the small classes. The largest gains were for minorities and children who attended inner-city schools. Gains were equal for boys and girls.

The achievement gains were long-term. Even when children went back to standard-sized classes in the upper grades, they maintained the advantage (Biddle & Berliner, 2002).

Perhaps the best indication came later with the realization that the benefits were truly lasting. By the time students had reached high school, children who had been in small classes had better grades, fewer grade retentions, and fewer dropouts than children who had been in the standard classes of 20 or more. In addition, the small class students took more advanced-level courses and enrolled in more foreign language classes. Compared to others, more of the small class students took the SAT and ACT tests for college entrance, and more of the small class size students were in the top quarter of their high school classes. And, adding frosting to the cake, the positive effects of small classes were largest for children who had been considered disadvantaged (Finn & Achilles, 1990).

> **Did the small-class children maintain their gains, or did the effects wash out once they got older and went back to larger classes?**

The study is respected as a strong, well-designed experiment. However, it is just one study, and we know that it is unwise to make decisions based on the results of one experiment. We also need to keep in mind that Tennessee schools are not a nationally representative sample. It could also be that schools where people willingly volunteered to participate in the study were different from schools where people did not volunteer and that difference could have affected the results. It is also possible that participants could have been influenced by news reports proclaiming the gains in achievement during the first year or two of the study (Biddle & Berliner, 2002). Though those concerns should be kept in mind, there is general respect for the results of the rigorous STAR study.

> **Was there any downside to the STAR study?**

Small classes bring academic and social advantages.

Have other states or districts experimented with class size?

There have been similar studies undertaken on a smaller scale in North Carolina, Michigan, New York, and Nevada. Even though the studies had fewer children and fewer districts, the results of decreased class size were similar to the positive results from the STAR project. In Wisconsin, the SAGE project pilot study, which reduced K–3 class size to 15, was so successful that the legislature hot-wired the project and went statewide with small classes. Indiana's Project Prime Time did the same with the entire state reducing K–3 classes to 18 children. When small-class students were compared to children in districts that did not participate in Project Prime Time, students who had been in the smaller classes scored better in both reading and math (Biddle & Berliner, 2002).

Florida passed a constitutional amendment requiring the state to fund reductions in class size. Maximum sizes are being reduced by 2 each year so that by 2010 preK–3 classes will be at 18; grades 4–8 at 22; and grades 9–12 at 25 (Rose, 2003).

Spurred by Tennessee's success with project STAR, California jumped on the smaller classes bandwagon. However, California's experience was problematic, moving quickly without a pilot study or ample time to implement a huge program allocating $1 billion a year to reduce all K–3 class sizes. Begun in the fall of 1996, California's class-reduction program saw only small gains in test scores. Whereas Tennessee had conducted a controlled experiment, California jumped in full speed ahead without ample preparation time and without the necessary qualified teacher pool (Stecher, Bohrnstedt, Kirst, McRobbie, & Williams, 2001). In addition, California's school population is much more diverse and requires more special services for non-English speakers than does the school population in Tennessee.

Why do small class sizes work? What do teachers do differently?

Though there have been several proposals and multiple opinions to explain the connection between smaller classes and improved achievement, we are not able to explain the why. Classroom climate is a multifaceted, complex factor. We do understand that most studies indicate an association between reduced class size in the early grades and long-term achievement gains, particularly when the student has spent longer times in small class placements (Biddle & Berliner, 2002). Are teachers changing what they are doing in the classroom? It does not appear so. A study of California teachers indicated that they did not change their teaching strategies or the content they covered when the size of their classes was reduced (Stecher et al., 2001; Achilles, 1999). Some authorities have called for professional development training prior to reducing the size of classes so that teachers will be prepared to take full advantage of learning opportunities associated with small class sizes.

If small class size is an advantage, is small school size also an advantage?

SCHOOL SIZE

School size is an issue that has been related to history in the United States. Before 1948 most schools in the country were small, with about 30 students and 1 teacher at the elementary school level (Howley, 2002). Gradually consolidations changed the scene. When roads improved and districts considered the academic advantages of more central locations, the economic benefits won out, one by one closing the doors of the smallest schools.

But it took a national shock wave to put the consolidation movement into full swing. When the Soviet Union launched Sputnik in 1957, the event was received in this country with a sense of national disappointment, fear, and doom. There was disappointment that another nation could be more technologically advanced than ours, and fear that the same technology that launched the first satellite would be used by our enemy against us. But we were not to take the insult lying down. The space race was on. The nation was determined to beat the Soviets at their own game.

As an issue of national defense, the schools were called upon to prepare scientifically savvy students. We needed science labs, more math classes, and foreign language labs in order to win the race and defend ourselves. School consolidation appeared to be the answer. Large schools could more easily provide advanced subjects, offer variety, allow for ability tracking, and save educational dollars. The influential Conant Report of 1959 called for consolidation in the name of efficiency and effectiveness. The call was heard, and more small-school doors were closed.

Large schools became even larger. Some educators began to wonder whether students had become detached, lost, just a number in such large settings. Like so many issues in education, the question of school size has been raised again. But this time the question is not "How large can we go?" but rather "How small is small enough?"

The movement toward smaller schools has found both popular and financial support as indicated by the $250 million allocated by the Bill and Melinda Gates Foundation specifically to reduce high school size. The current trend to reduce school size has focused mostly on the secondary school level, but there are also implications for primary schools.

What is the best size school?

A California study (Friedkin & Necochea, 1988) reported that students living in low socioeconomic status communities did better in small schools. But students living in high socioeconomic status communities did somewhat better in larger schools. Supporting those findings, Huang and Howley (1993) reported that small elementary schools provided a positive achievement advantage, and that advantage was most pronounced for children who were disadvantaged.

A group of researchers who understood the value of replicating, or repeating, research to give strength to our understanding and interpretations undertook a huge project. They wanted to know the answer to the question: Is there a relationship between school size and student achievement? If so, what is the best size for a school? A series of studies called the Matthew Project was undertaken to examine the effects of school size in a systematic manner and replicate the research in a number of locations and regions to validate the findings (Howley, Strange, & Bickel, 2000). The study encompassed every school in Montana, Georgia, Ohio, and Texas.

Did the size of the school have any relationship to students' achievement?

After examining all those schools in all those places, researchers discovered—like those mentioned earlier—that the optimal size of the school is different for different communities. The best size to promote student achievement depended on the socioeconomic status of the community

(Howley et al., 2000). If the community was affluent, students did better academically in larger schools. But if the community was impoverished, students did better academically in smaller schools. For optimum achievement, the poorer the community, the smaller the school should be.

How small is small enough?

To reduce the effects of poverty, Lee and Smith (1996) recommended limiting school size to 300 or fewer students at the elementary level. The current elementary school average enrollment is 477. Optimum size for high schools was set between 601 and 900 students. Others have set similar limits (Howley et al., 2000). Nevertheless, optimum size is probably more complex than setting a number based on poverty or wealth of the community. Other factors such as the location (urban or rural), curricular focus (comprehensive or special purpose), sector (public or private), and span of grades in a building all need to be considered as part of the building size issue (Howley et al., 2000).

How does the span of grades in a building change the size of the school? Isn't school size just head count?

There are two ways to determine school size. One way is to count heads. Another way is to look at grade span and its implications. Grade span has to do with how many grade levels are in a school. When the grade span is reduced, the number of students at each grade level increases. It has been proposed that the school then takes on characteristics associated with a large school (Howley, 2001). It is an interesting concept to consider, but has not been verified in the research base.

Is there a best way to group grades?

There are a number of popular grade configurations, with K–5, K–6, 6–8, 7–9, and 9–12 among the most common (Howley, 2002). However, there is no firm foundation of research to guide decision-making. So we cannot say with certainty that any one plan is better than another.

We do have evidence that moving from one school to the next may have a negative effect on achievement (Alspaugh, 1998). When grade span is reduced, there are more transitions as the student progresses from kindergarten through high school. According to Alspaugh (2000), as the number of school-to-school transitions increases, so does the rate of dropping out. Furthermore, Alspaugh determined that there is a loss of achievement in the year of the transition, followed by a year of recovery to the level before the move. In that study there was less achievement loss in the students who entered high school after attending a K–8 school. There was more achievement loss for students who had attended a middle school prior to high school.

Alspaugh's findings were supported by research in Texas and Louisiana where the K–12 school configuration was associated with achievement gains, particularly for lower socioeconomic status students (Howley, 2002). The term "elemiddle" was coined to describe this combination elementary and middle grades configuration that appears to connect the stability and continuity of continuous placement with increased achievement (Hough, 1995).

It appears that the transitioning, or school-to-school movement, may be detrimental academically and socially (Gregg, 2003). Children who are in one building for a short time have less chance to build a sense of school spirit and pride. There is little time to build a sense of community, a social unity. When grade configurations are narrow, the number of transitions increases, and so do the negative effects. It has been suggested that to improve achievement, we need to use smaller schools and a broad grade span (Gregg, 2003).

In their review of grade-span configurations, Coladarci and Hancock (2002) suggest that rather than ask which grade configuration is best, we should ask whether grade configuration matters at all, and if so, why. Howley (2002) cautions that we should ask how best to organize, not which grade span or grade configuration is best.

The lack of definitive research may not be important to school district officials who must deal with school building location, population distributions, building space, community preferences, and financial considerations when determining grade configurations. Because there are so many practical limitations on organization, decisions about grade configuration may need to be made on factors other than what might be the best pattern to promote achievement.

SUMMARY

Environmental factors affect student achievement and behavior in the school building and schoolyard. Color use, temperature, ventilation, noise levels, lighting, and space can affect learning and emotion. Comfort zones for personal space vary by culture and need to be considered when planning size of classrooms, use of space, and activities. Density is the key factor in determining whether or not space is adequate. Overcrowding influences behavior negatively and interferes with achievement.

Research on schoolyard environmental influences is limited but indicates that environmental influences may change children's play and socialization practices, using different areas of the schoolyard to satisfy different social and emotional needs.

There is no one perfect class size, but there are strong indications that small class sizes in the primary grades are correlated with increased achievement both in the short term and over time, even being correlated with better high school performance and lower dropout rates. The success of Tennessee's project STAR spurred other states to implement class size reductions. Although class size reductions benefit both boys and girls, there appears to be particular benefit for children of poverty.

Small schools may also provide an achievement advantage, and that advantage may be greater for children who are otherwise disadvantaged. Children living in middle-class neighborhoods, however, may do better in larger schools. School size is impacted by the span of grades located in a building. Reducing the span of grades increases the number of children at a given grade level, creating a climate more similar to large schools. Children who attend schools with small grade spans are faced with more school-to-school transitions, which some researchers have reported have negative effects on achievement and increase stress.

Grade configurations are often determined based on population and other factors unrelated to achievement. When students attend K–8 or K–12 schools, there is some indication that achievement is strengthened. As in many areas of educational concern, we need more empirical evidence before we can make definitive choices about important environmental factors affecting children in and around schools.

Key Terms

class size
pupil/teacher ratio

Using What You Know

1. Find out the average class size for a local elementary school. How does it compare to national figures? What local characteristics impact class size?

2. Survey your friends to find out what grade configurations they experienced in their K–12 education. Which are most popular? What do friends report as positive or negative features of those grade configurations?

3. Observe children and teachers working in classrooms and on playgrounds. What environmental factors do you see impacting achievement and behavior?

4. Compare the density of learning spaces in two different schools. Do you observe effects of overcrowding?

For additional information on research-based practice, visit our Web site at http://www.earlychilded.delmar.com.

Chapter 10

What Do We Know About Guidance and Discipline?

Portions of this chapter are excerpted from an article written by Sandra Crosser and published in *Early Childhood News*, September/October 1997, pages 6–12. Copyrighted by Excelligence Learning Corporation and reprinted with permission.

I don't know much about the game of football. But my son plays, so it is time to learn. The table between us becomes a football field as he coaches me in the basics. When the waitress arrives with our order, number 61 calls a time out.

"What about time-outs?" I ask. "Is that when you rest?"

"No, Mom," he laughs. "There is a strategy to calling time outs."

At once I am learning more than either of us intended. I think back to Ralph, a kindergarten boy I observed over several months. Ralph was stuck in a permanent time out beside the teacher's desk. Ralph learned a lot during his isolation. For example, he learned how to scoot his chair swiftly across the tile floor to sit beside me and whisper important stuff. When asked why he wasn't sitting with the other children, Ralph admitted that he was being punished. He didn't know why.

That is terrible for Ralph! But the teacher does need to maintain discipline. Is there a better way to deal with children who misbehave?

In this chapter we look at some of the research that might inform decisions about guidance and discipline. We examine how particular styles of adult/ child interaction may impact behavior. And we consider how the concepts of punishment, reward, and praise fit in the guidance and discipline picture.

GUIDANCE VERSUS DISCIPLINE

discipline—managing children's behavior

The term **discipline** has come to be equated with punishment. We speak of a parent needing to discipline a child who behaves in inappropriate ways. We call for more discipline in the classroom. We speak of a teacher having good discipline and children who need it. The yoke of discipline will make the unruly stay in line as they plod along the path of compliance. We keep a good supply of discipline on the pantry shelf, mete it out, and serve it up as needed.

guidance—helping children learn to manage their own behavior

Over the past decade, the harsh and punitive connotation associated with discipline has led some educators to favor the term **guidance** instead. Whereas the discipline approach creates the image of the teacher as policeman and judge, the guidance approach presents the teacher more in the role of a coach or trainer. The view of the child is quite different as well. The discipline approach casts children in the role of herds of cattle in need of constant patrol and control to avoid the feared stampede. The guidance perspective envisions children in the role of athlete in training.

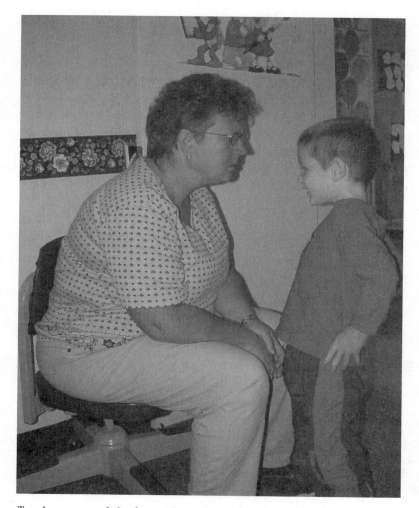

Teacher as coach in the guidance approach.

The difference between the discipline approach and the guidance approach can be illustrated by Ralph's situation in time-out. In response to some error in behavior, the teacher determined that Ralph should be isolated from the group activities where his unacceptable behavior was somehow being reinforced—perhaps through attention from other children.

Time-out reduces aggressive behavior, decreases self-injury behavior such as head banging, and reduces noncompliant behavior or refusal to do what the adult requests (Turner & Watson, 1999). From the discipline perspective, time-out is effective. Time-out prevents children from engaging in an activity that has the effect of reinforcing, or making the child feel good. Time-out is supposed to be uncomfortable because the child would rather be engaging in ongoing activities. Isolated and bored, the child should repent, change his wicked ways, and once again become an acceptable member of the group.

What is Ralph instructed to do in time-out? "Ralph, go to time-out. You sit there and think about what you did!"

Although Ralph can get himself to the dreaded chair, he will not logically analyze what he did because he cannot (Katz, 1984; Schreiber, 1999). It is beyond Ralph's developmental level to independently engage in logical analysis.

If we look at time-out from a guidance perspective, we see the strategy through different glasses. The child might be removed from a situation to cool down, but not as punishment. The teacher helps the child examine the troublesome behavior the child exhibited. Together the child and teacher

Should time-out be thrown out?

search for alternate, acceptable behaviors the child could use next time the situation arises. The child is empowered, learns self-discipline, and has a tool to use next time. This represents the guidance perspective.

But the discipline perspective has translated the concept of time-out from the world of sports to the world of the classroom in a different sense, and something has been lost in that translation. Teachers, as well as coaches, need a strategy for calling time-out. Let's look at those strategies.

TIME-OUT STRATEGIES

In the world of football, there is a limit on the number of time-outs that may be called, and there is a set, short timeline during which they must be concluded. There is always a purpose to the time-out, and the team huddles together to plan how to achieve the goal. A time-out may be called by an official when an injury has occurred, by a quarterback when he finds the defense has confounded the planned play, or by a coach. When a coach calls a time-out, it is for one of three reasons: to tell the team what they are doing wrong, to plan what to do next, or to pump up the players. Coaches never call a time-out when their team has momentum. However, calling a time-out may work to break the opponent's momentum. Therefore, a time-out is a strategic maneuver used to advance the team's effectiveness.

Just as in football, there should be a strategy for calling a time-out.

In Football, Time-outs Are Limited in Number and Duration

On the field, players and coaches must use time-outs frugally. The allotted time is short, so there is no time for punishment. Just like football players, young children are often aware immediately after an infraction that they have done something wrong. Newman and Newman (1997, p. 409) caution that "extensive punishment or shaming at that point serves only to generate a child's anxiety and further disorganize thinking rather than to reinforce the child's internal recognition of an inappropriate act." Time-out is an opportunity for a child to learn social skills. It is not an appropriate time to punish.

Any disciplinary strategy that is overused becomes ineffective. Time-out should never become the answer to every problematic situation and most certainly should never become permanent as in Ralph's case. If she chooses to use the time-out technique, the teacher must be selective in deciding when time-out is appropriate. If things are getting out of hand in the block area, perhaps the teacher could call all the block players together for a time-out huddle to solve the problem. This positive use of time-out stops the negative momentum and gives children the opportunity to regroup.

On the other hand, it would seem important to note that calling a time-out might be terribly inappropriate on those occasions when children have built up a positive learning momentum. If minds are clicking and exciting discoveries are being made, adult interruption would interfere with the child's growth. Never call a time-out when your team has momentum.

Never call a time-out when your team has momentum.

In Football, Time-out Is Purposeful

Because classroom time-out is a disciplinary tactic, we need to think about the purpose of discipline in the early childhood setting. If the purpose is to maintain a safe environment for children, then certainly a time-out similar to an official's time-out may be appropriate, especially when children are about to engage in dangerous behavior or if someone has been injured.

However, the larger, more encompassing goal for discipline must be to promote the development of self-regulation or self-control. The goal is for the child to rely more and more on her own inner resources and less and less on external control of her behavior.

According to Kopp (1987), self-regulation first becomes possible during the second year when the child has developed a sense of herself as a separate person with individual control over her actions; has reached a level of cognitive maturity that permits her to remember and internalize what adults have said; and has applied the stated rules of behavior to her own actions. As these abilities develop, the child will show evidence of compliance with adult requests. If the child willingly complies with adult directives, we know she is cognitively mature enough to benefit from strategies directed at developing self-control (Kaler & Kopp, 1990).

As language abilities develop, the child may use private speech to inhibit her own behaviors (Luria, 1961) as she tells herself, "No! No!" (Kochanska, 1993). If the child has reached a cognitive level that permits the development of self-control, then disciplinary strategies should be carefully selected to further that development.

Is time-out a strategy that can foster self-control?

That depends on how it is used. If the child is simply isolated on a time-out chair or sent to sit in his cubby for a few minutes, he may learn something, but he will not learn self-control. He will not have learned to apply socially acceptable alternative behaviors in future situations. In addition, he will not have learned to show empathy or to explain why what he did was wrong. However, he may have learned to avoid the punitive adult.

In order for discipline to teach self-control and morality, it must incorporate four elements (Newman & Newman, 1997):

1. Assisting the child in stopping the undesirable behavior

2. Helping the child discover an acceptable alternative behavior to use in the future

3. Providing understandable reasons for the wrongness or rightness of an act

4. Helping the child take the perspective of those who were wronged by his/her actions

Traditional time-out for misbehavior addresses only the first element. It stops or interrupts the undesirable behavior, but it does nothing to build self-control or moral understanding. Therefore, for time-out to be an effective disciplinary tactic, it must be followed by time-in—time spent with the child developing understanding, empathy, and alternative behaviors.

Baumrind (1971) and Martin (1975) found that if children did not understand why they were being punished, their level of aggression increased. Children need to understand the reasons for their punishment.

In time-out, children feel disliked, ignored, and under stress.

In Football, the Team Huddles for Time-out

Just as group problem-solving on the football field involves all the football players, so should group problem-solving involve all the classroom players. When conflicts arise, all involved players benefit from being guided as they negotiate a solution. At times, it may be beneficial for the whole group to problem solve together. Children who are bystanders can often offer helpful suggestions.

In Football, Time-out Is an Opportunity to Coach

In football, the coach calls a time-out to help the players see where they are going wrong or what they need to do next. He may use a time-out simply to pump up the players. These strategies are also appropriate in the classroom. Children often solve their problems without adult intervention. However, there are other times when it becomes necessary for the adult to call a stop to the action in order to coach or guide children as they learn the rules of socialization. Self-regulation is a learned behavior. Therefore, the teacher must coach children in self-discipline as surely as she must coach them in mathematical concepts.

In Football, the Quarterback Can Call a Time-out

If the quarterback steps up to the line and sees the defense set up in such a way that the planned play just will not work, the quarterback may call a time-out. Yes, one of the players may see a need to stop the action and make another plan.

Should children, as classroom players, be permitted to make the same judgment? Could children call their own time-out? Could children and teachers agree on a signal to be used when a child feels the need to stop the action and regroup for the good of the participants? Children can be taught the importance of planning together and changing plans in socially acceptable ways if the teacher coaches them in how and when to call a time-out appropriately. In this way, independence and autonomy are fostered as children learn they have increasing control over and responsibility for their actions.

Is time-out a developmentally appropriate practice?	Time-out may be an appropriate alternative to more coercive disciplinary tactics. If a child is out of control, a time-out may serve as a period for her to calm down and regain composure. A short period of time away from the conflict may provide the space necessary for her to regain self-control so that she will be receptive to more effective guidance techniques. But it is important that the child does not perceive the time-out as punishment. The child may need to be quietly rocked or gently held while she regains composure. This form of time-out is soothing and helps the child become ready to think and talk about the problem calmly. If the child is not receptive to physical comfort, she may be told, in a matter-of-fact manner, to get a drink of water or go to a quiet place for a few moments and get ready to talk about the problem.

In cases where time-out is not a particularly appropriate strategy to use with young children, what strategies could be effectively substituted?	Research gives us several clues.

- Engage the child in reasoning combined with warmth and loving care (Zahn-Waxler, Radke-Yarrow, & King, 1979).

- Give explanations that appeal to the child's concern for others, their pride, and acting grown up (Eisenberg, 1992).

- Explicitly model and teach the behaviors children are expected to imitate (Fukushima & Kato, 1976).

- If punishment is used, it should be accompanied by a verbal rationale that the child understands (Berke, 1997).

- Avoid demanding and controlling strategies that increase defiance (Kucsynski, Kochanska, Radke-Yarrow, & Girnius-Brown, 1987).

How do children view time-out?	Readdick and Chapman (2000) interviewed young children after they had been placed in time-out. Most of the children had been sent to the chair for not complying with a teacher request. Over half the children said that they believed they deserved to be in time-out, and most knew what they needed to do to get out. Though children reported that they felt safe when they were in time-out, they also felt all alone, disliked by the teacher, and ignored by their peers.

Some of the children, like Ralph, experienced time-out more frequently than others. The frequent visitors reported different feelings. They reported being more alone, more scared, sadder, and more disliked. Those children said they knew why they were in time-out, but only about half were able to supply answers that accurately reflected the reasons as recorded by observers.

PUNISHMENT

When punishment is administered, the purpose is to stop a behavior and someone other than the child is in control. Though punishment may bring momentary or situational compliance, the behavior may reappear when the punisher leaves. For example, the children may be working quietly until the teacher steps out of the room. Then rules are broken, and children act in ways they would not act if the teacher were present.

The teacher then returns and administers punishment. The punishment works to stop the misbehavior while the teacher is around. Therefore, the teacher is likely to continue to use punishment as a regular technique because he has been reinforced (Kohn, 1993). Because punishment brings temporary behavior improvement, the teacher perceives punishment as an effective strategy and continues to use it. Nevertheless, punishment alone does nothing to teach alternative, appropriate behavior. The child who is punished for misbehavior has learned to avoid the punisher or not get caught. He has not learned self-discipline. He has not learned anything about controlling himself. He has not learned what he might do next time.

Young children are developmentally, or naturally, egocentric. This puts them at particular emotional risk because children who are egocentric tend to label themselves. According to Elkind (1976) this developmental egocentrism causes children who are harshly punished to internalize shame and conclude that they are not good people. The younger the child, the less he understands about social behavior and the less capable he is of connecting the punishment to his actions rather than to his self-definition. Children do not have a stable sense of their moral identity before they are about six or seven years old. That means that it is particularly important for four- and five-year-olds to experience guidance rather than harsh punishment as they are learning social skills and developing a healthy sense of themselves as good people.

Very young children may actually define right and wrong by whether or not one would be punished for the act (Kohlberg, 1968). For example, it is wrong to hit your brother because you will get sent to your room. The child defines morality on the basis of whether or not the behavior will be punished. Therefore, if a child is to gain an internal understanding of morality, he must be helped to see the reasoning behind labels of right and wrong. Punishing a child for an infraction does not promote moral understanding. On the other hand, the guidance approach pairs reasoning, or induction, with appropriately high standards for behavior. The guidance approach assumes that the child is in the process of learning to be socialized.

Children learn how to navigate social expectations best when standards are clear and are consistently enforced. The effects of consistency in reprimanding children for behavior infractions was studied by Acker and O'Leary (1996). Moms all talked on the telephone for 12 minutes while their toddlers played with toys nearby. Of course the researchers expected the toddlers to do what toddlers normally do: interrupt the telephone

> It is sad to think about young children being excluded and left feeling scared, sad, and disliked. But don't children need to be punished when they do something wrong?

conversations. And that is just what they did. The toddlers banged toys, climbed on mom, cried, and pulled on the telephone cord.

But moms were instructed to respond in specific ways. There were three conditions: moms who reprimanded every inappropriate demand of the toddlers; moms who reprimanded half of the demands and ignored the other half; and moms who reprimanded half of the demands and gave in to the other half.

Children displayed the most negative and intrusive behaviors when mothers were inconsistent. The worst behavior occurred when moms reprimanded half of the time and gave in the other half of the time. It appears that children need to be able to predict what the caregiver will do on a consistent basis or they become confused.

If punishment is used, it should be consistent and combined with reason. Then a child can make the connection between the act and the consequence and learn how to behave appropriately if circumstances present themselves again. Reason and mild punishment reduce misbehavior (Larzelere, Schneider, Larson, & Pike, 1996).

However, some children endure harsh punishment in their homes. When children experience strong punishment at home, they tend to exhibit high levels of aggressive and defiant behavior outside of the home (Strassberg, Dodge, Pettit, & Bates, 1994). They have learned, or become socialized, to behave in aggressive ways. When aggression is modeled by real people who are perceived as powerful, children tend to imitate that aggression (Bandura, 1977).

> I think it must be better for children to be positively motivated. Is it good practice to give children stickers and other little tokens?

REWARDS

Teachers engage in rewarding children to motivate them, to praise them, to obtain compliance, to make children obey, and to entice other children to obey. Because rewards are so frequently handed out in early childhood classrooms, it is particularly important for teachers to examine the implications of such a seemingly innocent and well-intended gesture as giving a child a sticker.

Mike may be motivated to run a race because he truly wants to do it. He enjoys the training and gains satisfaction from completing the challenge. That is intrinsic motivation. Dave enjoys other activities and does not want to run in the race. However, Dave is broke and needs money. Mike offers Dave $50 to train and race with him. That is external motivation. The reward entices Dave to do what he otherwise has no desire to do.

It has been suggested that rewards are simply efforts at control—control by seduction (Kohn, 1993). Teachers need to examine the issues surrounding rewards and then decide the wisdom and ethics involved in purposefully manipulating the behavior of other individuals.

In a review of the literature, Kohn (1993) reported that rewards had been found to

- undermine creativity.
- result in immediate, but not lasting change.
- drag down performance level when promised in advance.

■ create competition and anxiety if there are not enough rewards for everyone.

■ discourage risk-taking.

■ affect the relationship between person rewarded and person handing out rewards.

■ reduce intrinsic, or internal, motivation.

In addition, Kohn (1993) concluded that when people are rewarded for a behavior, they tend to choose easier tasks. Work becomes less productive and more stereotyped. For example, if children are rewarded for reading library books, they tend to select short, less challenging books to get them to the reward as quickly as possible. The bigger the reward, the easier the selected task. The child heads straight for the reward, does just what is necessary to obtain the reward, and does not explore side roads, take chances, or look at possibilities along the way.

There is an ongoing debate about the relationship between extrinsic rewards and intrinsic motivation. There is some indication that extrinsic rewards may reduce a person's intrinsic desire to engage in the activity or do the task. If Miranda likes to read and we offer her a reading incentive like free pizza, will the reward decrease her desire to read?

A researcher observed Head Start children playing learning games. The children were rewarded for playing the games, but they lost interest when the rewards were gone (Lepper, Greene, & Nisbett, 1973). The same researcher visited different Head Start sites and noticed that children were playing eagerly with the same games, but they had not been rewarded for their play. This was one of the first of many investigations into the question of any relationship between rewards and decreased interest in tasks. The researchers continue to argue one way and the other.

Intrinsic motivation   **Extrinsic motivation**   **Reduced effort**

Extrinsic motivation in the form of rewards may reduce effort.

Cameron and Pierce (1994) used the meta-analysis technique to explore the issue. They concluded that

■ rewards do not decrease intrinsic motivation.

■ praise increases intrinsic motivation.

■ when rewards are given just for doing a task and do not specify any level of quality, there is a small negative effect on intrinsic motivation.

Cameron and Pierce included praise as a reward. Does praise have the same effect as other more tangible rewards?

PRAISE

There is no indication that praise and achievement are correlated, but results are mixed on praise and intrinsic motivation (Kohn, 1993). Some studies reported that subjects were more interested in the task when they were praised, but other studies reported either no change or less interest in the task.

We do know that praise needs to be sincere, particularly after third grade. Before third grade, children tend to see achievement as a result of the interaction of effort and ability, but as children grow older they become more aware of the limits of ability. So, when older children are praised for a task they consider to be fairly simple, they may misinterpret the praise as an indication that they are not smart enough to do something harder (Henderlong & Lepper, 2002).

Doesn't the whole issue of discipline and guidance boil down to individual differences? Don't punishment and rewards and praise have different effects on different individuals?

temperament—individual style of interaction with others and the environment

difficult temperament—individual is intense, irregular, negative, approaches cautiously, dislikes change

easy temperament—individual is regular, positive, adjusts to change

slow-to-warm-up temperament —individual is shy, quiet, cautious, slightly negative

TEMPERAMENT

Individual differences in personality, or **temperament**, are evident even soon after birth and continue to affect our interactions throughout life. We tend to approach the world with a particular pattern of interaction. Some babies cry and fuss a good deal of the time, whereas others seem content to go anywhere, put up with their parents, and eat and sleep quite regularly. Those differences in how individuals adapt to and interact within their environment tend to be fairly stable over time.

Thomas and Chess (1977) were the first to describe subjects in terms of temperament. Through observations and interviews, the researchers identified characteristics that were common to three general classifications. Thomas and Chess identified three temperament types: **difficult**; **easy**; and **slow-to-warm-up**.

Difficult children tend to be irregular in their body rhythms. They seldom follow a routine for eating, sleeping, and eliminating. Difficult temperament types approach the world cautiously, with an overall negative attitude and resistance to change. They adapt slowly, may be persistent, but respond with intensity. The difficult child may laugh extra hard, cry extra hard, and throw an impressive tantrum.

The slow-to-warm-up temperament type enters into new situations only after checking everything out. She may hesitate or observe before entering into activities, and may be uncomfortable meeting new people or trying new things. She approaches the world with a slightly negative attitude and demonstrates rather mild emotional reactions.

The easy personality is into routines for sleeping, eating, and eliminating. He likely awakes at about the same time each morning with a smile on his face. He is positive, quickly adapts to change, is eager to try new things, smiles, and laughs frequently.

Not all the Thomas and Chess subjects were easy to classify, as some were inconsistent and could not be placed in any of the three categories. Nevertheless, it is commonly recognized that differences in temperament do exist and are important components of personality, affecting and being affected by our environment.

The child's way of interacting impacts others and affects how they will respond to her, in turn. If the child is shy and withdrawn, she will not be the friend magnet that an easy child might be. Without many occasions to play with friends, strong social skills may not develop. Whereas the slow-to-warm-up child's temperament may put others off, the easy child invites interaction. Outgoing, adaptable, pleasant children are responsive and fun to be with, so parents want to engage them in play and take them on outings. Children reciprocate the smiles, encouraging more parent interaction.

> How could a child's temperament affect the environment?

Parents, as well, bring their own temperaments to bear on interactions with children. Sometimes the fit is good, sometimes it is not. Imagine the goodness of fit between a difficult child and an easy parent. Now imagine the fit between a difficult child and a difficult parent.

PARENTING STYLES

> Some parents are stricter than others. How do parent standards and expectations affect children?

Researchers have found some interesting correlations between parenting characteristics and behaviors of children. Those correlations are related to the everyday, common pattern of overall interactions, style, and expectations used by parents. Single incidents or isolated acts may differ, but in general, interactions take on a characteristic blend of warmth and control that comes to characterize the parenting style. Baumrind (1971; 1991) identified specific parenting styles considered by some to be discipline styles.

When these differing parenting styles are consistently applied, we see similarities in the behaviors of children. Child behavior is correlated to parenting style, but this is a group correlation, so there will be individual variations. However, in general we can predict child behavior when we know the parenting style (Darling, 1999). Research comes from a variety of sources including child reports, parent interviews, and observations. Results are consistent.

The **authoritarian** parent is in control. The parent makes the decisions and hands them down without explanation. Communication is one way—from parent to child. Standards are set high, and they are inflexible. The child is expected to do what he is told "because I said so." Obedience is demanded, and when rules are broken, the punishment may be harsh. The authoritarian parent may also use psychological control including inducing guilt, shaming, and withdrawing love (Darling, 1999). Though the

authoritarian parenting—low in warmth and high in control authoritarian parent may love the child dearly, there is little open demonstration of warmth. It is not a huggy relationship.

As a result, children and youth may be withdrawn, discontented, distrustful, or depressed. School behavior and academic performance tend to be acceptable, but social skills and self-esteem are low. The child may have difficulty deciding the merit of behavior and may have trouble making wise decisions. After all, the child has not had experience making decisions and living with the consequences. Adults have made the decisions for them.

The permissive parent exerts little control, but motives differ. **Permissive indulgent** parents are child-centered, warm, and responsive, but low in control. **Permissive negligent** parents are adult-centered, unresponsive, and low in control. Parents are accepting, lax, and do not closely monitor activities of their children and youth. Impulsive expressions are permitted. Because the permissive negligent parent is uninvolved, the child may feel rejected or stressed.

As a result, children may be aggressive and throw temper tantrums. As adolescents, behavior may be hostile, selfish, and rebellious, but self-esteem and social skills may be high. School performance and behavior may be problems. Children of permissive parents have difficulty following rules. They do not internalize the concept that rules apply to them, so they break rules at will.

Authoritative parents combine control with encouragement. The standards are there and must be met, but the standards are individualized

permissive indulgent—child-focused parenting style high in warmth and low in control

permissive negligent—adult-focused parenting style low in warmth and control

authoritative parenting—parenting style high in warmth, combines control with encouragement

PARENTING STYLES AND CHILD BEHAVIOR

Parenting Style			Behavior
Authoritative			
Control and encouragement			Independent
Two-way communication			Assertive
High expectations			Makes good decisions
Reasonable standards			Good achievement
Mild punishment			Secure
Induction, explains reasons			Self-reliant
Warm			Exploratory
Authoritarian			
Control oriented			Withdrawn
Harsh punishment			Uncertain
Top-down communication			Trouble making wise decisions
Rigid standards			Difficulty deciding behavior choices
Little demonstration of affection			Distrustful
Permissive			
Indulgent	or	Negligent	Views rules as applying to others
Child-centered		Adult-centered	Uncertain
Overinvolved		Uninvolved	Anxious
Undemanding		Ignore, neglect	Lacks self-control

rather than being the same for every child. Compliance is expected, but reasons are explained and there is room for reasonable negotiation. Communication is two-way, and demands are reasonable. Parents are warm and accepting. Punishment is mild. It is expected that children will participate in family work and family fun. The child's opinions, thoughts, and points of view are respected, and the child is treated in such a way that he may maintain his integrity. Children are encouraged to make appropriate decisions and live with the consequences of those decisions.

As a result, research has found amazing consistency in behavioral outcomes. Children and youth are independent, assertive, responsible, and full of confidence. They make wise decisions and exhibit lower levels of problem behavior. They have good social skills and positive self-competence. In a review of the literature, Darling (1999) generalized that the benefits of authoritarian parenting held true from preschool through adulthood and were equally beneficial for boys and girls and all economic backgrounds.

Authoritative parenting is most common among two-parent, middle-class families (Darling, 1999). Social class distinctions have been reported (Maccoby, 1980; McLoyd, 1990; Vuchinich, Bank, & Patterson, 1992; Arnett, 1995) along with the explanation that stress of poverty and different skill levels may be at the heart of the trend for lower socioeconomic status parents to use a more authoritarian parenting style. Financial stress may cause parents to be more aloof and coercive.

Although we need more definitive research, it appears that authoritative adults are actually embracing the guidance approach to living and working with children. So far as the teacher builds a sense of family in the classroom, uses developmentally appropriate practice, and institutes a guidance approach, the positive social climate created by the teaching style may result in students who have similar characteristics to those associated with authoritative parenting (Jambunathan, Burts, & Pierce, 1999).

> Do the parenting styles work the same way for teachers?

RECESS AS A GUIDANCE STRATEGY

Recess is the favorite part of the day for most school children. It is fun, time to talk to friends, time for self-chosen activity, a welcome break. But recess is more than time to giggle and wiggle. In her review of the research, Jarrett (2002) indicated that recess provides time for children to practice and refine social skills. They learn to negotiate, take another perspective, share materials, and take turns. Recess promotes health and creates a more active lifestyle for a population confronting childhood obesity. Recent research indicates that there may also be academic advantages related to physiological changes that occur during recess.

There is some indication in memory research that the brain works more efficiently when study sessions are broken into spaced units of time (Toppino, Kasserman, & Mracek, 1991). Recall is better when learning is spaced, and recess may provide that space. Not only does recess provide space between learning episodes, but it also provides some novelty that appears to be necessary for maintaining attention (Jensen, 1998). Jensen

(1998) also proposed that attention may be cyclical, following a 90- to 100-minute pattern as brain chemicals recycle. If so, what a perfect time for recess.

When recess is late, children become progressively less attentive. Then, when they finally get to the playground, they play harder and are more active than when they had recess on time (Pellegrini & Davis, 1993; Pellegrini, Huberty, & Jones, 1995). Jarrett and colleagues (1998) found that the fourth graders they observed were on task more often, appeared calmer, and engaged in less fidgeting on days they had recess. Although all children appeared to benefit, hyperactive children gained the most benefit.

> **If recess has the potential benefits you described, should children be punished by loss of recess time?**

Do we ever consider punishing a child with, "That's it, Sonny. No math for you today!"? Children need recess for their physical needs just like they need math for their academic needs.

SUMMARY

Guidance and discipline represent two different approaches to dealing with behavior in the classroom. Discipline has become equated with punishment; guidance is associated with reasoning and teaching. Control techniques such as time-out and punishment are effective at stopping the undesirable behavior as long as the person who controls the rewards and punishments is present. There are consequences associated with punishment. The child may learn to avoid the situation, the punisher, and the punishment. The child will not learn alternative behaviors. Inconsistency is the undoing of any system of punishment or rewards.

As a strategy, time-out relies on moving a child from a troublesome situation to a boring situation. The danger is that, due to age and developmental level, the child will internalize the punishment and label himself as a bad person. There are strategies that may be used to alter time-out so that it will become an effective strategy for guiding behavior.

For long-term benefit, it is not enough to simply stop unwanted behavior. The adult needs to help the child discover an acceptable alternative behavior to use in the future, provide understandable reasons for the wrongness or rightness of an act, and help the child take the perspective of those who may have been wronged by his actions.

There is disagreement in interpreting the research on the effects of rewards, or extrinsic motivation. Some experts contend that rewards decrease inner desire, or intrinsic motivation. Others disagree. Rewards may drag down performance, reduce creativity, and interfere with quality of performance. More definitive research is called for.

Children bring their individual personalities and temperaments to school with them. Temperament, or style of interacting, can influence others to respond in positive or negative ways. Based on general interaction style, temperaments have been classified as difficult, easy, and slow-to-warm-up. Some individuals do not fit into any category. The child develops best when there is a good fit between the child's temperament and the requirements of the environment. The adult's temperament may either work with or work against the child's own personal temperament.

Authoritarian, authoritative, and permissive parenting styles have been identified as patterns used by parents. Each style results in particular childhood personality traits. The dimensions of responsiveness and control appear at different levels in each of the parenting styles, with authoritative parenting resulting in positive outcomes that can be traced into adulthood. Authoritative parenting generally results in children who make wise decisions, are independent, assertive, confident, and socially skilled. Authoritative parenting has been associated with guidance.

Recess has the potential to positively influence social, cognitive, and physical development. Spaced study optimizes learning and attentiveness. Recess provides a vehicle to promote the child's well-being in social/emotional, cognitive, and physical development.

Key Terms

authoritarian parenting
authoritative parenting
difficult temperament
discipline
easy temperament

guidance
permissive indulgent
permissive negligent
slow-to-warm-up temperament
temperament

Using What You Know

1. Review the parenting styles and related child characteristics. Analyze the style your parents used when raising you.

2. How would you classify your temperament type? Why?

3. Survey your classmates to determine which temperament type is most common.

4. Review the characteristics of the child with a difficult temperament type. As a teacher, what steps could you take to make school life more manageable for the child with a difficult temperament?

5. As a teacher, what steps could you take to make school life more manageable for the slow-to-warm-up child?

For additional information on research-based practice, visit our Web site at http://www.earlychilded.delmar.com.

Chapter 11

Does Delivery of the Curriculum Affect Learning?

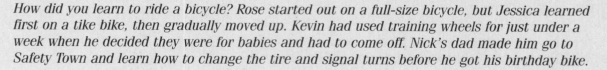

How did you learn to ride a bicycle? Rose started out on a full-size bicycle, but Jessica learned first on a tike bike, then gradually moved up. Kevin had used training wheels for just under a week when he decided they were for babies and had to come off. Nick's dad made him go to Safety Town and learn how to change the tire and signal turns before he got his birthday bike.

Ramon watched the older kids run and jump on, then skid to a stop. It looked like fun, so Ramon watched closely to see how they did it. He watched and practiced and fell. Ramon watched and practiced, and fell again until finally, one day, Ramon could run and jump on, then skid to a stop just like the older kids. Ramon taught himself how to ride a bike.

Klaire was fearful, so she had a runner—an angel who ran along side, holding her up when she lost her balance and started to tip. First Klaire's angel held the handlebar in one hand and the back of the seat in the other, running beside her as she peddled and tried to steer, righting her time and again as she learned just how far to lean with each push on the peddle. As Klaire gained confidence and ability, her helper released the hold on her handlebars and just held to the seat. When Klaire increased in skill, her runner angel let go and just ran along beside. Then one day Klaire's angel runner simply stopped running and went inside to do the dishes.

The children learned using different methods, but all the children eventually learned how to ride their bikes. Was one method more efficient? Did one method result in more accomplished bikers? In this chapter, we look at what research has to say about how methods of learning are related to efficiency and accomplishment in schools. We examine influences of program models, homework, and questioning techniques. We also take a quick look at the research base concerning individual learning preferences.

CURRICULUM MODELS

A curriculum model is a structure or organizational framework that is used to make decisions about everything from policies and priorities to teaching methods and assessment procedures. The conceptual model is grown from a philosophy or theoretical tradition. So we see some models rooted in behaviorism and others from social learning theory or constructivist theory, or any other theoretical orientation.

Just as there are different models of automobiles that can be used to deliver people and goods, there are different instructional models that can be used to deliver the curriculum. Any two teachers could teach, or deliver, the same content in two very different ways. For example, Mr. Flack believes that children learn best when the teacher organizes the material for them and directly presents the information. So when Mr. Flack teaches about the concept of friction he tells students what he wants them to learn, perhaps demonstrating as he lectures. Mr. Rush, on the other hand, comes from a philosophical orientation that believes children learn best in social situations, so he teaches the concept of friction through small group experiments.

There are numerous models for delivering the curriculum, and variations within the approaches, as well. Educators have been interested in looking at the outcomes associated with different curriculum models.

> **Which curriculum model produces the highest achievement?**

Most of the research has been limited to just two or three of the most popular curriculum delivery models. Marcon (2002) conducted an important longitudinal study, which compared a child-initiated model to an academically directed model and a third model that was a combination of the other two. The child-initiated model was based on a **constructivist philosophy**, which emphasizes active, hands-on learning so that children can build their own understandings. Children select and initiate their own activities, projects, and problems in a carefully prepared setting emphasizing play.

constructivist philosophy—children learn through active experiences, building their own understanding

behaviorist philosophy—learning occurs as a result of reinforcement

In contrast, the academically directed model comes out of the **behaviorist philosophy** in which the teacher selects and directs activities. Children take a more passive role in their learning, typically working individually on skills. The academically directed model tends to be teacher-centered with formal instruction, whereas the child-initiated model tends to be child-centered with informal instruction.

The third model in the study was a combination of both approaches. Subjects were preschoolers when they experienced the three different models. Marcon followed their progress through the end of fourth grade.

Marcon's 183 subjects were 96 percent Black, 75 percent lived at or below poverty level, and 73 percent came from single-parent homes. Subjects were randomly sampled, but they all came from one school district. Report cards, grades, retention rates, and special education placements were used as measures of achievement. At the end of the preschool year, the children in the child-initiated program demonstrated greater mastery of basic skills even though the children in the academically directed model had received formal skills instruction. The combination model did poorly in all areas except for measures of self-help and social coping.

Did the advantage last over the next few years?

At the end of third grade, there were no differences in achievement scores or special education placements. However, fewer of the academic model children had been retained. Then, by the end of fourth grade, there were differences in achievement once again, and those differences were significant. Children who had been in the academic model earned significantly lower grades than children who had been in the child-initiated model.

Marcon's subjects were from just one school district. Have other larger studies found similar results?

The High/Scope Preschool Curriculum Comparison Study is another longitudinal project that compared curriculum delivery models (Schweinhart & Weikart, 1998). These subjects were also followed from preschool, where they experienced three different instructional models: direct instruction; traditional nursery school; and High/Scope.

The direct instruction model came from the behaviorist tradition and used scripted academic lessons and positive reinforcement for correct responses. The traditional nursery school model, based on psychoanalytic theory, was child-centered and child-initiated. Teachers responded to interests of children and organized curriculum by themes from the everyday world. There was emphasis on free play. The High/Scope model came out of the constructivist and developmental traditions emphasizing an open framework where teachers and children planned together, engaged in activities, then reviewed what had been done in a plan-do-review cycle.

Children in all three programs attended school for two and one half hours, five days each week. Groups were similar. The High/Scope and traditional nursery school groups had similar results. The direct instruction group had no advantage over the other two models. Children in the direct instruction group increased intelligence test IQ scores up to 5 points, while children in the High/Scope group were reported to have IQ gains up to 23 points, a most impressive gain. Schweinhart (1997) suggested that the

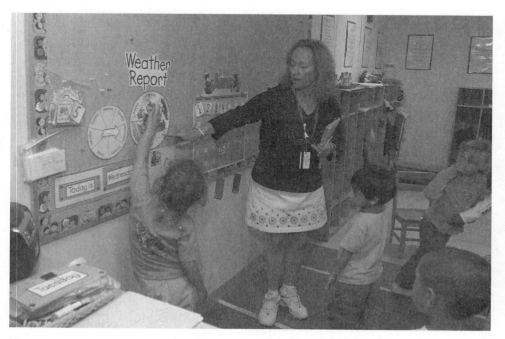

The direct instruction academic model is teacher dominated.

direct instruction model has better results in elementary school than in prekindergarten because the methods are inappropriate for the typical preschooler's developmental level and are better suited to older children.

In a review of three longitudinal studies comparing curriculum delivery models, Banks (2003) reported that the High/Scope Preschool Curriculum Comparison study, Louisville Head Start study, and University of Illinois study all found academic gains of up to one year for the direct instruction model, but no advantage for that model after the initial year. Some other related findings for the Louisville study included improved ambition and higher verbal and social participation scores for children who had participated in the nursery school group. But that group's advantages were not all positive, as they also scored higher than the direct-instruction group in aggressiveness (Banks, 2003). The University of Illinois study reported that the nursery school group had a 78 percent graduation rate, but the direct-instruction group had a graduation rate of only 48 percent.

Results from these three longitudinal studies are generally respected, and smaller studies tend to support those findings. Didactic, teacher-directed program models tend to show early academic gains that are short-lived. There is some evidence that the teacher-directed program is associated with less motivated children (Marcon, 2002) who may be less creative, have poorer verbal and receptive language skills, and exhibit less divergent thinking than subjects in child-initiated programs (Banks, 2003; Marcon, 1992; Hyson, Hirsh-Pasek, & Rescorla, 1990; Dunn, Beach, & Kontos, 1994).

Though we cannot say that the program delivery model caused children to behave in certain ways, some researchers have uncovered a relationship or correlation between certain behaviors and specific program models. For example, although Hart, Charlesworth, Burts, and DeWolf (1993) found no academic differences, there were behavior differences associated with children who had been in didactic, teacher-centered programs. Teachers rated those children as being more distractable; having poorer work and study habits, poorer conduct, fewer prosocial behaviors; and being less willing to follow directions.

Academics are only one part of any child's development. Do program models impact social or emotional development?

Positive emotional adjustment has been related to child-initiated programs. For example, at age 23, High/Scope and nursery school subjects grew up to engage in more volunteer work, and had fewer arrests than the direct-instruction group (Schweinhart & Weikart, 1998). Stipek and colleagues (1995) found that self-concept was related to program, as children in child-centered preschools and kindergartens were more independent, rated their abilities higher, and had higher expectations for their own success than subjects who participated in didactic, highly academic programs.

Direct instruction models have also been related to more stress behaviors particularly during workbook and group times and especially for males and Blacks (Burts, Hart, Charlesworth, & Kirk, 1990; Burts, Hart, Charlesworth, Fleege, Mosley, & Thomasson, 1992). When children had little opportunity to choose or make decisions about their own activities, they made more complaints, reported feeling sick, stuttered, fought, exhibited tremors, engaged in inappropriate laughter, and bit their nails more frequently than children in child-initiated programs. Burts related these behaviors to stress. Others have suggested that stress is induced by formalized schooling when it takes place at an age too early for the child's developmental level (Marcon, 2002; Katz, 1999).

Early childhood organizations have emphasized the need for activity in childhood. The Association for Childhood Education International's position paper on the child-centered kindergarten states, "The activity/experience-centered environment, which is essential if young children are to reach their maximum potential, provides for a far richer and more stimulating environment than one dominated by pencil-and-paper, teacher-directed tasks" (Moyer, 2001, 162). The National Association for the Education of Young Children has lobbied for developmentally appropriate practice and active learning for more than a decade.

Do we need to choose between academic and social/emotional advantages?

Both academic and social/emotional long-term advantages have been consistently associated with child-initiated program models. Early, short-term gains in achievement are tied to the academic, direct-instruction model, but the gains do not persist over time and may be creating stress in the lives of children. According to Katz (1999), "Most young children willingly do most things adults ask of them. But their willingness is not a reliable indicator of the value of an activity. The developmental question is not only, 'What can children do?', but also, 'What should children do that best serves their development and learning in the long term?'"

Differences in achievement seem to be measured most often in the areas of reading and math. Aren't there other kinds of achievement that would be important to consider when evaluating the success of any curriculum delivery program?

Verbal and mathematical abilities are often tested to make comparisons about achievement. Any other area of the curriculum could be measured as well. But there are some people who believe that when we study differences in achievement, we are really looking at differences in intelligence. If achievement is only measured in terms of verbal and mathematical abilities, perhaps we are being too limited in our thinking about the scope of intelligence. Perhaps there are different kinds of intelligence that result in a broader range of achievement than just reading- and mathematics-related accomplishments.

Child-initiated models offer choices and are associated with academic and social gains.

MULTIPLE INTELLIGENCES

In 1983 Howard Gardner proposed a theory of multiple intelligences, or separate abilities, each with their own developmental course and each governed by distinct areas of the brain. Gardner initially proposed seven intelligences, which he termed frames of mind (Gardner, 1983). Gardner later added an eighth intelligence to the list. The frames of mind are linguistic, musical, logical-mathematical, spatial, bodily-kinesthetic, interpersonal, intrapersonal, and naturalist intelligence. See Figure 11-1 for a fuller description.

GARDNER'S EIGHT FRAMES OF MIND

1. **Linguistic intelligence:** Mastery of language by using words to convey meaning, knowing the meaning of words, understanding ideas presented in words (author writes poetry, novels, instruction booklet; creates metaphors; interprets symbolism).

2. **Logical-mathematical:** Understanding objects, the actions that can be done with them, the relationships among objects, and the logical and mathematical operations that can be performed on objects such as ordering and counting (code breaker uncovers or creates complex pattern in sequences of numbers).

3. **Spatial:** Ability to precisely perceive objects in space and later accurately reproduce them through memory, imagining the appearance and transformations of objects in the "mind's eye" (coach mentally envisions how both teams would move in relation to one another during a specific football play; architect envisions completed building).

4. **Musical:** comprehending musical relationships and producing or reproducing musical tone, pitch, rhythm, and mood (musician mentally hears the music when reading a score).

5. **Bodily-kinesthetic:** Skillful use of one's body and objects in space as dancer, athlete, craftsman (ice skater executes difficult jump with grace and control of body).

6. **Interpersonal:** Accurate interpretation of feelings, motivations, intentions, temperaments of others (diplomat mediates an argument with insight into unspoken needs of both parties).

7. **Intrapersonal:** Knowing oneself and accurately interpreting own emotions, feelings, being aware of own strengths and weaknesses (adolescent selects a career that realistically matches personal capabilities).

8. **Naturalist:** Makes discrete distinctions in details among plants, animals, man-made objects (car buff identifies the type, year, model, country of manufacture of Volkswagen Beetle based on minute design and mechanical characteristics).

Figure 11-1 Gardner's Eight Frames of Mind

It makes sense that there is more than one kind of intelligence. People seem to excel in more areas than reading and math, so shouldn't we value talents such as musical skills and athletic capabilities as well as the traditional skills measured by IQ tests?

It does make sense, particularly to teachers who are aware of the vast differences individual children display. The theory of multiple intelligences has become accepted generally by the education community on an intuitive basis. Workshops have been conducted to help teachers identify characteristics of children with particular intelligences, and many pages have been written debating how to accommodate the differences.

Educators have been willing to jump on the multiple intelligences bandwagon because it sounds logical, fits into the ways teachers have been trained to view individual differences, and takes on the robes of science. Furthermore, when a term enters into the common jargon of the profession, the need to question the validity of the concept seems to fade. After all, those who should know talk about the concept as if it has been documented in research and there is no longer a question of truth. Thus the theoretical becomes part of popular language and popular culture. The problem comes when we attempt to find scientific evidence to support the theory.

What does science tell us about multiple intelligences?

The evidence cited in support of the concept of multiple intelligences comes from inferences made by theorists, rather than from experimental studies. For example, one of the proofs Gardner and others use in support of the theory arises from the study of individuals who have been subjected to brain injuries. Some brain trauma may result in the loss of function in the injured area. Depending on which area of the brain is affected, the victim may suffer loss of speech or sight, for example. Proponents of multiple intelligences theory reason that different areas of the brain are responsible for very specific types of thinking and doing. If there is a specific area of the brain dedicated to a given ability, and injury to that area results in loss or interference with that capability, then there must be a distinct intelligence related to the site. Therefore, there must be many intelligences, rather than one single intelligence.

Is that inference the only evidence that there are multiple intelligences?

Richard Wawro is an accomplished Scottish artist, first exhibiting when he was 17 years old and now internationally known for his detailed, intense landscapes in wax oil crayons. Richard is severely mentally retarded. Tim Baley is a concert pianist so skilled he was invited to play at the White House. Tim cannot read music, but he can play anything if he hears it once. Tim's mental capacity has been described as that of a 10-year-old. Richard and Tim are savants.

A **savant** exhibits particular skill that is far beyond the level most people can achieve with dedication, practice, and instruction. But a savant's skill is not learned. The Dustin Hoffman character in the movie *Rain Man* serves as an example of a savant. He had exceptional skill remembering baseball statistics, whole sections of the telephone book, and cards in Las Vegas, but functioned mentally at a level so low that he was unable to maneuver the everyday tasks of life. There are artistic savants, musical savants, and even calendar savants who can accurately name the day of the week for any given date within an 8,000-year span.

savant—individual with mental deficiencies exhibits high level of unlearned and specialized skill

What does the savant have to do with the idea of multiple intelligences?

Theorists reason that the savant gives evidence that there are, indeed, particular areas of the brain wired for specific abilities, such as drawing or playing music or remembering and calculating numbers. If there are differentiated areas of the brain, those areas could represent the sites of potential intelligences.

Critics of multiple intelligences theory have been quick to point out that some individuals have a broad range of talents, perhaps exhibiting particular expertise in several areas such as art, music, and spatial tasks (Winner, 1996; Feldman & Goldsmith, 1991). The evidence is not clear and more likely represents supposition rather than firmly grounded research. Other critics look at the physiology of the neurological system. They point out that for some kinds of thinking, several areas of the brain are interrelated or brought into play at one time. For example, depending on the task, logico-mathematical ability may be linked to spatial intelligence as well as other areas of the brain. It may be that intelligence is more complex than indicated in the multiple intelligences theories. Nevertheless, theories such as Gardner's have served as catalysts to broaden the education community's thinking about intelligence and how narrowly it is defined and valued in Western cultures.

According to Brualdi (1996), everyone is born possessing the intelligences. Nevertheless, all students will come into the classroom with different sets of developed intelligences. This means that each child will have his own unique set of intellectual strengths and weaknesses. These sets determine how easy (or difficult) it is for a student to learn information when it is presented in a particular manner. This is commonly referred to as a **learning style**.

learning style—concept that individuals have preferred ways of learning

LEARNING STYLES

Over the past several decades, there has been general acceptance of the concept that people have preferred ways of learning. It was even suggested that some people prefer to think with one or the other half of their brain. This led to the fad of classifying individuals based on whether they tended to use the left side or right side of the brain in their style of thinking. The ideas caught on in the popular press, so they soon became part of the popular culture. People took learning style inventories in magazines and compared learning style preferences over coffee.

Many teachers and teacher educators embraced the concept of learning styles. After all, if there are multiple intelligences, it follows that our individual intelligences would lead to our preference for learning in ways that correspond to our intelligence. We would be most comfortable and learn most efficiently if we were to learn using our own preferred style of learning. For example, if Jenny's brain were endowed with artistic intelligence, then she should be given the opportunity to learn geography or science or math by interpreting the lesson through art—perhaps by drawing or making a model. Or if Max were endowed with musical intelligence, his preferred learning style would probably be auditory. Max should have the opportunity to learn geography or science or math by listening and perhaps by singing songs about the content.

Teachers were urged to identify the learning styles of pupils and teach to their strengths. Some proponents of learning styles suggested that teachers could not possibly teach every lesson using all the preferred learning styles of all students, so it would be good practice to at least target every learning style at some point during the school day or week. Others suggested that children be urged to use their less preferred learning styles in order to practice and become more adept at learning in a variety of styles.

There may be multiple intelligences. There may be different learning styles. Both ideas may have led to the use of good teaching strategies. Even so, there is not sufficient evidence to support either claim. Nevertheless, the education community ignores the lack of research base and continues to operate as though there were solid evidence that multiple intelligences and learning styles do, in fact, exist (Ojure & Sherman, 2001).

It seems safe to conclude that simplistic answers are not particularly well suited to the complex and awesome workings that make up even the youngest of human beings. Even so, it is tempting to look for simple solutions to raise achievement levels. During the last half of the 1980s another simplistic solution appeared on the scene in the form of—just give them more homework.

HOMEWORK AND ACHIEVEMENT

The brouhaha over homework erupted partly as the result of various national reports that one after another criticized and continuously called into question the quality of public education. The schools were blamed for everything but adolescent pimples, so once again we looked for the simple fix. This time the fix was to toughen up and give those kids more homework.

> **That seems like a reasonable response to low achievement. Does homework work to improve achievement?**

Chen and Stevenson (1989) looked at first and fifth graders in Japan, the United States, and China. Time spent doing homework was compared to test scores in reading and math. Chen and Stevenson found no relationship between time doing homework and achievement scores. The researchers wondered whether student achievement would improve if they had help with their homework. So Chen and Stevenson looked at correlations between homework time and achievement test scores when Mom helped with the homework. Of 27 correlations, 10 were significant, and those were negative.

Although single studies offer some insight, it can be more helpful to look at the effects of a practice through the meta-analysis technique. Cooper (1989) conducted a meta-analysis of over 100 research studies on the topic of homework. Was there a homework/achievement link? Cooper concluded that the answer to that question is related to the child's grade level. In middle school and high school there was a positive correlation between the time students spent doing homework and their achievement scores. But at the elementary school level that link was missing. Homework was related to achievement above fourth grade, but not below.

> **Then how much time should students spend doing homework?**

Cooper's (1989) synthesis of the research led to the conclusion that the amount of time spent on homework is not all of equal value. The first 15 minutes is more profitable than the last 15 minutes. Homework time follows the law of diminishing returns. The National Parent Teacher

Association (PTA) and the National Education Association (NEA) both recommend that homework follow the 10-minute rule. First graders should have 10 minutes of homework, second graders should add 10 minutes more, third graders should add another 10 minutes, and so on through twelfth grade. These are not magic numbers, and there is no research evidence that would lead one to conclude that a specific amount of time is appropriate for homework. The nature of the homework assignment must be considered when evaluating the outcomes associated with homework time. In addition, we need to conduct studies with students randomly assigned to differing homework conditions because, according to Cooper (1989), we cannot prove that homework is the cause of higher achievement scores.

> **Could it be that children who are academically successful are just more likely to complete homework?**

Children with high intelligence are apt to succeed at school and may be more prone to complete homework assignments. We do not know whether failure to complete homework causes lower achievement scores, or whether some other factor, such as ability, is involved.

Proponents of homework have suggested that assignments should be made for reasons other than academics. According to Janine Bempechat, who wrote *Getting Our Kids Back on Track: Educating Children for the Future*, homework should be assigned even in the elementary school grades because it helps children to learn responsibility, organization, diligence, delay of gratification, and tolerance for boredom (Vail, 2001). Although responsibility, organization, and diligence might be characteristics we would hope to instill in our children, it just might be that some of those homework assignments are boring and intellectually unsatisfying. Don't we want children to find education so stimulating and exciting that they will want to continue to learn throughout their lives? What value could there be in learning to tolerate boredom?

Homework may be causing stress in households across the country (Begley, 1998; Vail, 2001; Silvis, 2002). Parents responding to a Public Agenda survey (Vail, 2001) revealed that 50 percent had argued with their child over homework during the past year. Homework was seen as a source of stress and struggle by 34 percent of the respondents, and 22 percent of the parents admitted that they had completed part or all of their child's homework either because the work was too hard or the child was too tired to complete it.

CLASSROOM QUESTIONING

Questioning is the second most popular curriculum delivery method, taking a back seat only to the lecture. It has been observed that 35 to 50 percent of teaching time is spent questioning (Cotton, 2001).

> **Do teachers lecture in elementary schools?**

The lecture does not need to be done standing behind a formal podium. In early grades, teachers are still giving a form of lecture when they stand in front of the group and tell. Direct instruction, or telling, is a form of lecture. The students are passive while the teacher is active.

recitation—teaching strategy that incorporates telling and questioning

Teachers often combine the lecture with questioning. This interactive lecture is sometimes called **recitation**. The teacher instructs, questions, instructs in a predictable cycle. Teachers use questions to lead thinking, maintain attention, and assess understanding. To promote understanding, it is better for teachers to ask questions than to not ask questions (Rothkopf & Billington, 1974), and oral questions are more effective than written questions (Cotton, 2001).

How do teachers know whether the questions they are asking are too easy or too difficult?

That is the Goldilocks question that plagues teachers as they plan for individual pupils: What level is just right? Brophy and Evertson (1976) were interested in that question. How does a teacher judge the "just right" level of questioning? When they looked at recitation questions, the researchers found that on average, a 75 percent correct answer rate was optimum. But they found something more. The optimum level of correct responses during recitation differed by the socioeconomic status of the children. Children of low socioeconomic status did best with an 80 percent correct answer rate, but high socioeconomic status indicated a need for more challenge. Brophy and Evertson concluded that a 70 percent correct answer rate was most appropriate for higher socioeconomic status pupils.

But not all questioning is oral. Teachers also require children to answer questions about what they read. The problem then is one of placement. When should the teacher pose the questions? Rothkopf and Billington (1974) conducted a classic experiment to determine the most effective placement of questions to facilitate comprehension of written text. Rothkopf and Billington set up four conditions:

1. No questions

2. Questions to be answered after reading

3. Questions to be answered before reading

4. Questions interspersed with the reading

Rothkopf and Billington concluded that questions focus attention. The three groups with questions comprehended more than the group with no questions. Best overall comprehension was associated with questions interspersed with the text. It seems important for the questions and the textual explanations to be close together.

Is that why I am here asking questions in the middle of the text?

That is your purpose in life.

What happened to the groups with questions placed before or after reading?

Subjects in the group that had questions to read before doing the reading assignment also improved comprehension, but they were aided by the questions in a different way. Questions prior to reading improve comprehension considerably, but there is a catch. The increased comprehension is only for the content related to the questions. That is an important point. It seems that prereading questions target specifics so much that the remaining content is more or less ignored. So if the teacher's purpose is to target specific information, prereading questions would be in order.

Rothkopf and Billington found that questions after reading were the least effective placement. One way to counteract that effect would be to have students read end-of-chapter questions first, before reading the assignment. Then those same questions would function like prequestions.

In a review of the literature, LeNoir (1993) reported general agreement about the effects of questions interspersed or prior to reading. Prequestions have been found to be particularly beneficial to older students who have high ability and high interest in the topic (Cotton, 2001). However, for very young pupils and for poor readers, prequestions may be too limiting, focusing attention too narrowly (Cotton, 2001).

> **Textbooks are frequently designed with end-of-chapter questions. How does that impact comprehension?**

There has been particular interest in levels of questioning since Benjamin Bloom created a classification system in 1956 (Bloom et al., 1956). Six levels of questions were identified. The levels required different types of thinking (see Figure 11-2). The lowest levels revolve around facts specifically stated, memorized, and handed back to the teacher. Higher levels require the student to manipulate and use the information by applying it in a new situation, analyzing relationships, synthesizing information into a new form, or making judgments and evaluations based on a standard or criteria. When educators talk about higher level thinking or questioning, they are generally making reference to application, analysis, synthesis, and evaluation levels.

> **Some teachers ask questions that are like Trivial Pursuit. They are just facts. Other teachers ask questions that require more thought. Are these differences in types of questions related to achievement?**

BLOOM'S TAXONOMY

LEVEL	SKILL	ACTION
Knowledge	Recall information	List, tell, describe, identify, tabulate, name, label
Comprehension	Understand information	Compare, chart, predict, summarize, estimate
Application	Use information in a new situation	Use, relate, solve, classify, compute, illustrate
Analysis	Break down structure into parts	Categorize, separate, order, graph, diagram, subdivide
Synthesis	Put together in another way	Summarize, design, invent, plan, rewrite, modify
Evaluation	Critique or judge based on criteria	Critique, defend, justify, grade, rank, select

Figure 11-2 Bloom's Taxonomy

Researchers have been interested in the relationship of achievement gains to the levels of questions students are asked to answer. Does asking higher-level questions result in greater achievement? Part of the answer must lie in how achievement is measured. If it is measured by tests that require factual-level information, then students who have learned factlets will be at an advantage on the test. If, on the other hand, the assessment poses questions that require processes such as analysis, synthesis, and evaluation, then students who have had experience using those processes will be at an advantage.

A number of studies have reported on frequencies and levels of questioning used in classrooms across the country. Most questions are lower level (Wilen, 1990; Brualdi, 1998). During class recitation sessions, 60 percent of the questions are lower level, 20 percent are higher level, and 20 percent are about procedural matters (Cotton, 2001). Findings such as these have led for calls to increase the cognitive level of questioning in the classroom and in textbooks. However, there is not general agreement in the research base about any relationship between levels of achievement and levels of questions (Cotton, 2001).

There is an observed tendency for higher-level questions to elicit higher-level answers (Klinzing; Klinzing-Eurich, & Tisher, 1985). Nevertheless, students do not always respond to high-level questions with high-level responses. For example, the teacher may ask a student to read accounts of a Civil War battle from both Northern and Southern perspectives, then compare and contrast the accounts and identify which account is from the perspective of the North and which account represents the perspective of the South. The student may respond by analyzing the accounts and synthesizing prior knowledge to produce a high-level response. On the other hand, the student might simply take an uneducated guess.

Nevertheless, there is a positive, but not perfect, correlation between achievement and the frequency with which higher-level questions are asked (Redfield & Rousseau, 1981; Samson et al., 1987). However, there is also a positive correlation between achievement and the frequency with which low-level questions are asked (Brophy & Good, 1986). Surprisingly, Brophy and Good also report that the frequency with which low-level questions are asked is positively correlated with achievement on assessments that require higher-order thinking.

To further complicate the matter, there is debate about whether it might be better to stop questioning and start using alternative strategies to foster more involved and deeper discussion among students. It has been suggested that questions may actually interfere with discussion (Dillon, 1991). Cotton (2001) has proposed that when looking at cognitive levels of question research, we should consider the subject matter, the students, and the teacher's purpose. We need more definitive research.

WAIT TIME

wait time—the amount of time a teacher waits between asking a question and calling on a student for a response

Another aspect of questioning came under study when Mary Budd Rowe became interested in how long teachers waited for responses after asking a question. She called this span **wait time** (Rowe, 1986).

Rowe had observed that teachers tended to avoid dead time. Whether to make efficient use of time, to maintain classroom control, or to avoid a long silence, the tendency is for teachers to quickly call on one of the first people to raise a hand in response to a question. The average wait time is 0.7 to 1.4 seconds (Stahl, 1994). And, Stahl continues, if the teacher calls on a student who is slow to answer, the teacher tends to reduce wait time to 0.7 seconds before calling on someone else.

> **Why would Ms. Rowe want to know how long it takes a teacher to call on someone to answer a question?**

If the question is clear and well phrased, increased wait time is correlated with positive effects (Stahl, 1994). In fact, the list of positive effects of increased wait time is very similar to the positive effects resulting from asking higher-level questions. Rowe (1974) observed that teachers were using less than 1 second wait time, so she trained teachers to wait from 3 to 5 seconds before calling on someone to answer a question. Teachers found it difficult to wait even that short period of time, but many did eventually increase their wait time. When wait time lasted just 3 to 5 seconds, Rowe found that the quantity and quality of responses improved. See Figure 11-3 for a list of specific results of increased wait time.

> **That hardly gives time for students to think through their answers. Does increasing wait time improve the quality of responses?**

In a review of related research, Cotton (2001) reported that increasing wait time beyond 3 seconds also resulted in some changes in teacher behaviors. Teachers tend to listen more. They were more flexible in their responses, asked a greater variety of questions, asked more higher cognitive questions, and increased their expectations of students they previously considered to be slow.

Although reported benefits of increased wait time may be impressive, Riley (1980) found that increased wait time in first through fifth grade science lessons was positively related to achievement only after asking a high cognitive level question. But increased wait time after asking a low cognitive question actually decreased achievement. Anshutz (1975) also studied

RESULTS OF INCREASING WAIT TIME BEYOND 3 SECONDS

- Longer responses
- More responses
- More speculation
- Greater variety of responses
- More questions posed by students
- More student-to-student comparisons of information
- Higher achievement
- Improved retention of information
- Increased frequency of high-level cognitive responses
- Fewer student interruptions

(Cotton, 2001; Rowe, 1974)

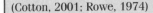

Figure 11-3 Results of increasing wait time beyond 3 seconds

wait time in science lessons for grades 3 and 4 but found no achievement differences related to wait time. It would seem important to study the matter more fully with primary grade pupils, particularly because most research related to achievement and wait time has focused on settings in which older students were learning abstract content.

SUMMARY

Delivery of the curriculum is related to theoretical and philosophical orientations. In early childhood, there are numerous program models, which tend to fall somewhere along a continuum of teacher-directed to child-initiated. The teacher-directed programs with focus on direct instruction sometimes show short-term achievement advantages, but the child-initiated program delivery models tend to be related to long-term academic advantages, motivation, creativity, and language skills. Positive social behaviors and work habits have been related to the child-initiated program model as well.

There has been a trend for program models to emphasize use of a variety of strategies to help children learn through their most preferred intelligence or learning style. The education community has warmly embraced the concepts of multiple intelligences and learning styles. Brain differentiation and savant characteristics have been used as arguments in support of multiple intelligences, but at this point in time the empirical research evidence that would support such concepts and related practices is not sufficient. Perhaps further evidence will be uncovered as science progresses.

The use of homework as a strategy for delivery of the curriculum has been both praised and criticized. Meta-analysis indicates that homework is related to achievement above fourth grade, but not below. Homework follows the law of diminishing returns, with productivity decreasing as time increases. The PTA and NEA both recommend that homework follow the 10-minute rule. But in the end, the value of the homework assignment depends in great part on the quality of the assignment. Homework has been praised for teaching responsibility and criticized for adding stress to already overburdened household schedules.

As a strategy to deliver curriculum, questioning has been related to higher achievement regardless of the level of the question. High-level thinking is related to high-level questioning, but student responses do not always rise to the level of the question. Both questioning and increased wait time are related to positive academic advantages. Though it is difficult for teachers to increase wait time, the possible positive outcomes of stretching the wait to 3 to 5 seconds are worth the effort. Increased wait time is generally related to increased quantity and quality of responses.

Key Terms

behaviorist philosophy   recitation
constructivist philosophy   savant
learning style   wait time

Using What You Know

1. Using a familiar story such as *Goldilocks and the Three Bears,* make up questions at each of Bloom's cognitive levels. Which questions are easiest/hardest for you to create? Why?

2. In a local school or in your college classroom, monitor wait time. Do the average wait times you observe confirm research indicating short wait times?

3. As you observe in your college classrooms, do you find an increase in the quantity and quality of responses when professors allow more wait time? Are the results the same in the elementary school setting?

4. Conduct an Internet search for Bloom's taxonomy. Read several explanations and examples of the cognitive levels. Try to make up questions at all levels.

For additional information on research-based practice, visit our Web site at http://www.earlychilded.delmar.com.

Chapter 12

How Does Family Involvement Impact Education?

The curriculum guide said the children must study Australia. The teachers wondered how their five-, six-, and seven-year-olds could understand anything meaningful about a country so far removed from their own life experiences. The children were just learning to understand the concept of community. How could they grasp the concept of country, a country so distant it was even in a different hemisphere? The children lived in the Midwest, an agricultural countryside dotted with woods and great fields of corn and soybeans. How could they comprehend the Great Barrier Reef, the outback, the opal mines? Who wrote this curriculum? Did they know anything about the ways young children think?

Teachers have little choice about what content to teach, but they have all the choice in the world about how to teach it. So at the next faculty planning session, the teachers decided that they would do what they had to do, and they would do it with class. If the curriculum content were inappropriate for the ages of the children, the teachers would make the best of the situation. They would study Australia. But because young children learn best through real experiences, the teachers decided that they would need to take the children to Australia, all 280 of them. Knowing they could not do it by themselves, the teachers enlisted the help of the parents.

Working as partners, parents and teachers transformed the west hall into the Great Barrier Reef with sand and shells, looped video, real objects, and aquariums. Sea life dangled from the ceiling, books about reef life lured passersby, photos of the reef lined the walls. Classroom doors were replaced by shimmering fish shower curtains. A rowboat offered comfortable seating for settling down with a book about the island continent.

The front hall became a sheep farm. Children could card wool, see demonstrations of spinning, sit on the fence, and tend the sheep. Some real sheep came to visit; they were petted, counted, and keenly observed for a few days.

The gym was the outback. A visiting Australian citizen taught songs, dances, and Australian expressions. She served as a real-life resource to make the abstract concepts more concrete. Teachers used the visitor to check information for accuracy. Children in every classroom had time to chat casually with their visitor and explore how they were like Australian children. Children gathered information to answer their own questions.

The opal mine was located in the east hallway. It was dark in the mine, so one needed to wear headgear with lights. There was a guide in the mine, explaining, showing, inviting youngsters to touch. Words like natural resource, tunnel, export, shaft, and transport came to life as they explored the mine and posters on its walls.

If the children were going to travel to Australia, they decided they would need to know about the weather so that they could pack appropriately. They would need travel documents—passports with photos, tickets for the flight, maps to use after landing. Parents and teachers worked in concert to facilitate the children's work.

Everything in order, the children arrived at school in shorts and sunglasses because they had researched the weather and found that even though it was winter in the Midwest, it was summer in Australia. The atmosphere was electric. Passports ready, tickets out, find your seat, and buckle up. The long south hall had magically become a 747, their airplane with rows of seats on either side of the center aisle, belts to buckle, magazines to read.

It was a long flight. Airline attendants offered Australian word searches to passengers. Australian style meals were served to the passengers, and of course there was an in-flight movie. Upon deplaning, small groups of children cycled through the centers, visiting the reef, outback, sheep ranch, opal mine. There was kangaroo jumping complete with tape measures to compare the length of the jumps. There was dancing, singing, history, storytelling, and map reading.

The plane ride back was a bit shorter, but time enough to relax, compare experiences, and debrief. Children had learned. And they would remember this day, the day they went to Australia.

Teachers had "taught Australia" with class. But it could not have happened without the parents and families of the children. Family members had become flight attendants, sheep ranchers, scuba divers, dancers, singers, miners, and pilots. Families and teachers worked together to build the outback, reef, ranch, and mine. Parents and teachers worked together toward a common goal, enriching the education of the children, enhancing learning by making school an intriguing, exciting place to be.

> **It would have required many parent volunteers to put the Australia trip together. Is this a wealthy school in an affluent district?**

The school is rather ordinary with a mix of socioeconomic status families including a number who qualify for free or reduced price lunches. Many of the families are working class and middle class. The school has a history of fairly high levels of parent involvement, but the family involvement did not happen either quickly or by accident. The administration and teachers have worked diligently over the years to build a strong volunteer program because they believe it is valuable to have families involved in the everyday life of the school.

PARENT INVOLVEMENT

> **There are many busy families with both parents working full-time these days. Families are short on time. Is it really important for parents to be involved in their children's education?**

Parent involvement has received enormous support at the national, state, and local levels. Goal number 8 of *Goals 2000: Educate America Act of 1994* challenged educators to create "school partnerships that will increase parent involvement and participation in promoting the social, emotional, and academic growth of children." In fact, parent involvement provisions are at times required by law. For example, if a district receives more than one half million federal dollars in one year, the *Improving America's Schools Act of 1994* requires that at least 1 percent should be spent on parent involvement activities. Mandated parent involvement is also an integral part of all Head Start programs, with parents volunteering in classrooms and serving on advisory boards.

The National Board for Professional Teaching Standards includes a parent involvement standard that must be met in order for a teacher to be nationally certified. Standards for teacher education institutions accredited

When parents are involved, children do better in school.

under the National Council for the Accreditation of Teacher Education (NCATE) also include parent involvement components. For more than a decade, the California Education Code has required teachers "to serve as active partners with parents and guardians in the education of children" (California Education Code 44291.1, 1993). And a survey of 200 school districts in 15 states revealed that over 90 percent of the school districts had at least one parent involvement policy in place (Kessler-Sklar & Baker, 2000).

Early childhood and primary teachers use parent involvement techniques most often (Caplan, Hall, Lubin, & Fleming, 1997b). Activities tend to focus on encouraging parents to read to children at home and help in the classroom (Caplan et al., 1997b). The highest level of parent involvement occurs when children are young; the involvement decreases as children move up through the grades (Caplan et al., 1997b; Izzo, Weissberg, Kasprow, & Fendrich, 1999). It has been suggested that family involvement decreases during middle school and high school due to the child's growing need for autonomy, because there are more teachers, and because in upper levels of school there is not usually one teacher responsible for tracking an individual student (Caplan et al., 1997b).

Overall, parent involvement tends to decrease as the child grows older. However, fathers who are highly involved during the early years of school tend to stay highly involved through elementary school and middle school. It isn't until the child enters high school that the previously involved father significantly reduces his activity level (NCES, 1997).

Parent Involvement and Achievement

Parent involvement has been correlated with higher achievement, improved attitudes, increased attendance, fewer discipline problems, fewer grade retentions, higher aspirations, and fewer dropouts (Caplan et al., 1997b; Epstein, Clark, Salinas, & Sanders, 1997; Henderson & Mapp, 2002; Shaver & Walls, 1998; Fan & Chen, 2001; Hara & Burke, 1998; Miedel & Reynolds, 1999). In their meta-analysis, Fan and Chen (2001) reviewed quantitative studies examining parent involvement and achievement of children. They found a moderate relationship. Fan and Chen pointed out that they found parent expectations for their child's achievement to be an important factor. It is not clear, but Fan and Chen found indications that parent expectations may be related to the frequency and type of involvement parents choose for themselves. Carter (2003) analyzed and summarized a decade of parent involvement research. She confirmed the conclusion that parent involvement is related to numerous positive outcomes for students.

Do children do better academically when their parents are actively involved?

When parents are involved, children tend to do better in school, regardless of age, economic status, gender, or any other known factors. For example, findings from the Miedel and Reynolds (1999) study that investigated parent involvement in an inner-city Chicago setting indicated a relationship between parent involvement and reading achievement, lower numbers of grade retentions, and fewer special education referrals.

Hara and Burke (1998) also studied inner-city elementary students and found significant student reading gains. There were several facets to the

Does parent involvement affect achievement of children who are at risk?

parent involvement model that was developed and implemented by one school. Though the study was small, the reported parent outcomes are intriguing and deserve further study. Not only did the children make achievement gains, but the parents also appeared to develop more positive attitudes toward education, teachers, and their own interest in learning for themselves. Similar findings relating involvement in school to more positive attitudes toward teachers were reported by Caplan, Hall, Lubin, and Fleming (1997b). Parents who were actively involved rated the teacher's teaching ability higher after they became involved.

In their survey of 200 superintendents in 15 states, Kessler-Sklar and Baker (2000) found that parent involvement activities were reported more frequently by superintendents of districts with high numbers of at-risk students. That is an encouraging finding because numerous studies have indicated that parent involvement is correlated with positive transitions to kindergarten, particularly for children who are disadvantaged and at risk of school failure (Kreider, 2002; Marcon, 1999; Miedel & Reynolds, 1999; Starkey & Klein, 2000). The effects may be long-term, as well, as indicated by a longitudinal study of 1,205 urban kindergarten through third grade students (Izzo, Weissberg, Kasprow, & Fendrich, 1999). Children and their parents' involvement levels were followed for three years. Teachers then rated frequency of parent-teacher contact, quality of parent-teacher interactions, participation in educational activities at home, and level of participation in school activities. Although all the variables were moderately correlated with children's achievement, the strongest relationship to academic success was parent participation in educational activities at home.

Levels of Parent Involvement

Does helping children at home count as parent involvement, or do parents need to be in the schools helping in order to be considered involved?

Epstein (1998) identified six levels of parent involvement which include activity both in and out of the classroom. The levels are parenting, communicating, volunteering, learning at home, decision making, and collaborating with the community.

At the parenting level, schools help families to understand child development and appropriate parenting to promote the child's development. Schools learn from families, as well, with the duty to understand the family culture, values, and ways of interacting.

At the communicating level, Epstein indicates that two-way communication is preferred to one-way communication in which the school simply tells or notifies parents. Two-way communication may include such methods as phone calls, conferences, e-mail.

The volunteering level brings parents into direct contact with schools and children in a variety of active and passive roles. Parents may volunteer to monitor or even direct an activity, or simply act as an audience for an impromptu puppet skit or listen to a child read.

The learning at home level brings children and parents together to work on curriculum projects or supervise and assist with homework. Parents may be provided with literacy bags or suggested activities for learning activities at home. Parents may be encouraged to read to their children or complete activities such as math puzzles.

The advisory council is acting at the decision-making level.

Leadership as a member of an advisory council, Parent/Teacher Organization, or school committee would qualify as decision-making level involvement. For example, parents may sit on textbook selection committees or take active roles in helping to develop a parent handbook. By law, Chicago schools must elect a local school council with parents making up the majority of the members. The councils are responsible for selection of the principal and development of an annual improvement plan. Moore (1998) reported a correlation between high reading scores and schools with strong local school councils. More research is called for in this important area of parent involvement.

The level of collaborating with the community revolves around coordinating services for families within the community. For example, a parent committee might arrange for health department nurses to offer immunizations at the school site, notify parents with children who are eligible, and promote the program.

Parent Involvement Programs

No one model seems to meet the needs of all parties (Jordan, Orozco, & Averett, 2001). However, taken together, research indicates that any level of involvement is better than no involvement. For example, dropping out has been associated with parents who are less involved, seldom attending events or helping with homework and, instead, punishing poor grades (Caplan et al., 1997b). A National Center for Education Statistics survey of a nationally representative sample of 900 public schools indicated that schools are making the effort to involve parents by offering a wide variety of options for involvement (NCES, 1998). Schools reported making the

Which type of parent involvement brings the best results?

effort to communicate regularly with parents and facilitating that communication by providing interpreters for parents with limited English proficiency. Other activities reported on the survey included providing information on parenting and child development through resource centers, workshops, and publications such as newsletters. Opportunities for participation in decision making were reported less often. Parent involvement tended to decrease in schools with high poverty and high minority enrollment.

There is little definitive research indicating that one particular model of involvement is better than another, but we do have bits and pieces of information about different levels of involvement and results from specific studies. For example, Shaver and Walls (1998) reported on a project that offered parent-training workshops to parents of elementary school children. Compared to the control group, standardized achievement test scores were better for children when parents had completed the workshop training. The results were similar regardless of income level or the educational level of the parents.

There are many model parent involvement programs reporting positive effects. Project EASE (Early Access to Success in Education) is an example from Minnesota (Jordan, Snow, & Porche, 2000). Low- and middle-class parents came to school to be trained in helping their kindergarten children to develop literacy skills. When the training was complete, parents were given materials to take home and practice what they had learned. The results? Scores increased as the amount of work done at home increased. The more parents worked with children, the higher the children's scores rose. That result could be expected, but there was a surprise in the bottom of the package. Children who scored lowest at the beginning of the study turned out to make the greatest gains in the end.

Whereas Project EASE found positive results associated with parent training, another parent-training program reported mixed results. Project HIPPY (Home Instruction Program for Preschool Youngsters) worked with

Community members may volunteer.

parents of four- and five-year-olds from poor and immigrant families. During biweekly home visits, trainers modeled skills that would support language and learning. The first group of children showed positive gains when parents were trained, but the second group showed no significant differences compared to control groups (Baker, Piotrkowski, & Brooks-Gunn, 1998). When results are mixed, it is important to examine the study to look for any design flaws and then conduct additional evaluations of the program.

Parent training was the subject of a large study of 3,000 infants and toddlers from low-income homes who attended 17 different Early Head Start sites (Mathematica, 2001). Children were randomly assigned to experimental and control groups. Experimental group parents were trained in diverse topics such as parenting, health and family support services, and activities to stimulate mental, physical, and emotional development. When the children were two years old, the control group lagged behind the experimental group in language skills and cognitive development. In addition, families that had received training were more supportive of children's development and literacy.

Latino and African-American families were subjects in an experimental examination of parent training to help children with mathematics. Starkey and Klein (2000) assigned children to experimental and control groups. Following four months of classes, experimental group parents were provided with packets of related math materials to use at home with their own children. Results of the study indicated that parents were able and willing to use their training to work with their children. As a result, children's achievement in mathematics knowledge and skills was superior to that of the control group.

Diversity Issues

Ethnic and cultural values impact how parents think about education and what they believe their role should be in promoting the education of their children. Those values and beliefs color the nature of parent involvement, making it more diverse and unique. The parents' concept of involvement may not include the traditional committee work, library clerking, or room mother role offered by the schools (Mapp, 2002; Martinez & Valazquez, 2000; Peng & Wright, 1994; Henderson & Mapp, 2002). The family's concept of education may be different from the school's view. Parents may consider education in a broader context. In some cultures, education might be more about character development, morals, citizenship, and values and less about spelling, reading, and math.

> Do ethnic and cultural differences affect how parents become involved in their children's education?

Lopez (2001b) interviewed parents of children who were academically successful but from marginalized migrant families. Parents identified themselves as being highly involved in their children's education, but not in traditional ways. Parents in the study reported that they believed usual forms of involvement such as attending PTO meetings, volunteering in the schools, and teacher contacts were positive things to do. However, they did not believe those activities were important to the academic success of their children. Lopez (2001a) recommends that schools identify and recognize nontraditional ways parents may become involved.

Lopez (2001a) also described how an Hispanic immigrant family introduced children to the drudgery of hard manual labor in order to educate children to the value of education as a path to a better life. It seems important for schools to recognize and value the diverse ways families become involved in the education of their children.

Low-income families tend to be involved more in their child's education at home whereas affluent families tend to become more involved at the school level (Lareau & Horvat, 1999). There may be a language barrier, educational barrier, and/or social barrier. More affluent, better-educated parents tend to feel more comfortable with teachers and consider them equals. Lareau and Horvat (1999, 44) observed that White, middle-class families share "social and cultural capital," allowing for more trust and comfort in the school environment where parents and teachers are more likely to share values, expectations, and vocabulary.

In their synthesis of the research literature Henderson and Mapp (2002) concluded that "families of all cultural backgrounds, education, and income levels encourage their children, talk with them about school, help them plan for higher education, and keep them focused on learning and homework. In other words, all families can, and often do, have a positive influence on their children's learning."

> **Does the research indicate any particularly good strategies for promoting parent involvement?**

Promoting Parent Involvement

Effective strategies for forming and maintaining parent involvement have been studied, but both the studies and the samples tend to be small. Whether or not the strategies for involving parents are successful appears to depend on communication and building and sustaining connections with families.

Communication

Communication is a common thread running throughout the studies devoted to promoting parent participation. The most widespread communication is the old standby—the report card (Hiatt-Michael, 2001). Report cards are not particularly good forms of communication because the stream of communication goes only one way—from the teacher to the parent. Two-way communication is facilitated by the parent/teacher conference, which is the second most widespread communication strategy used by schools (Hiatt-Michael, 2001).

Analysis of data at the national level (Westat, 2001) indicated that low-income children in Title I programs demonstrated better reading and math scores in elementary school when teachers made a high-level effort to communicate face-to-face with parents on a regular basis. Communication was not limited to problem times. Parents were regularly contacted by phone and received ideas to help the child at home. When standardized achievement test scores were compared, scores were higher for the high-outreach school, compared to schools where there was low outreach to families.

From their survey of the related literature, Henderson and Mapp (2002) generalized that even though there is little evidence about the impact of specific strategies on improving parent involvement, what was important was how the strategies were implemented. When parents understood that their involvement could be linked to improving achievement, families were more engaged.

In order to be effective, communication needs to be frequent, almost continual (Caplan et al., 1997b). Effort to improve communication can be very worthwhile for the school. When communication is frequent and effective, parents evaluate the teacher higher, have a "sense of comfort" with the school, and are more involved with school activities (Caplan et al., 1997b). If the teacher is communicating suggested activities for parents to do at home with their children, parents are more likely to participate when communication is

- frequent.

- varied.

- about the content children are studying.

- enthusiastic.

Building and Sustaining Relationships

Mapp (2002) interviewed 18 parents in a low-income neighborhood in Boston. Parents reported that they were highly interested in their children's education and knew that their own involvement in the process was important. Some of the ways they involved themselves were nontraditional and were not always valued by school personnel. Those 18 parents listed the factors that affected their willingness to be involved. Based on those recommendations, schools need to

- welcome parents.

- build trust.

- show care and concern.

- honor parents.

- focus on being partners working to help children.

A different group of researchers identified reasons parents were uninvolved (Ritter, Mont-Reynaud, & Dornbusch, 1993). When parents have a history of negative experiences in schools, they may not want to spend time in a school environment. Parents may have a distrust of institutions in general, or schools in particular. Some parents reported that when teachers questioned them about their child, the questions were interpreted as being disrespectful. Other parents reported that they were not involved because they felt they lacked the necessary language skills.

However, parents were more likely to increase their involvement when the teacher was committed to and excited about initiating a parent involvement activity (Ritter, Mont-Reynaud, & Dornbusch, 1993). Parents actually rated the teacher higher when they understood more about what was being taught and when they believed that they should help their children at home.

Parents were more likely to come to school training programs when consideration was given to facilitating needs such as child care and transportation (Starkey & Klein, 2000). Effective strategies include providing child care on site, arranging carpools, encouraging families to send substitutes when they were unable to attend, and providing materials to take home and use with children (Starkey & Klein, 2000).

Are fathers and mothers equally involved in their children's education?

Mothers and fathers are involved in somewhat different ways. When there are two parents in the home, mothers appear to be more involved than fathers. One study revealed that in two-parent homes, 27 percent of fathers are highly involved compared to 56 percent of the mothers (NCES, 1997). When mothers were highly involved, children had higher achievement, but when fathers were also highly involved, children had higher achievement yet (Viadero, 1997).

Almost half of moms and dads who were heading up single-parent homes were involved in school activities (NCES, 1997). They appear to rise to the occasion. Noncustodial fathers are more likely to become involved in educational activities if the mother is highly involved, but in one study, 69 percent did not participate (NCES, 1997). In another study, when noncustodial fathers were involved in parent activities, children were more likely to be involved in extracurricular activities and fewer children were retained, suspended, or expelled between sixth and twelfth grades (NCES, 1997).

According to one report (NCES, 1997), fathers are more involved during the elementary school years if

- the child attends a private school.
- mother is employed full-time.
- parent education level is high.
- mother is highly involved.
- there is a stepmother.

Involved fathers boost achievement.

In general, Fagan and Palm (2004) reported that fathers are less involved than mothers. They communicate less with the teacher and are less likely to participate in activities or committee work. Fathers appear to be more interested in parent education and support activities. More than anything else, fathers are more likely to attend family activities at school (Turbiville, Umbarger, & Guthrie, 2000).

The overarching theme of findings from studies of parent involvement is one of relationship building. When parents are honored, treated with dignity, and viewed as assets rather than liabilities, parent involvement is promoted (Henderson & Mapp, 2002). Simple, but effective strategies that make parents feel welcomed can be implemented. For example, Caplan and colleagues (1997a) reported that parents volunteered more and attended PTO meetings more frequently when a school welcoming committee made home visits. The small, but special personal touch made a difference.

SUMMARY

Parent involvement has been positively related to achievement, attendance, improved attitudes, fewer discipline problems, fewer grade retentions, higher aspirations, and fewer dropouts. Involvement is highest in elementary school and then tends to drop off through middle school and high school. When parents are involved, children tend to do better in school regardless of age, economic status, or gender.

Epstein identified six levels of parent involvement: parenting, communicating, volunteering, learning at home, decision making, and collaborating. Although it is not clear that one level is better than another, research indicates that involvement at any level is better than no involvement at all.

Ethnic and cultural values impact how parents think about education and what they believe their role should be in promoting the education of their children. Therefore, parent involvement may not include the traditional activities promoted by schools.

There may be differences in how socioeconomic factors play into parent involvement. Low-socioeconomic-status parents tend to be more involved in educational activities at home, whereas more affluent parents tend to be more involved at school. Mothers and fathers appear to prefer different kinds and amounts of involvement. Good communication and sensitivity are necessary to build the strong relationships necessary for parents and teachers to work collaboratively for the success of the children.

Using What You Know

1. Interview a principal, a teacher, and a parent from one school. What are their perceptions of the value of parent involvement? What barriers do they see to full involvement?

2. Interview the president of the local parent/teacher organization. How does the organization promote parent involvement?

3. Access the National Parent Teacher Organization at http://www.ptotoday.com. What are the hot topics? What resources are available to promote parent involvement?

For additional information on research-based practice, visit our Web site at http://www.earlychilded.delmar.com.

Chapter 13

What are the Most Appropriate Ways to Assess Young Children?

Cole's mother is concerned that he might not be ready for kindergarten. Though Cole turned five in time to meet the September 1st cutoff date for his school district, he has not shown much interest in academic activities such as learning the alphabet or writing his name. Cole's preschool teacher suggested that he might not be ready for school and could benefit from another year of preschool. Cole's parents hope that when he undergoes kindergarten screening, the school will tell them whether or not he is ready for kindergarten. Like most parents, Cole's mother wants her child to have the best start possible, but is faced with the question of how to determine readiness for school.

Cole's mother takes him to kindergarten screening to be tested. She wants to know whether Cole is ready for school. Readiness is just one of the reasons we commonly assess young children. But that will not be the end of it. Assessments will continue throughout Cole's education. He will be assessed informally throughout each school year, and he will be formally assessed at a number of points in his school career. He may be tested to determine whether or not he has met certain academic benchmarks or perhaps to determine whether or not he will be promoted to the next grade, or even permitted to graduate.

In this chapter, we examine issues surrounding assessment. We look at types of assessments and which ones are most appropriate for young children. In particular we look at the issues surrounding kindergarten screening and readiness testing.

ASSESSMENT

You mention assessment and testing. Aren't they the same things?

assessment—documentation of children's work to make educational decisions

I have read headlines in the newspaper about high stakes testing. What is that?

Tests are **assessments**, but not all assessments are tests. "Assessment is the process of observing, recording, and otherwise documenting the work children do and how they do it, as a basis for a variety of educational decisions that affect the child" (National Association for the Education of Young Children & National Association of Early Childhood Specialists in State Departments of Education, 1990). Assessment may take the form of a test, or it may take another form. Because of the national emphasis on testing, many people have come to equate assessment with testing.

Some assessments have consequences attached to them. For example, Chicago's third graders must pass a proficiency test before they are permitted to move up to fourth grade. Ohio students must pass a graduation examination. There are significant rewards and punishments attached to scores on those tests, so they are termed high stakes. Assessment is also high stakes if outcomes are reported individually for a person, classroom, or school. There are significant perks and public embarrassments attached to classroom, building, or district report cards published in the local papers and discussed at the corner coffee shop.

There are important reasons to test. In some cases, testing is tied to funding. If the state or district wants the dollars, they must pay the piper in the form of test results. The No Child Left Behind Act is just one example. The act mandates that children be tested in reading and mathematics every

Copyright 2002 Joel Pett. Reprinted by permission.

year in grades 3 through 8, and even more testing requirements are built into the law. School districts are required by law to report proficiency test results to the states, and the states are required to aggregate and forward the information on to federal officials.

In fact, there are so many assessments being required of children and schools that the issues surrounding them have become quite hot topics debated from the barn to the ballroom. Yet there are solid educational reasons for assessment. Katz (1997) listed a number of reasons to assess students:

- To determine the rate of progress

- To make placement and promotion decisions

- To identify learning and teaching problems

- To assist in making decisions about curriculum and instruction

- To gather information for reporting to parents

- To enable the child to assess her own progress

The National Association for the Education of Young Children (NAEYC, 1987) and the Association for Childhood Education International (ACEI, 1991) have both published position papers expressing great concern with the inappropriate torrent of tests being given to young children. As advocates for children, both organizations have called for appropriate assessments rather than high stakes testing programs. Standardized tests have been particular targets of the organizations' concern. It has been strongly suggested that standardized tests should only be used when they can result

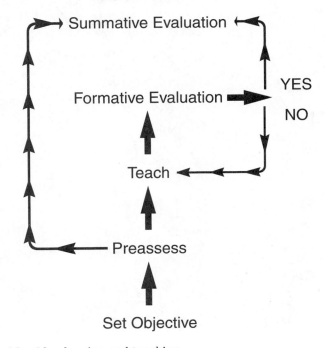

Objective Met?

Assessment should guide planning and teaching.

in improving services and outcomes beneficial to the child (NAEYC, 1987). In addition, both organizations have stipulated that no single test should be used to make important decisions for any child. A battery of assessments, rather than a single test, is a more appropriate strategy for assessment and decision making.

In general, assessment of any kind should relate to the goals and objectives of the program, and the results of the assessment should guide planning and teaching. Therefore, assessment may take three forms: **preassessment**, **formative evaluation**, and **summative evaluation**.

Preassessment takes place prior to teaching. The teacher uses the information from the preassessment to determine the student's current level of skill or understanding. Formative evaluation takes place as the learning process proceeds. Summative evaluation is the final assessment and determines whether or not the goals and objectives have been met.

As an example, if the task were for a child to learn to ride a bicycle, the teacher would first conduct a preassessment. The teacher may observe the child's bicycle-riding skill or even ask the child whether she can ride a bicycle. Formative assessment would take place as the child was learning to ride the bike. The teacher might run beside the bicycle as the child learned to peddle, balance, and steer. As the child made errors and gained competence, the teacher would mentally assess the status and make adjustments by giving more or less assistance. Summative evaluation occurs at the end of a teaching/learning process. After the child had learned to peddle, balance, steer, and had practiced with help, the teacher would determine whether or not the child could ride the bicycle independently.

preassessment—determines the child's knowledge before teaching content

formative evaluation—monitors understanding during the learning process

summative evaluation—determines whether or not objectives have been met

Assessment is ongoing.

Preassessment, formative evaluation, and summative evaluation can be informal or formal. **Informal assessment** may take the form of observations, checklists, portfolios, or rating scales. Observation is particularly appropriate in early childhood settings because the ongoing activity can continue while the teacher is making observations. Observation may take several forms. For instance, the teacher may jot down anecdotal records as single events of significance occur throughout the day. The teacher may also write a running record, which is more like a story with a sequence of related events. Another observational strategy is time sampling. In time sampling, the teacher records the frequency of an event or behavior over a certain period of time. Event sampling is similar in that frequency of behavior is recorded. However, event sampling is related to one type of event, such as biting or thumb sucking. The assessment takes place as the teacher uses the information gained from observation to look for patterns that may be occurring.

Checklists are informal assessments using a yes/no format. Checklists must, of necessity, be used for assessing all or nothing categories. Can the child identify letters of the alphabet, tie her shoe, or count 10 objects accurately?

For behaviors or understandings that are subject to levels of quality, rating scales might be used. The teacher observes the child performing a task and then rates the level of success. Philip is gaining proficiency in speaking Spanish but has not quite mastered the language. His skill level may be rated on a scale.

Portfolio assessment uses documentation to demonstrate growth and understanding. Real objects, recordings, project work, photographs, original writing, and other artifacts are selected as representative of a student's progress through a learning cycle. The student, teacher, parents, or others can evaluate the work. Though portfolios are planned exhibits, they are considered informal assessments.

Formal assessments are generally considered to be tests. Standardized tests are normed based on a representative sample, and the student's score is compared to the scores of the norming group. Achievement tests attempt to measure what a person knows or can do. Ability tests attempt to measure capability to learn, or intelligence. Developmental tests are measures that compare a child's score to the typical score of others at a particular developmental level. For example, speech can be assessed based on how the child's spoken language compares to that of other children the same age. Readiness tests are a snapshot in time that attempts to capture the child's level of skills and abilities compared to a standard determined prior to testing.

informal assessment—level of skill or understanding is measured as the child completes learning tasks

formal assessment—level of skill or understanding is measured by a test

Young Children and Tests

There certainly are considerations when administering formal tests to young children. If there are too few items on a test, there can be no clear indication of what the child knows. On the other hand, if there are too many test items, the child may become tired, restless, and disinterested in the task. More interesting events, activities, or people in the environment may easily distract children.

I saw a teacher trying to give a test to a group of kindergarteners. Some of them just did not think it was important to pay attention. Are test scores accurate for young children?

Other children might mistakenly see the test as a creative effort. For example, Richard, a very bright first grader, was taking a test that required him to mark certain pictures. The teacher read from the test manual, "Mark the picture of the animal that can fly." Richard looked over the pictures and marked the elephant rather than the obvious answer, a bird. Overwhelmed with curiosity, the teacher had to ask, "Richard, why did you mark the elephant?" Of course Richard had a reason. "Dumbo can fly."

Ann's teacher was perplexed when the scores for the Metropolitan Achievement Test came back very low. Ann had been at the top of her class all year. What had happened? When the teacher and Ann's mother compared notes, they were able to map out what had happened. Ann had been treated for an ear infection the day after the test, and the pediatrician later estimated that Ann had a 50 percent hearing loss at the time. The directions for the test were all oral, spoken by the teacher because tests for kindergarten children do not have written directions. Sometimes young children neglect to tell the teacher if they are not feeling well—even on the day of the big test.

Use of standardized tests with young children has been subject to criticism. According to Shepard, Kagan, and Wurtz (1998), it is "not technically defensible to administer formal, standard measures to hold children to grade level standards before third grade." Meisels (1995a) also raised questions about the use of group administered standardized tests below third grade because they generally contain abstract content, have the potential to be biased toward middle-class test-takers, and are verbally mediated.

SCREENING TESTS

In the chapter introduction we left Cole going off to kindergarten screening. Are screening tests also inappropriate for young children?

screening test—identifies children who may need special services or interventions

Cole was going off to kindergarten screening. However, his mother was worried about whether or not Cole was ready for kindergarten. **Screening tests** and readiness tests have different purposes. Screening tests are in place to identify children who may need special services (Costenbader, Rohrer, & Difonzo, 2000) and are mandated in some states for all new entrants.

Does the child seem to have difficulty hearing? seeing? speaking? Does the child's development seem to be off track?

Costenbader, Rohrer, and Difonzo (2000) have identified a list of domains that they suggest are appropriate to test at kindergarten entrance, including

- physical health.
- hearing and visual perception.
- cognitive development.
- knowledge of basic concepts.
- speech and language development.
- gross and small muscle development.
- socialization.
- self-help.

If a screening instrument catches any irregularities or unusual behaviors indicating possible problems in development, the child should be referred for more specific developmental testing. That testing must be done by trained professionals.

As part of a large, national longitudinal study reported by Prakash, West, and Denton (2003), administrators were surveyed about testing prior to kindergarten. Administrators of 61 percent of the schools reported that they do test prior to kindergarten. The reported purposes of the testing were twofold: first, to identify children in need of further testing; and second, to guide instruction. Schools were more likely to conduct prekindergarten testing if the schools were public and had enrollment larger than 300. Some reporting schools enrolled only preschool and kindergarten children. Of those schools, only 21 percent tested children before they entered kindergarten.

Figure 13-1 indicates how test results were used. Most often the results were used to plan for and individualize instruction. The second most frequent use of the information was to screen for children who might need special services. It is interesting to note that 27 percent of the reporting administrators indicated that prekindergarten testing was used to make recommendations that some children delay entry to kindergarten. We examined academic redshirting as a practice in chapter 5 and drew the conclusion that redshirting is not grounded in research. As we can see, the educational research base does not always filter into the daily practices of the schools.

> **If 61 percent of the reporting schools conduct tests prior to kindergarten, they must find the information valuable. How do they use the test results?**

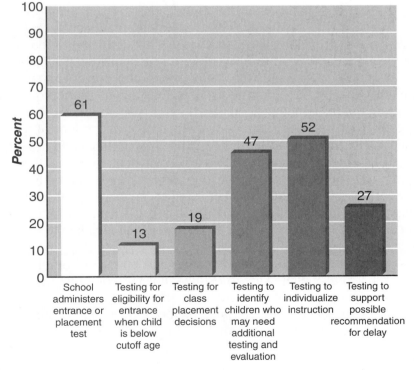

Note: Statistics are for U.S. schools with one or more kindergarten classes.
Source: U.S. Department of Education, National Center for Education Statistics, Early Childhood Longitudinal Study, Kindergarten Class of 1998–99, Public-use Base Year Data File.

Figure 13-1 Percent of schools that give a kindergarten entrance or placement test prior to kindergarten and how the test information is used, 1998–99.

In a survey of 385 schools reported by Costenbader, Rohrer, and Difonzo, (2000), 25 percent of the survey respondents spent less than 20 minutes with each child during their screening. It is particularly important to consider the impact on testing results when children are young, separated from parents, and in an unusual situation with strangers asking them to perform at their best and given 20 minutes to do it. Do we want to make decisions on the basis of this kind of testing?

READINESS TESTS

readiness—commonly used term without an agreed-upon definition

Parents worry over their child's **readiness**. Parents may even prep their children for kindergarten testing so that they will "pass" the test. Anxiety surrounding the readiness issue is fed by "Is your child ready for school?" articles regularly published in the popular press along with checklists parents are invited to use in order to gauge their child's degree of readiness. If, for some reason, the child is evaluated as unready, the implication is that the child is deficient and in need of being fixed.

Americans seem to be alone in their preoccupation with readiness. Nationally the concept came to the forefront during the late 1970s when the kindergarten curriculum began to take on the academic flavor of first grade. Readiness continued to garner attention during the 1980s as educators attempted to get back to the basics and reform education. The concept of readiness once again gained momentum in the 1990s showcased as the first of the National Education Goals: "By the year 2000 all children will start school ready to learn" (Shepard, Kagan, & Wurtz, 1998).

Kagan (1999) explained that for Americans, starting school represents an important entry rite. Therefore, the American tendency to find the idea of readiness so compelling is related to the value ascribed to the entry rite or new beginning. We tend to fuss. However, in countries where preschool education is universal, people tend to be less preoccupied with the concept of readiness because kindergarten is viewed as a continuation of schooling rather than a starting point.

Kagan (1999) also discriminated between two conceptions of readiness: readiness to learn and readiness for school. Research in child development reveals that human beings are able to learn even prior to being born. Therefore, given normal intelligence, one cannot argue that children need to reach a certain state of readiness before they can learn. On the other hand, readiness for school implies that there is some set of knowledge or skill that a child must possess in order to be successful in school.

What are the skills children need in order to be ready for school?

At the present time we know of no agreed-upon set of readiness skills. If, indeed, there are such skills, they have not yet been identified. In fact, the term "readiness" was held in such poor regard that the Goal 1 subgroup of the National Education Goals panel deliberately avoided using the term (Shepard, 1997). Assigned to study how to measure readiness, the group acknowledged the complex and nebulous nature of the term by purposefully failing to use it.

There are several possible explanations, but the primary obstacle is most likely the lack of an agreed-upon definition of readiness. Meisels (1995b) referred to readiness as a maze, reflecting the general frustration felt when attempting to make sense of the construct.

A survey of state early childhood policies revealed that no state had developed a definition of what readiness might be (Saluja, Scott-Little, & Clifford, 2000). Nevertheless, teachers and parents were certain about what it means to be ready for school. However, teachers and parents disagreed among themselves about what it means to be ready. Whereas teachers want to know if the child is healthy and rested, able to follow directions and conduct herself appropriately, parents consider readiness to be an academic criterion (U.S. Department of Education, 1993). The task of defining readiness is further complicated by factors such as theoretical orientation, curriculum design, teacher expectations, and school district policies.

Differing theoretical orientations, or beliefs about how children develop and learn, paint differing pictures of what it means to be ready (deCos, 1997). For example, for the maturationist, readiness is simply a matter of time. Children's skills will unfold like the petals of a flower, but not until the child has matured to the necessary level. Therefore, maturationists tend to sit back and wait for the child to become ready.

The view is quite different for developmentalists who see value in intervention. According to the developmentalist, if children have normal

Why is it so difficult to identify readiness skills?

How do we know they are ready for school?

intelligence and typical life experiences, they will progress through a series of stages that are hierarchical, invariant, predictable. As children pass through the stages, their development will reflect the qualitatively different characteristics of each stage. In developmental theories, experience is vital because the child's interactions with the environment build background skills and knowledge necessary for constructing new understanding. If a child has many rich experiences, he will develop maximally. If experiences are limited, the child's development will reflect the lack. In this way, heredity and environment interact so that there is a range of possible outcomes for each individual.

For the maturationist, readiness is static, but for the developmentalist, readiness can be enhanced or impeded depending upon the nature of the child's environment and experiences. Whereas the maturationist gives the child the gift of time to flower, the developmentalist sees a need to water, weed, and fertilize.

In addition to theoretical orientation, curriculum design has the potential to impact our understanding of readiness. Because there is no centralized system of education in the United States, each state holds the authority to determine the content that will be taught at each grade level. Some states further delegate curricular decisions to the school district level, making for a great deal of curricular variation across the country. That situational diversity makes it very difficult to identify any specific set of knowledge or skills a child would need in order to be successful in school. As long as there is no single, national curriculum, there cannot be one single definition of readiness.

Teacher expectations are also situational. As individual teachers set their own guidelines for acceptable levels of classroom behavior as well as acceptable academic performance, the child's chances for success are impacted. Although Enrique may be deemed ready for a year of kindergarten with teacher A who values play and hands-on experiences, he may not meet the readiness standard for a year of kindergarten with teacher B who expects children to learn through more passive, teacher-directed methods.

School district policies also have the potential to impact a definition of readiness. If the school district policy sets benchmarks for entry, then the child who cannot meet those benchmarks may be labeled as not ready for school. Criteria for entry may be related to the child's language, cognitive, physical, or emotional status, depending on individual school district practices and policies.

If readiness is situational, how do schools determine which children are permitted to enroll?

Given the lack of a strong readiness research base that would allow for school entry decisions to be made scientifically (Crnic & Lamberty, 1994), states have opted to make entrance to kindergarten a function of the child's chronological age. In the name of equity, the National Association for the Education of Young Children (NAEYC) and the National Association of Early Childhood Specialists in State Departments of Education have taken the strong position that chronological age should be the only criterion used to determine whether or not a child may attend kindergarten (NAEYC, 1995; NAECS, 2000). If the child is age-eligible, parents or guardians may opt to delay entrance, but legally entrance may not be denied.

Nationwide, children may legally attend kindergarten at age five, but states have legislated differing cutoff dates by which a child must have turned five. Cutoff dates vary across the country from June to December, but there is no clear basis for establishing age five as an optimal time for either developmental or instructional reasons (Crnic & Lamberty, 1994).

We test and guess. We offer opinions and try to gauge readiness, then counsel parents about the degree of readiness the child exhibits.

As part of the 1980s reform movement, some states mandated readiness testing but allowed local districts the discretion to make decisions about what and how to test. Readiness testing has been mandated in 17 states with the purpose of identifying special needs or for planning instruction (*Education Week*, 2003). Six states report using tests to determine preparedness for schooling (*Education Week*, 2003). The assumption appears to be that if we measure the skills children have acquired prior to formal schooling, we will be able to determine which children will be able to complete program goals by the end of the kindergarten year—and we want all children to be goal-completers.

LaParo and Pianta (2000) addressed the readiness testing controversy in a meta-analysis looking at effect sizes of both cognitive and behavioral assessments. The researchers examined 70 studies and compared assessments completed before or during kindergarten to assessments completed in first or second grade. Across time, readiness assessments were found to be poor predictors of behavior and social development. For cognitive comparisons, the meta-analysis showed small to moderate effect sizes. The research team concluded that "we should not make too many decisions based on children's performance prior to school entry. It reinforces the notion that young children's skills are unstable and dependent on exposure to stimulating settings" (Little, 2002).

Readiness tests are snapshots in time that may be measuring exposure to life experiences. Because children have unequal access to early experiences like visits to libraries, museums, and zoos, some children may be at a disadvantage when they take the readiness test. If a child does not know the name for an object because she has had limited experiences, readiness tests may actually be measuring socioeconomic status.

The use of readiness tests is not supported by research, but the results of such tests are often used to make important decisions about children; and those tests may, in fact, obscure factors outside that child such as socioeconomic status, preschool attendance, or home experiences that may be better at predicting school success.

Readiness tests are purported to predict success in school. However the high rate of false positives associated with readiness tests means that children may be misidentified and perhaps misplaced in school (Costenbader et al., 2000). NAEYC (1990) reported that readiness tests should be able to stand up to the highest standards of reliability and validity. Reliability means that a test results in similar scores when the same person takes the test on different dates. Validity is a technical term indicating that the test actually measures what it says it measures. For instance, a math achievement test is only valid if it truly does measure

> **Is there an age when children are ready to begin school?**

> **If we don't know what it means to be ready and if experts cannot agree on any specific set of readiness skills, how are decisions made about the readiness status of individual children?**

> **How effective are readiness tests at predicting academic success?**

math achievement. According to NAEYC, there are no readiness tests that meet high standards of reliability and validity (NAEYC, 1990).

What kinds of items are on readiness tests?

Because there is no scientific basis for identification of readiness skills that determine success in school (Crnic & Lamberty, 1994), the tests have taken on an eclectic, choose-your-own-flavor diversity. The tests themselves tend to assume a separate skills orientation. The NAEYC official position on school readiness cautions that interpreting readiness as mastery of isolated skills oversimplifies growth and may lead to mislabeling as "inadequate" some children who are actually developing normally (NAEYC, 1995).

SUMMARY

Assessment should keep the child's best interests in mind. Assessment may take a variety of forms and need not be formal testing. High stakes tests have significant rewards or punishments attached to scores, so they are termed high stakes. Assessment is also high stakes when outcomes are publicly reported. Individual educational decisions should be made on the basis of multiple inputs, never one single test.

When assessments are related to curriculum goals and objectives, they may become important tools for planning and instructional decisions. Preassessments, formative evaluation, and summative evaluation can provide vital instructional insights. These assessments may be formal, or they may be conducted informally using strategies such as teacher observation, anecdotal records, event sampling, running records, and time sampling. These assessments provide the basis for the teacher to analyze events and look for patterns of behavior.

Checklists, portfolios, and rating scales provide insights into student learning, but they also open the door to documenting student interests, work, and growth. More formal assessments such as standardized achievement and ability tests compare the child to a norming sample. Developmental tests compare the child's score to others at particular developmental levels.

There are cautions advised when administering formal tests to young children. Length of the test, student factors, and environmental factors can all impact a child's test performance. Particular caution should be used when administering standardized tests and interpreting test results for children younger than third grade.

Many school districts report conducting kindergarten screenings, and many states require screening prior to kindergarten to determine whether special services are needed. Screening is valuable when it targets gross physical, social, and cognitive difficulties.

We cannot agree on what it means to be ready for school. There is no accepted definition. Experts do not agree on any specific set of skills that one would need to possess to be deemed ready.

"Ready for liftoff" means all systems are running properly.

"Ready, set, go" means position your feet in the blocks, assume the position, then run.

"Ready, aim, fire" means position yourself and the gun, then take aim and shoot.

Frequently we ask, "Are you ready?" In that context we are asking whether that someone is prepared for what comes next. But we do not ask children whether they are ready for school. Instead, we test and guess. We offer opinions and try to gauge readiness, then counsel parents about the child's degree of readiness.

Key Terms

assessment

formal assessment

formative evaluation

informal assessment

preassessment

readiness

screening test

summative evaluation

Using What You Know

1. Observe kindergarten screening at a local school. How can you relate your observations to the text?

2. Go to your state department of education Web site and find out what testing requirements exist for grades K–3.

3. Go to the NAEYC Web site and read the position statement on standardized testing. Compare your local school district policy to the NAEYC guidelines.

For additional information on research-based practice, visit our Web site at http://www.earlychilded.delmar.com.

Part Three

Connecting Research to Practice

In the third division of this book, you are invited and challenged to apply what you read in the first two sections. Part I provided background to help when reading and interpreting educational research. Part II summarized research findings about school issues. In Part III you are invited to participate in the often messy but ultimately rewarding process of sorting out what we know from what we need to find out, and what we need to discard as unfounded. Finally, you are challenged to apply the research base to decision making in the practical, day-to-day world of children in schools.

Understanding and accurately applying what we have read can be a difficult task, but it is a necessary professional ability. As we have seen, most problems in the education profession are multifaceted, seldom isolated to a single issue with a simple answer. The case scenarios in chapter 14 are designed for working with others. The projects and activities suggested in chapter 15 are designed for individuals and small groups to delve deeper into key educational issues.

Chapter 14
Case Scenarios to Explore

This chapter contains case scenarios based on real situations where names and places have been disguised to protect the innocent—or in some cases, the guilty. Use what you have learned in prior sections of this book as you read and discuss the cases with others. You may need to draw on information from several different chapters as you analyze and evaluate the numerous issues involved in each scenario.

SCENARIO I: SISTER SCHOOLS

The Fairfield School Board will meet tonight to discuss best use of buildings within the small, city school district. The school-age population has become uneven across the district, making it difficult to fully utilize classroom space in some buildings and causing overcrowding in others. The six elementary buildings, which are spread out across the city, are of most concern.

Currently the elementary buildings serve kindergarten through sixth grade in individual neighborhoods. People take pride in their neighborhood schools where most children walk to school with their friends. The Parent/ Teacher Organization is active in most of the schools, and in the more affluent neighborhoods parents tend to volunteer in their children's schools.

The buildings themselves vary in age and appearance. Newer buildings are located in newer, upper middle class subdivisions, and the older buildings are located in the older, central areas of the city. All buildings have been kept in good repair, but older buildings are discernibly in need of updating and modernization.

Fairfield citizens tend to support their schools financially with good voter turnout to pass school levies and bond issues. Fairfield is known as a great place to raise children, though in recent years several pockets of poverty have developed and drugs have been identified as a problem at the high school. The community is not diverse, as most residents are Caucasian. The school district has a good reputation for quality, though schools located near two large, fairly new mobile home parks have poorer academic achievement than do the other elementary schools.

The school board is considering a plan that would create three pairs of sister schools at the elementary level and place grades 5 through 8 in middle schools. The elementary schools would become either grades K–2 only or 3–5 only. Each K–2 building would feed into a sister building of grades 3–5. That way children would stay together as they moved from one sister school to the next. Neighborhood school attendance lines would be erased, as children would be located in K–2 buildings or 3–5 buildings, depending on age.

Parents have been invited to phone the school board office if they would like to be placed on the agenda to speak to the board. The attendance at tonight's meeting is expected to be high because interest in the issue is high and personal. The local newspaper has received numerous letters to the editor on the topic. The superintendent of schools, Jack Jeffry, is focusing on the cost savings such a plan would permit. Superintendent Jeffry also emphasizes that the plan would make it easier for grade level teachers to plan together because they would be physically housed in buildings with other teachers at the same grade level.

Related Activities

1. Imagine that you are a parent of a child who will enter kindergarten next year. What questions do you have concerning the plan?

2. Evaluate the plan based on what you have learned about class size, school size, and the parent connection.

3. How might implementing this plan affect the parents and other members of the community?

4. Are there other benefits or considerations the school board should think about?

5. You and your spouse borrowed to the hilt in order to finance a home purchase in a specific area of Fairfield specifically because you wanted your children to attend the excellent elementary school in that neighborhood. The new plan would change the school your children would attend. You have asked to address the school board at the meeting tonight. What points will you make?

SCENARIO II: KINDERGARTEN SCHOOL

As a large city school and a sizable population of families with children living below the poverty level, San Gabriel has been plagued with poor achievement test scores for a number of years. However, the new superintendent is determined to target achievement problems early with particular focus on the kindergarten level.

The district has adopted a teacher-directed kindergarten curriculum with a strong academic thrust. If a child begins to fall behind, the plan calls for immediate individual tutoring in specific skills lessons until the child catches up. This early intervention program is aimed at remediating children when their problems are small and manageable.

It has been determined that kindergarten school buildings will be set up throughout the city. All San Gabriel kindergartners will be in one of the kindergarten schools where teachers will plan and work together closely. Only kindergarten children will attend these schools, removing them from possible negative influences of older children. Class sizes will be kept small at a pupil teacher ratio of approximately 17:1. After the kindergarten year, children will be tested to determine whether they will be promoted to first grade or placed in a pre-first grade class for an additional year where they will receive more intense intervention.

Related Activities

1. Evaluate the plan in light of current research.

2. Imagine that you were hired by the San Gabriel School District as a research consultant. Your job is to determine whether or not the new plan is resulting in greater academic achievement. In a small group, discuss how you would design the study.

3. What changes would you recommend to make the plan come into line with current research?

SCENARIO III: QUESTIONING

After reading the section on questioning in chapter 11, read the following selection from the Judy Blume book, *Blubber*. Analyze what is happening in the scene and lead a discussion of how teachers can avoid the problem depicted by Ms. Blume.

When she finished her song she was right next to Wendy. "Wendy . . . can you tell me what was coming out of my mouth as I sang?"

"Out of your mouth?" Wendy asked.

"That's right," Miss Rothbelle told her.

"Well . . . it was . . . um . . . words?"

"No . . . no . . . no," Miss Rothbelle said.

(continued)

Wendy was surprised. She can always give teachers the answers they want.

Miss Rothbelle moved on. "Do you know, Caroline?"

"Was it sound?"

"Wrong!" Miss Rothbelle said, turning. "Donna Davidson, can you tell me?"

"It was a song," Donna said.

"Really Donna . . . we all know that!" Miss Rothbelle looked around. "Linda Fischer, do you know what was coming out of my mouth as I sang to the class?"

Linda didn't say anything.

"Well, Linda . . ." Miss Rothbelle said.

"I think it was air," Linda finally told her. "Either that or breath."

Miss Rothbelle walked over to Linda's desk. "That was not the correct answer. Weren't you paying attention?" She pulled a few strands of Linda's hair . . .

She walked up and down the aisles until she stopped at my desk . . .

"We'll see if you've been paying attention . . . suppose you tell me the answer to my question."

I had no idea what Miss Rothbelle wanted me to say. There was just one thing left that could have been coming out of her mouth as she sang, so I said, "It was spit."

"What?" Miss Rothbelle glared at me.

"I mean, it was saliva," I told her.

Miss Rothbelle banged her fist on my desk. "That was a very rude thing to say. You can sit in the corner for the rest of the period.". . .

At the end of the music period Robby Winters called out, "Miss Rothbelle . . . Miss Rothbelle . . ."

"What is it?" she asked.

"You never told us what was coming out of your mouth when you sang."

"That's right," Miss Rothbelle said. "I didn't."

"What was it," Robby asked.

"It was melody," Miss Rothbelle said. Then she spelled it. "M-e-l-o-d-y. And every one of you should have known." She blew her pitch-pipe at us and walked out of the room.

Excerpt from Simon & Schuster Books for Young Readers, an imprint of Simon & Schuster Children's Publishing Division, from *Blubber* by Judy Blume. Copyright 1974 Judy Blume.

SCENARIO IV: HOMEWORK POLICY

The Piscataway Township School District in New Jersey created a media feeding frenzy when the school board adopted a new homework policy. The 7,000-student district had increased homework demands on students but had not seen an expected rise in achievement. Parents complained that students had no time left for other activities, and there was concern that students whose parents were unable to help with their homework were at an increased disadvantage (Vail, 2001). The result was a new district-wide homework policy that contained provisions to limit homework. Go to http://www.asbj.com. Using the "Search asbj" button, do a search for the "April 2001 cover story" and read the "Homework Problems" article in the *American School Board Journal*. Then click the link to read the homework policy, looking for any uncommon provisions.

Related Activities

1. Take the role of the following characters and from each perspective, evaluate the homework policy.

   a. Student

   b. Parent

   c. Spanish teacher

   d. English teacher in middle school and high school

   e. Math teacher

   f. Soccer coach

   g. Scout leader

SCENARIO V: TEXAS AND FLORIDA RETAIN THIRD GRADERS

When 43,000 Florida pupils and 11,700 Texas pupils failed to pass state reading assessments at the end of third grade, schools offered special summer reading remedial courses so that children could then retake the test, hopefully pass it, and move on to fourth grade. At the end of the summer, there were reports in local Florida newspapers that an estimated 32,000 third graders would be retained because they were not able to pass the reading test even after summer school. The number represents 16 percent of Florida's third graders. Texas did a little better, with just under 4 percent of the state's third graders being retained in grade.

Senator Frederica S. Wilson, a Democrat from Miami warned, "We're gambling with these children. We will be sorry, because we have lost a group of children that could have been saved" (Reid, 2003).

The Florida State Department of Education spokesperson explained that children could not be promoted because they would fall further behind. Without solid reading skills, children would not be able to succeed in fourth grade. Pupils may take the test multiple times, and parents have the right to appeal the decision to retain their child another year.

Related Activities

1. Write a letter to the editor explaining your professional opinion about whether or not the pupils should be retained. Give reasons based in research.

2. Go to the Florida State Department of Education Web page and find out whether the "pass the test to pass the grade" policy is still in effect. If not, is there any indication why not?

SCENARIO VI: ACADEMIC REDSHIRTING

Rob will celebrate his fifth birthday on July 4th and is excited about the prospect of attending kindergarten at the big school where his older brother and sister are enrolled. A tall, slim child, Rob approaches new situations and new people with caution until he gains a degree of comfort. Then he wins over most people with his shy smile and calm personality.

Rob comes from a stable middle-class home with an electrical engineer father and mother who works part-time at the public library. Rob likes to play soccer and catch with his older brother and sister and his dad. He helps his mother with chores and is responsible about caring for his pet turtle. Rob knows almost everything there is to know about his turtle. He became an expert by begging his mother to bring home turtle books from the library.

Rob likes any kind of sport and is often seen with a ball in his hands. Though Rob enjoys physical activities, his coordination is just average for his age and developmental level. He takes turns, plays fair, and has made several close friends in his preschool class.

During free choice time, Rob usually selects blocks and cars, construction sets, or the science center, and his friends follow his lead. He seldom selects crafts, books, puzzles, or writing activities. In fact, Rob is not interested in formal academics and becomes easily distracted when the teacher is in front of the class teaching letter sounds or mathematical concepts.

During parent/teacher conferences, Rob's preschool teacher, Mrs. Washington, suggested that he might not be ready for kindergarten. Mrs. Washington pointed out that Rob's lack of interest in academics might be a problem in the academic-focused curriculum of the local kindergarten. It might be good for Rob to wait out a year to give him more time to mature. After all, Rob's July birthday would make him one of the youngest children in the kindergarten class because the cutoff date for kindergarten entrance is September 1. Mrs. Washington reassured Rob's parents that they would never regret giving Rob the gift of time.

Related Activities

1. Rob's parents come to you for your professional advice. Based on research and Rob's individual characteristics, what do you tell them?

2. Academic achievement is only one piece of the entrance age puzzle. In your opinion, what are the other pieces?

SCENARIO VII: THE TASK FORCE

You are a teacher in a suburban school district attached to a large urban area. Your district has become a transition place for parents to move as a step out of the inner city. As a result, the influx of students has led to a dramatic decline in test scores. The school superintendent has appointed you to a task force to solve the problem of declining test scores. In preparation for the first meeting, each member of the task force has been asked to come prepared to make at least one sound recommendation. What will you recommend?

Chapter 15
Projects and Activities

The projects and activities in this chapter are intended to help you think deeply about the research reported in Part II. Rather than work systematically through each item, it is suggested that you skim through the suggested projects and activities, then choose items to pursue that interest you. Suggested projects vary in complexity and the amount of time they require to complete. It is hoped that the projects and activities raise additional questions about the early childhood research base and entice you to design additional projects and activities of special interest to you.

1. How do the following quotes relate to, uphold, or call into question the research described in Part II of this text?

   a. "What we want is to see the child in pursuit of knowledge, not knowledge in pursuit of the child."—George Bernard Shaw

   b. "Not everything that can be counted counts, and not everything that counts can be counted."—Albert Einstein

2. Review the research on transition programs, redshirting, and readiness. Then read *'I Need Time to Grow': The Transitional Year*, reprinted here. Construct several key questions about the article as it relates to the research base.

'I NEED TIME TO GROW': THE TRANSITIONAL YEAR

Not every student is developmentally ready to move on to first grade after a year of kindergarten. The best gift we can give is to those who aren't, Ms. Harris has found, is an extra year to mature—mentally, socially, and emotionally—in a nurturing environment.

By Barbara S. Harris
Associate Headmaster, Presbyterian Day School, Memphis, Tennessee

While watering my plants near the kitchen window one morning, I noticed that one particular plant, though healthy in appearance, was not flourishing like the others I had rooted at about the same time. All had received the same amount of sunlight, well-prepared soil, water, and pruning, and since I had not moved them, the temperature was the same for all. Yet the green leaves of this plant had not matured as rapidly, the stems were not as strong, and the overall size of the plant was much smaller. As I continued to ponder these differences, it occurred to me that perhaps this one plant just needed more time before its roots took hold in that growth spurt that leads to maturity.

Isn't that just the way it is with children? When I see the kindergarteners spilling into our school each fall, I'm always struck that they are alike in so many ways, yet different in so many others. We provide all of them with a bounty of care, nurturing, and attention, and it seems that they should master these skills, soak up everything teachers can pour out for them, and mature at an ever-quickening pace. Yet, as they near the end of that kindergarten year, many of the children do not seem to possess the maturity, both academic and social, that they will need for their "replanting" in first grade.

At my school and others throughout the country, educators long ago saw the need for the transitional classroom, a place where normal children would be given the time they need to acquire maturity, to master work habits, to refine skills, and to develop the attention span that is so critical to success in the early grades.

I recently came upon an old cartoon that I had been keeping. It showed two kindergarten boys coming out of their classroom. One was saying to the other, "I plan to take a year off between kindergarten and first grade to find myself." I suspect that more than just a few kindergarteners need to "find themselves" during an extra year's time between kindergarten and first grade—a year that can stimulate them to further learning and support their development of positive self-esteem.

When I think back over the years about students I've known who seem to succeed with ease in the early years and compare them to those who struggled, the major difference that I see has to do with readiness—developmental readiness. In *All Grown Up and No Place to Go,* David Elkind writes, "In New Hampshire children are not hurried. It is one of the few states in the nation that provides 'readiness' classes for children who have completed kindergarten but who are not yet ready for first grade."[1]

Yes, we are a society that is in a hurry, but where are we going, and what will we get there with, if our young children are not fortified and nurtured in

(continued)

the early years of growth? As Nancy Bohl so clearly put it many years ago in her special message to parents, the step between kindergarten and first grade is a *giant* one, and for those who are not developmentally ready, it can lead to frustration and failure.[2]

I recently participated in a panel discussion with several kindergarten teachers who bear the responsibility of recommending (or requiring) that students in their classes attend a transitional class for a year rather than passing directly into first grade. In the case of *recommending* transition, parents have the option of choosing whether the student moves on to first grade or goes to the transitional year. If a student is *required* to attend the transitional class, there is no option, and the child must be enrolled in the transition program.

These are not easy decisions that teachers make overnight. They think long and hard and observe the children in their kindergarten classes closely as they work throughout the entire year to evaluate each child's readiness for first grade. That readiness is measured in several ways:

- using handwriting samples for assessment,
- testing letter/sound recognition,
- using checklists for mastery of skills in reading and math,
- evaluating journal writing,
- observing the student and peer group,
- judging the student's ability to work in groups versus independently,
- evaluating how well students listen to and follow directions,
- assessing work habits and organizational skills,
- using one-on-one testing, and
- using standardized testing.

Of course, as any kindergarten teacher would recognize, this list is just a partial one. We know that the most important evaluative tool is the teacher, who must work patiently each day as he or she interacts continually with each young child.

The kindergarten teachers with whom I spoke mentioned several factors that influence their decision to recommend students to the transition program. All agreed that a lack of maturity is one factor that is usually noted early in the school year. Other factors that they felt are important in identifying readiness for first grade include attentiveness, ability to focus, listening skills, blending sounds, understanding math concepts, ability to process skills, responsiveness, developmental readiness in written work, independence, and skill mastery. The kindergarten teachers unequivocally determined that poor behavior related solely to conduct would *not* be a reason to recommend a student to the transition program. Reading readiness was the number-one academic area that most influenced their decision to require a student to move into a transitional class.

Ever since the late 1950s, there has been considerable debate in the education community as to whether the transitional class is a valuable program that actually improves academic performance. It does seem clear that transitional classes have a beneficial effect on social growth and the growth of self-esteem. Anthony Coletta argues that "supporters [of transitional classrooms] view them favorably because they help children who might do poorly in a rigid, academic curriculum by providing instead the opportunity to be successful in a more relaxed, developmentally appropriate environment. Extra-year programs are therefore seen as a clear alternative to grade retention."[3]

I recently interviewed Laurel Childs, teacher of a successful transitional class in an all-boys elementary school. Years before, she had also been a kindergarten teacher who evaluated students in her own class and recommended to transitional classes those students who needed an extra year. I asked her to identify some of the specific strengths that make her transitional class so successful. Here are some of the factors that she mentioned:

■ smaller class size (between 11 and 13 students),

■ individual attention to meet the specific needs of students,

■ time for extra reinforcement of skills,

■ building on the successes and strengths of students,

■ whole-language exposure, as well as strong phonics approach, and

■ extra patience on the part of the teacher in dealing with students' repeated mistakes.

Childs mentioned that the slower-paced curriculum of the transitional class allows students to move at their own rate. One of her goals is building character and self-esteem. She said that she makes a great effort to develop a team whose members work with and for one another. Each child has a basic individualized plan to help work on strengths and weaknesses. "My classroom is set up to be a place that is nonjudgmental. Students can make mistakes in a safe and trusting environment. Administration and special-area personnel give much attention to the students, giving praise and reinforcement. Enrichment activities include special field trips, unique projects, and lots of parent involvement. Parental concerns and needs are recognized and addressed through extra communication," says Childs. I asked her to share some of the feedback that she has received from parents, teachers, and children.

> Former parents praise the program and testify to what it has done for their children. Last year, one mother told me that they came in "kicking and screaming" and did not want this transitional year, but now she feels that it has been a wonderful year. I have seen former students go on to become successful because of that gift of another year. Current students often want to stay in the same classroom and not move on to a new grade because it is a safe and successful place for them. Teachers who teach the transition child the following year praise the program because they feel it gives the child a boost that is needed for the child to be successful in first grade.

Anthony Coletta described published research in which Jonathan Sandoval of the University of California studied high school students who years earlier had completed the transitional (junior) first grade. Students placed in the transitional class were superior to a control group on three out of four indicators of academic progress. The students exhibited positive attitudes about having been in the program and stated that the experience helped them to do better socially and emotionally, as well as academically.

(continued)

In three case studies that I conducted on former transitional class students, I found some similarities regarding their progress following the transitional year.

Case Study A. A boy was recommended for an extra year because he had difficulty writing letters and numbers, cutting, and coloring, and he was unable to follow a story silently while another child read. He also exhibited a lack of self-control, as well as an inability to complete work carefully within a reasonable period of time. By the end of the transitional year, reading, math, and language development showed marked improvement, and the student had received an "E" for excellence in his ability to complete work.

Case Study B. A boy was recommended for the transitional class because he had difficulty with his work habits. He was unable to complete work in a reasonable period of time, could not follow directions, and was unable to continue an activity without constant help. The lack of reading readiness became a concern as the year progressed. He was unable to blend sounds; sequence objects, pictures, and events; and follow a story silently while another child read. He was also unable to solve number sentences in math by the end of the kindergarten year. However, reading skills were the main focus of the transitional year for this student and he made marked improvement in all areas.

Case Study C. This boy had difficulty following directions, listening, and working independently. Some reversals were noted in numbers and letters throughout the year. Following the year in the transitional class, he exhibited marked improvement in all areas.

All three students appeared to have benefited from the transitional class. At the time that these case studies were completed, student A had completed the first grade, student B was finishing his third-grade year, and student C was finishing fifth grade in a departmentalized setting. Student B was the only one who appeared to be leveling off academically. It is interesting to note that all three of the students had a positive feeling about having been in the transitional class. They exuded confidence, and their self-esteem was strong.

Educators need to remember that each child has his or her own time line. Even though schools use chronological age to determine a child's legal readiness for school, age is not always a reliable indicator of readiness for learning. Giving students the opportunity to mature physically, socially, and emotionally in a nurturing environment that is intellectually stimulating, relatively free of stress, and has a low pupil/teacher ratio can provide them with the opportunity to build their developmental readiness and so offer a better chance for academic success.

---

[1] David Elkind, *All Grown Up and No Place to Go* (New York: Addison Wesley, 1996).
[2] Nancy Bohl, "A Gift of Time: The Transition Year," *Early Years*, January 1984, p. 14.
[3] Anthony Coletta, *What's Best for Kids* (Rosemont, NJ: Modern Learning Press, 1991).

3. Lead or participate in a group discussion of the article. As an alternative, solicit classmates to help you reenact the scene.

4. After reading the section in chapter 11 about homework, write five tips for teachers to make the most of homework assignments. Then compare your tips to those suggested by Cooper on the Northwest Regional Educational Laboratory Web site http://www.nwrel.org (Summer 2002 issue in the take-home section). Search the term "Take-Home Lessons" and then click #27. Then click "Take-Home Lessons."

5. Create an analogy or a metaphor to help explain the concept of looping or multiage grouping.

6. Create a short questionnaire and conduct a survey of guidance and discipline plans used by area early childhood teachers. Analyze the results and draw any conclusions.

7. Observe in at least two early childhood classrooms to identify the curriculum delivery model being used by the teachers. What characteristics led to your conclusions? Do your observations agree or conflict with the research evidence?

8. Interview several teachers about the practice of academic redshirting. Do they ever recommend that a child be held out of kindergarten in order to give a year to mature?

9. Observe in a classroom for the way the teacher uses praise. Make a chart to help you record important characteristics. Here are some suggested headings: frequency, the circumstances, whether it is specific or general praise, male or female receiving praise, child's response to praise. Jot down a list of praise phrases the teacher uses. Summarize what you charted. What generalizations can you make from your observations?

10. The following Web sites are related to working with parents. Review each site then write a description for each site in 25 words or less.

   http://www.projectappleseed.org

   http://www.pta.org

   http://www.ncpie.org

   http://www.croton.com

   http://www.educationpolicy.org

11. Evaluate the school board policy at http://unionps.org. Search the term "board policy." Click on "Sections 1–4.rev99-00". Discuss the implication of fundraising as part of parent involvement.

12. More than one hundred years ago Herbert Spencer wrote, "We dress our children's minds as we do their bodies . . . in the fashion of the day." Relate the quote to curriculum issues today.

13. Examine the illustration here. Discuss its meaning for education.

Illustration: Jim Hummel

14. Rose and her teacher cannot find Rose's reading paper. Rose rides the school bus, so she cannot stay after school. The teacher tells Rose to do the paper again during recess time. Discuss.

15. Visit a mall, church, or other place where families gather. Identify the parenting styles exhibited. Tell which characteristics led you to make your decisions. Do the behaviors of the children hold true to what you read in the textbook, or are they different?

16. Observe children on the playground at recess. What evidence do you see that children are developing social skills through recess?

17. Observe a parent and child interacting at a restaurant, ball game, or other gathering. Can you identify the temperament types? Is there a good fit? Why?

18. Interview parents about their discipline/guidance strategies. How many use the authoritative parenting style?

19. Observe the uses of rewards and punishments in primary classrooms. How do they affect behavior?

20. In your classroom observations, look for examples of intrinsic and extrinsic motivation.

21. With parental permission, interview a child or small group of children about time-out. "Tell me about time-out. How does that work?" What insights do you gain?

Glossary

A

abstract—summarized report.

academic learning time—part of engaged time when tasks are successfully completed because students understand.

academic redshirting—purposefully delaying kindergarten entrance so that the child will be older and more competitive.

accountability—assurance that resources spent on programs result in comparable learning outcomes.

allocated time—time scheduled for school to be in session.

assessment—documentation of children's work to make educational decisions.

attachment—nature of the love relationship between parent and child.

authoritarian parenting—parenting style low in warmth and high in control.

authoritative parenting—parenting style high in warmth, combines control with encouragement.

B

behaviorist philosophy—learning occurs as a result of reinforcement.

C

case study—research design to study in depth an experience or individual circumstance.

class size—ratio of children to teachers.

constructivist philosophy—children learn through active experiences, building their own understanding.

control group—in experimental research, the group receiving no treatment.

correlational research—research design that investigates the patterns of how variables move.

cross-generational problem—subjects who grew up during different periods of history may be different from one another in ways that might influence study results.

cross-sectional design—subjects are assessed at only one point in time.

D

database—collection of subject-related bibliographic references.

dependent variable—in experimental research, the variable that is not manipulated.

difficult temperament—individual is intense, irregular, negative, approaches cautiously, dislikes change.

discipline—managing children's behavior.

E

easy temperament—individual is regular, positive, adjusts to change.

effect size—statistical treatment to aid in determining the practical significance of a research finding.

engaged time—the part of instructional time when students are cognitively engaged and on task.

experimental group—the group receiving a treatment in experimental research.

experimental research—research design in which variables are manipulated and comparisons are made between groups.

F

formal assessment—level of skill or understanding is measured by a test.

formative evaluation—monitors understanding during the learning process.

G

guidance—helping children learn to manage their own behavior.

H

heterogeneous grouping—children with mixed levels of ability are grouped together for instruction.

homogeneous grouping—children who are academically similar are grouped together for instruction.

I

independent variable—in experimental research, the variable that is manipulated.

informal assessment—level of skill or understanding is measured as the child completes learning tasks.

instructional time—the part of the school day allocated to academics.

inter-rater reliability—observers are trained in recording observations to eliminate differences in interpretation.

L

learning style—concept that individuals have preferred ways of learning.

longitudinal design—the same subjects are followed over a period of time.

looping— the teacher stays with the same group of children for more than one year, then loops back to pick up another group.

M

meta-analysis—statistical analysis of numerous research studies focusing on the same problem.

multiage grouping—children of mixed ages are placed in the same classroom to facilitate interaction.

N

naturalistic observation—observations occur as subjects go about their activities in a real-world setting.

nongraded/ungraded grouping—mixed ages are grouped together to make groups homogeneous.

P

permissive indulgent—child-focused parenting style high in warmth and low in control.

permissive negligent—adult-focused parenting style low in warmth and control.

preassessment—determines the child's knowledge before teaching content.

primary source—the original research report.

pupil/teacher ratio—ratio of children to all professional school personnel.

R

random selection—subjects for studies are selected in a random manner such that all potential subjects have the same opportunity to be selected.

readiness—commonly used term without an agreed-upon definition.

recitation—teaching strategy that incorporates telling and questioning.

research base—body of professional knowledge supported by rigorous research evidence and the basis for making educational decisions.

S

same-sex grouping—children are grouped by gender to improve achievement.

savant—individual with mental deficiencies exhibits high level of unlearned and specialized skill.

scientifically based research—generally interpreted as results of rigorous research that has been statistically analyzed.

screening test—identifies children who may need special services or interventions.

secondary source—reports on or discusses aspects of the original research.

self-report—research design using subjects who tell about themselves.

sequential design—combines aspects of longitudinal and cross-sectional designs by studying separate groups over time.

slow-to-warm-up temperament—individual is shy, quiet, cautious, slightly negative.

structured observation—occurs in a laboratory setting or other prearranged environment.

summative evaluation—determines whether or not objectives have been met.

systematic observation—organized plan for observing subjects and recording observations in an orderly manner.

T

temperament—individual style of interaction with others and the environment.

transition classes—extra-year classes before kindergarten or first grade.

trickle-down curriculum—increased academic expectations have resulted in first grade curriculum taught in kindergarten.

W

wait time—the amount of time a teacher waits between asking a question and calling on a student for a response.

References

Achilles, C. M. (1999). *Let's put kids first finally: Getting class size right.* Thousand Oaks, CA: Corwin Press.

Acker, M. M., & O'Leary, S. G. (1996). Inconsistency of mothers' feedback and toddlers' misbehavior and negative affect. *Journal of Abnormal Child Psychology, 24,* 703–714.

Ainsworth, M. D. S. (1978). The development of infant-mother attachment. In B. M. Caldwell & H. N. Riccuiti (Eds.), *Review of Child Development Research,* (Vol. 3), Chicago: The University of Chicago Press.

Alspaugh, J. W. (1998). Achievement loss associated with the transition to middle school and high school. *The Journal of Educational Research, 92,* 20–25.

Alspaugh, J. W. (2000). The effect of transition grade to high school, gender, and grade level upon dropout rates. *American Secondary Education, 29,* 2–9.

Anderson, G. E., Whipple, A. D., & Jimerson, S. R. (2002). *Grade retention: Achievement and mental health outcomes.* Bethesda, MD: National Association of School Psychologists.

Andersson, D. (1992). Effects of day-care on cognitive and socioemotional competence of thirteen-year-old Swedish schoolchildren. *Child Development, 63,* 20–36.

Anne E. Casey Foundation. (2003). *Kids count databook.* [WWW document] http://www.aecf.org.

Anshutz, R. (1975). An investigation of wait-time and questioning techniques as an instructional variable for science methods students microteaching elementary school children (Doctoral dissertation, University of Kansas, 1973). *Dissertation Abstracts International, 35,* 5978A.

Arnett, J. J. (1995). Broad and narrow socialization: The family in the context of a cultural theory. *Journal of Marriage and the Family, 57,* 617–628.

Associated Press (2002, September 16). Current rules restrictive on single-sex education. [WWW Document]. http://cnnfyi.printthis.clickability.com.

Association for Childhood Education International. (1991). *ACEI position paper on standardized testing.* Wheaton, MD: ACEI.

Baker, A. J. L., Piotrkowski, C. S., & Brooks-Gunn, J. (1998). *The effects of the home instruction program for preschool youngsters (HIPPY) on children's school performance at the end of the program and one year later.* [WWW document]. http://www.futureofchildren.org.

Balzer, C. (1991). *The effect of ability grouping of gifted elementary students, combined with instruction modified for level and rate of learning on student achievement: A review of the literature.* ERIC Digest (ERIC Document Reproduction Service No. ED 345392).

Bandura, A. (1977). *Social learning theory.* Englewood Cliffs, NJ: Prentice-Hall.

Banks, R. (2003). *The early childhood education curriculum debate: Direct instruction vs. child-initiated learning.* ERIC Clearinghouse on Elementary and Early Childhood Education. [WWW document]. http://ericeece.org.

Baumrind, D. (1971). Current patterns of parental authority. *Developmental Psychology,* 1–103.

Baumrind, D. (1991). The influence of parenting style on adolescent competence and substance use. *Journal of Early Adolescence, 11*(1), 56–95.

Begley, S. (1998). Homework doesn't help. *Newsweek, 131*(13), 50–51.

Belsky, J. (1988). The "effects" of infant day care reconsidered. *Early Childhood Research Quarterly, 3,* 235–272.

Berke, L. E. (1997). *Child development.* Needham Heights, MA: Allyn and Bacon.

Biddle, B., & Berliner, D. C. (2002). Small class size and its effects. *Educational Leadership, 59*(5), 1223.

Binkley, M. E. (1989). *Transition classes. Evaluation report.* Nashville, TN: Nashville Metropolitan Public Schools.

Bloom, B., Englehart, M., Furst, E., Hill, W., & Krathwohl, D. (1956). *Taxonomy of educational objectives: The classification of educational goals.* Handbook 1, *Cognitive domain.* New York: Longmans Green.

Bracey, G. W. (1989). Age and achievement. *Phi Delta Kappan, 70,* 732.

Bracey, G. W. (1999). Failing children—twice. *Education Week, 18*(40), 42.

Bracey, G. W. (2001). At the beep, pay attention. *Phi Delta Kappan, 82*(7), 555–556.

Brophy, J., & Evertson, C. (1976). *Learning from teaching: A developmental perspective.* Boston: Allyn & Bacon.

Brophy, J., & Good, T. (1986). Teacher effects. In M. Wittrock (Ed.), *Third handbook of research on teaching* (pp. 328–375). New York: Macmillan.

Brualdi, A. C. (1996). *Multiple intelligences: Gardner's theory.* ERIC Digest. (ERIC Document Reproduction Service No. ED 410226).

Brualdi, A. C. (1998). *Classroom questions.* ERIC Digest (ERIC Document Reproduction Service No. ED 422407).

Burts, D. C., Hart, C. H., Charlesworth, R., Fleege, P. O., Mosley, J., & Thomasson, R. H. (1992). Observed activities and stress behaviors of children in developmentally appropriate and inappropriate kindergarten classrooms. *Early Childhood Research Quarterly, 7*(2), 297–318.

Burts, D. C., Hart, C. H., Charlesworth, R., & Kirk, L. (1990). A comparison of frequencies of stress behaviors observed in kindergarten children in classrooms with developmentally appropriate versus developmentally inappropriate instructional practices. *Early Childhood Research Quarterly, 5*(3), 407–423.

Byrd, R. S., Weitzman, M., & Auinger, P. (1997). Increased behavior problems associated with delayed school entry and delayed school progress. *Pediatrics, 100*(4), 654–661.

Byrnes, D. (1989). Attitudes of students, parents and educators toward repeating a grade. In L. Shepard & M. Smith (Eds.), *Flunking grades: Research and policies on retention* (pp. 108–131). New York: The Falmer Press.

Cameron, J., & Pierce, W. D. (1994). Reinforcement, reward, and intrinsic motivation: A meta-analysis. *Review of Educational Research, 64*(3), 363–423.

Cameron, M. B., & Wilson, B. J. (1990). The effects of chronological age, gender, and delay of entrance on academic achievement and retention: Implications for academic redshirting. *Psychology in the Schools, 27,* 260–263.

Campbell, F. A., & Ramey, C. T. (1995). The cognitive and school outcomes for high-risk African-American students at middle adolescence: Positive effects of early intervention." *American Educational Research Journal, 32,* 743–772.

Campbell, F. A., & Pungello, E. (2000). *High quality child care has long-term educational benefits for poor children.* Paper presented at the Head Start National Research Conference (5th, Washington, DC, June 28–July 1, 2000).

Caplan, J., Hall, G., Lubin, S., & Fleming, R. (1997a). *Parent involvement: Literature review and database of promising practices.* [WWW document]. http://www.ncrel. org.

Caplan, J., Hall, G., Lubin, S., & Fleming, R. (1997b). *Literature review of school-family partnerships.* [WWW document]. http://www.ncrel.org.

Carter, S. (accessed 2003). *The impact of parent/family involvement on student outcomes: An annotated bibliography of research from the past decade.* Consortium for "Appropriate Dispute Resolution in Special Education." [WWW document]. http://www.directionservice.org.

Chen, C., & Stevenson, H. W. (1989). Homework: A cross-cultural examination. *Child Development, 60,* 551–561.

Coladarci, T., & Hancock, J. (2002). *The (limited) evidence regarding effects of grade-span configurations on academic achievement: What rural educators should know.* ERIC Digest (ERIC Document Reproduction Service No. ED 467714).

Connell, P. H., & Evans, J. (1992). *The effects of extra year program after kindergarten on students' school achievement and self-esteem.* Paper presented at the Annual Meeting of the Mid-South Educational Research Association, Knoxville, TN, November 11–13.

Cooper, H. (1989). *Homework.* White Plains, NY: Longman.

Cooper, H., Lindsay, J. J., Nye, B., & Greathouse, S. (1998). Relationships among attitudes about homework, amount of homework assigned and completed, and student achievement. *Journal of Educational Psychology, 90*(1), 70–83.

Costenbader, V., Rohrer, A. M., & DiFonzo, N. (2000). Kindergarten screening: A survey of current practice. *Psychology in the Schools, 37*(4), 323–332.

Cotton, K. (2001). *Classroom questioning.* Northwest Regional Educational Laboratory. [WWW document]. http://www.nwrel.org.

Crnic, K., & Lamberty, G. (1994). Reconsidering school readiness: Conceptual and applied perspectives. *Early Education and Development, 15*(2), 99–105.

Crosser, S. (1991). Summer birth date children: Kindergarten entrance age and academic achievement. *Journal of Educational Research, 84*(3), 140–146.

Crosser, S. (1997). Time out: Insights from football. *Early Childhood News, 9* (September/October), 6–12.

Cryan, J. R., Sheehan, R., Wiechel, J., & Bandy-Hedden, I.G. (1992). Success outcomes of full-day kindergarten: More positive behavior and increased achievement in the years after. *Early Childhood Research Quarterly, 7*(2), 187–203.

Currie, J., & Thomas, D. (1999). Does Head Start help Hispanic children? *Journal of Public Economics, 74*(2), 235–262.

DaCosta, J. L., & Bell, S. (2000). *Full day kindergarten at an inner city elementry school: Perceived and actual effects.* Paper presented at the Annual Conference of the American Educational Research Association, New Orleans, LA, April 24–28, 2000.

Darling, N. (1999). *Parenting style and its correlates.* ERIC Digest (ERIC Document Reproduction Service No. ED 427896).

Datnow, A., Hubbard, L., & Woody, E. (2001). *Is single gender schooling viable in the public sector? Lessons from California's pilot program. Final report.* [WWW document]. http://www.oise.utoronto.ca.

DeCos, P. L. (1997). *Readiness for kindergarten: What does it mean?* California Research Bureau, California State Library CRB-97-014.

DeMeis, J. L., & Stearns, E. S. (1992). Relationship of school entrance age to academic and social performance. *Journal of Educational Research, 86*(1), 20–27.

Dillon, J. T. (1991). Questioning the use of questions. *Journal of Educational Psychology, 83*(1), 163–164.

DiPrima, D., Zigmond, N., & Strayhorn, J. (1991). Chronological age at entrance to first grade: Effects on elementary school success. *Early Childhood Research Quarterly, 6,* 105–117.

Dunn, L., Beach, S.A., & Kontos, S. (1994). Quality of the literacy environment in day care and children's development. *Journal of Research in Childhood Education, 9*(1), 24–34.

Dunn, L., Beach, S. A., & Kontos, S. (1997). What have we learned about developmentally appropriate practice? Research in review. *Young Children, 52*(5), 4–13.

Education Development Center, Inc. & Boston Schoolyard Funders Collaborative. (2000). *Schoolyard Learning: The Impact of school grounds.* Newton, MA: Education Development Center, Inc. and the Boston Schoolyard Funders Collaborative.

Education Week, 22(17), 97, Quality counts. (2003, January 9).

Eisenberg, N. (1992). *The caring child.* Cambridge, MA: Harvard University Press.

Elicker, J., & Mathur, S. (1997). What do they do all day? Comprehensive evaluation of a full-day kindergarten. *Early Childhood Research Quarterly, 12*(4), 459–480.

Elkind, D. (1976). *Child development and education: A Piagetian perspective.* New York: Oxford University Press.

Epstein, J. L. (1998). *School and family partnerships: Preparing educators and improving schools.* Boulder, CO: Westview Press.

Epstein, J. L., Clark, L., Salinas, K. C., & Sanders, M. G. (1997). *Scaling up school-family-community connections in Baltimore: Effects on student achievement and attendance.* Paper presented at the annual meeting of the American Educational Research Association, Chicago.

Evangelou, D. (1989). *Mixed-age groups in early childhood education.* ERIC Digest. (ERIC Document Reproduction Service No. ED 308990)

Fagan, J., & Palm, G. (2004). *Fathers and early childhood programs.* Clifton Park, NY: Thomson Delmar Learning.

Fan, X. T., & Chen, M. (2001). Parental involvement and students' academic achievement: A meta-analysis. *Educational Psychology Review, 13,* 1–22.

Feldman, D. H., & Goldsmith, L. T. (1991). *Nature's gambit.* New York: Teachers College Press.

Feth, L., & Whitelaw, G. (1999). *Many classrooms have bad acoustics that inhibit learning.* Columbus, OH: Ohio State University. [WWW document]. http://www.acs.ohio-state.edu.

Field, T. M. (1991). Quality infant day-care and grade school behavior and performance. *Child Development, 62,* 863–879.

Finn, J. D. (2003). *Full-day kindergarten: Answers with questions.* [WWW document]. http://www.temple.edu.

Finn, J. D., & Achilles, C. M. (1990). Answers and questions about class size: A statewide experiment. *American Educational Research Journal, 27*(3), 557–577.

Fletcher, M. A. (2002, May 9). Single-sex education gets boost: Bush plan would reverse key policy. *Washington Post,* A01.

Foster, J. E. (1993, Fall). Retaining children in grade. *Childhood Education,* 38–43.

Friedkin, N., & Necochea, J. (1988). School system size and performance: A contingency perspective. *Educational Evaluation and Policy Analysis, 10*(3), 237–249.

Fukushima, O., & Kato, M. (1976). The effects of vicarious experiences on children's altruistic behavior. *Bulletin of Tokyo Gakkuge University, 27* (Series 1), 90–94.

Fusaro, J. A. (1997). The effect of full-day kindergarten on student achievement: A meta-analysis. *Child Study Journal, 27*(4), 269–277.

Galley, M. (2002, January 10). State policies on kindergarten are all over the map. *Quality Counts 2002: Building Blocks for Success, 17.* Bethesda, MD: Editorial Projects in Education, 45.

Gardner, H. (1983). *Frames of mind: Theory of multiple intelligences.* New York: Basic Books.

Gaustad, J. (1998). *Implementing looping.* ERIC Digest 123 (ERIC Document Reproduction Service No. ED 429330).

Good, L. (1996). *Teachers' perceptions of the all-day, alternating day kindergarten schedule.* ERIC Digest (ERIC Document Reproduction Service No. ED396853).

Gorrell, J. L. (1998). *A study comparing the effect of multiage education practices versus traditional education practices on academic achievement.* [WWW document]. http://www.edrs.com.

Graetz, K. A., & Goliber, M. J. (2002). Designing collaborative learning places: Psychological foundations and new frontiers. *New Dimensions for Teaching and Learning, 92,* 13–22.

Gregg, K. (2003). *Elementary school grade span configuration: New evidence on student achievement, achievement equity, and cost efficiency.* [WWW document]. http://phkhome.northstarnet.org.

Grenninger, G. (1997). *An investigation of the relationship among kindergarten entry age, gender, intelligence, academic achievement, and classroom performance of Head Start graduates in the primary grades.* Unpublished master's thesis, The Pennsylvania State University, University Park, PA.

Greer-Smith, S. (1990). *The effect of a full-day kindergarten on the student's academic performance.* Unpublished master's thesis, Dominican University, San Rafael, CA. ED 318570.

Gullo, D. F., & Burton, C. B. (1992). Age of entry, preschool experience, and sex as antecedents of academic readiness in kindergarten. *Early Childhood Research Quarterly, 7,* 175–186.

Gullo, D. F. (2000). The long term educational effects of half-day vs full-day kindergarten. *Early Child Development and Care, 160,* 17–24.

Haag, P. (2000). *K–12 single-sex education: What does the research say?* ERIC Digest (ERIC Document Reproduction Service No. ED 444758).

Hampton, F., Mumford, D., & Bond, L. (1997, March). *Enhancing urban student achievement through family oriented school practices.* Paper presented at the Annual Meeting of the American Educational Research Association, Chicago.

Hara, S. R., & Burke, D. J. (1998). Parent involvement: The key to improved student achievement. *School Community Journal, 8*(2), 9–19.

Harker, R., & Nash, R. (1997, March). *School type and education of girls: Co-ed or girls only?* Paper presented at the annual meeting of the American Educational Research Association, Chicago.

Hart, C. H., Charlesworth, R., Burts, D. C., & DeWolf, M. (1993, March). *The relationship of attendance in developmentally appropriate or inappropriate kindergarten classrooms to first and second grade behavior.* Poster session presented at the biennial meeting of the Society for Research in Child Development, New Orleans, LA.

Hauser, R. M., Pager, D. I., & Simmons, S. J. (2000). *Race-ethnicity, social background, and grade retention. CDE working paper.* Paper presented at the Annual Meeting of the American Sociological Association, Washington, DC.

Hausken, E. G., & Rathbun, A. H. (2002). *Adjustment to kindergarten: Child, family, and kindergarten program factors.* Paper presented at the Annual Meeeting of the American Educational Research Association, New Orleans, LA, April 1–5, 2002.

Head Start Bureau, (2002, June 11). *Head Start history.* [WWW document]. http://act.dhhs.gov.

Helburn, S., Culkin, M. L., Howes, C., Bryant, D., Clifford, R., Cryer, D., Peisner-Feinberg, E., & Kagan, S. L. (1995). *Cost, quality, and child care outcomes in child care centers.* Denver: University of Colorado at Denver

Henderlong, J., & Lepper, M. R. (2002). The effects of praise on children's intrinsic motivation: A review and synthesis. *Psychological Bulletin, 128*(5), 774–795.

Henderson, A. T., & Mapp, K. L. (2002). *A new wave of evidence: The impact of school, family, and community connections on student achievement.* National Center for Family and Community Connections with Schools, Southwest Educational Developmental Laboratory.

Hestenes, L. L., Kontos, S., & Bryan, Y. (1993). Children's emotional expression in child care centers varying in quality. *Early Childhood Research Quarterly, 8,* 295–307.

Hiatt-Michael, D. (2001). *Preparing teachers to work with parents.* ERIC Digest (ERIC Document Reproduction Service No. ED 460123).

Hildebrand, C. (2001). Effects of three kindergarten schedules on achievement and classroom behavior. *Research Bulletin, 31.* Phi Delta Kappa Center for Evaluation, Development, and Research. [WWW document]. http://www.pdkintl.org.

Holloway, J. H. (2001). Understanding learning differences. *Educational Leadership, 59*(3), 84–85.

Horm-Wingerd, D. M. (1993). Teachers' perceptions of the effectiveness of transition classes. *Early Education and Development, 4*(2), 130–138.

Hough, D. L. (1995). The elemiddle school: A model for middle grades reform. *Principal, 74*(3), 6–9.

Hough, D., & Bryde, S. (1996, April). *The effects of full-day kindergarten on student achievement and affect.* Paper presented at the annual conference of the American Educatonal Research Association, New York (ED 345691).

Housden, T., & Kam, R. (1992). *Full-day Kindergarten: A summary of the research.* Carmichael, CA: San Juan Unified School District. ED 345868.

Howard, E. (1986). *A longitudinal study of achievement associated with participation in a public school kindergarten.* Unpublished doctoral dissertation, Mississippi State University, Mississippi State.

Howes, C. (1990). Can the age of entry into child care and the quality of child care predict adjustment in kindergarten? *Developmental Psychology, 26,* 292–303.

Howes, C., Smith, E., & Galinsky, E. (1995). *The Florida child care quality improvement study: Interim report.* New York: Families and Work Institute.

Howley, C. B. (2001, April). *The disappearing local school in two Appalachian states.* Paper presented at the annual conference of the Appalachian Studies Association. Linwood, WV. ERIC Digest (ERIC Document Reproduction Service No. ED 451018).

Howley, C. B. (2002, March). Grade-span configurations. *School Administrator.* [WWW document]. http://www.aasa.org

Howley, C., Strange, M., & Bickel, R. (2000). *Research about school size and school performance in impoverished communities.* ERIC Digest (ERIC Document Reproduction Service No. ED 448968).

Huang, G., & Howley, C. (1993). Mitigating disadvantage: Effects of small-scale schooling on student achievement in Alaska. *Journal of Research in Rural Education, 9*(3), 137–149.

Hyson, M. C., Hirsh-Pasek, K., & Rescorla, L. (1990). The classroom practices inventory: An observation instrument based on NAEYC's guidelines for developmentally appropriate practices for 4- and 5-year-old children. *Early Childhood Research Quarterly, 5*(4), 475–494.

Izzo, C. V., Weissberg, R. P., Kasprow, W. J., & Fendrich, M. (1999). A longitudinal assessment of teacher perceptions of parent involvement in children's education and school performance. *American Journal of Community Psychology, 27,* 817–839.

Jacobson, L. (1997, October 15). Looping catches on as a way to build strong ties. *Education Week, 16,* 19.

Jago, E., & Tanner, K. (1999). *Influence of the school facility on student achievement.* University of Georgia. [WWW document]. http://www.coe.uga.edu.

Jambunathan, S., Burts, D. C., & Pierce, S. (1999). Developmentally appropriate practice as predictors of self-competence among preschoolers. *Journal of Research in Childhood Eduation, 13,* 167–174.

Jarrett, O. S. (2002). *Recess in elementary school: What does the research say?* ERIC Digest (ERIC Document Reproduction Service No. ED 466331).

Jarrett, O.S., Maxwell, D.M., Dickerson, C., Hoge, P., Davies, G., & Yetley, A. (1998). The impact of recess on classroom behavior: Group effects and individual differences. *Journal of Educational Research, 92*(2).

Jensen, E. (1998). *Teaching with the brain in mind.* Alexandria, VA: Association for Supervision and Curriculum Development.

Johnston, R. C. (2000, September 20). Chicago study questions results of retention. *Education Week, 3.*

Jordan, C., Orozco, E., & Averett, A. (2001). *Emerging issues in school, family, and community connections: Annual synthesis 2001.* Austin, TX: Southwest Educational Development Laboratory.

Jordan, G. E., Snow, C. E., & Porche, M. V. (2000). Project EASE: The effect of a family literacy project on kindergarten students' early literacy skills. *Reading Research Quarterly, 35*(4).

Kagan, S. L. (1999). Cracking the readiness mystique. From our president. *Young Children, 54*(5), 2–3.

Kaler, S. R., & Kopp, C. B. (1990). Compliance and comprehension in very young toddlers. *Child Development, 61,* 1997–2003.

Karweit, N. (1988). Time-on-task: The second time around. *NASSP Bulletin,* February, 31–39.

Karweit, N. L. (1999). *Grade retention: Prevalence, timing, and effects.* Baltimore, MD: Center for Research on the Education of Students Placed at Risk.

Katz, L. (1984). The professional early childhood teacher. *Young Children, 39*(5), 3–10.

Katz, L. G. (1997). A developmental approach to assessment of young children. ERIC Digest (ERIC Document Reproduction Service No. ED 407172).

Katz, L. G. (1999). Curriculum disputes in early childhood education. ERIC Digest (ERIC Document Reproduction Service No. ED 436298).

Kennedy, M. (2001). Into thin air. *American School & University, 73*(6), 32.

Kessler-Sklar, S. L., & Baker, A. J. L. (2000). School district parent involvement policies and programs. *Elementary School Journal, 101*(1), 101–118.

Kinsey, S. J. (2001). *Research on multiage education.* ERIC Digest (ERIC Document Reproduction Service No. ED 448935).

Klinzing, G., Klinzing-Eurich, G., & Tisher, R. (1985). Higher cognitive behaviors in classroom discourse: Congruencies between teachers' questions and pupils' responses. *Australian Journal of Education, 29,* 63–75.

Kochanska, G. (1993). Toward a synthesis of parental socialization and child temperament in early development of conscience. *Child Development, 64,* 325–347.

Kohlberg, L. (1968). The child as a moral philosopher. *Psychology Today, 2,* 25–30.

Kohn, A. (1993). *Punished by rewards.* Boston: Houghton Mifflin Company.

Kopp, C. B. (1987). The growth of self-regulation: Caregivers and children. In N. Eisenberg (Ed.), *Contemporary Topics in Developmental Psychology* (pp. 34–55). New York: Wiley.

Kreider, H. (2002). *Getting parents "ready" for kindergarten: The role of early childhood education.* Amherst, MA: Harvard Family Research Project. [WWW document]. http://www.gse.harvard.edu.

Kuczynski, L., Kochanska, G., Radke-Yarrow, M., & Girnius-Brown, O. (1987). A developmental interpretation of time out: Young children's noncompliance. *Developmental Psychology, 23,* 799–806.

Kulik, J. A. (2001). *An analysis of the research on ability grouping: Historical and contemporary perspectives.* [WWW document]. http://www.ucc.uconn.edu.

Kuller, R., & Lindsten, C. (1992). Health and behavior of children in classrooms with and without windows. *Journal of Environmental Psychology, 12,* 305–317.

Kundert, D. K., May, D. C., & Brent, D. (1995). A comparison of students who delay kindergarten entry and those who are retained in grades K–5. *Psychology in the Schools, 32,* 202–209.

LaParo, K. M., & Pianta, R. C. (2000). Predicting children's competence in the early school years: A meta-analytic review. *Review of Educational Research, 70*(4), 443–484.

Lareau, A., & Horvat, E. (1999). Moments of social inclusion and exclusion: Race, class, and cultural capital in family-school relationships. *Sociology of Education, 71,* 37–53.

Larzelere, R. E., Schneider, W. N., Larson, D. B., & Pike, P. L. (1996). The effects of discipline responses in delaying toddler midbehavior recurrences. *Child and Family Behavior Therapy, 18,* 35–57.

Lawton, M. (1997, September 17). AFT report assails schools' promotion, retention policies. *Education Week.*

Lazar, I., & Darlington, R. (1982). *Lasting effects of early education: A report from the consortium for longitudinal studies.* Monographs of the Society for Research in Child Development, *47,* (2–3, Serial No. 195).

Ledingham, J. E. (1998). How playgrounds affect children's behavior. *Canadian Journal of Research in Early Childhood Education, 6*(4), 353–356.

Lee, V., & Smith, J. (1996). High school size: Which works best and for whom? *Educational Evaluation and Policy Analysis, 19*(3), 205–227.

Lee, V. E., & Lockheed, M. M. (1990). The effects of single-sex schooling on achievement and attitudes in Nigeria. *Comparative Education Review, 34*(2), 209–231.

Legislative Office of Education Oversight. (1997). *An overview of full-day kindergarten,* Columbus, OH: Legislative Office of Education Oversight.

LeNoir, W. D. (1993). Teacher questions and schema activation. *Clearing House, 66*(6), 349–352.

LePore, P. C., & Warren, J. R. (1997). A comparison of single-sex and coeducational Catholic secondary schooling: Evidence from the National Educational Longitudinal Study of 1988. *American Educational Research Journal, 34*(3), 485–511.

Lepper, M. R., Greene, D., & Nisbett, R. E. (1973). Undermining children's intrinsic interest with extrinsic reward: A test of the 'overjustification' hypothesis. *Journal of Personality and Social Psychology, 28,* 129–137.

Lewis, A. C. (2003). New hope for educational research? *Phi Delta Kappan, 84*(5), 339–340.

Lincoln, R. D. (1998). Looping in the middle grades. *Principal, 1,* 58–59.

Little, L. (2002). *AERA research award goes to NCEDL investigators.* [WWW document]. http://www.fpg.unc.edu.

Lloyd, L. (1999). Multiage classes and high-ability students. *Review of Educational Research, 69*(2), 187–212.

Lopez, G. (2001a). The value of hard work: Lessons on parent involvement from an immigrant household. *Harvard Educational Review, 71*(3), 416–435.

Lopez, G. (2001b). *On whose terms? Understanding involvement through the eyes of migrant parents.* Paper presented at the annual meeting of the American Educational Research Association, Seattle, WA.

Lou, Y., Abrami, P. C., & Spence, J. C. (2000). Effects of within-class grouping on student achievement: An exploratory model. *The Journal of Educational Research, 94*(2), 101–112.

Luria, A. R. (1961). *The role of speech in the regulation of normal and abnormal behavior.* New York: Liveright.

Maccoby, E. E. (1980). *Social development.* San Diego, CA: Harcourt, Brace Jovanovich.

Mapp, K. L. (2002). *Having their say: Parents describe how and why they are involved in their children's education.* Paper presented at the Annual Meeting of the American Educational Research Association, New Orleans, LA, April 1–5.

Marcon, R. A. (1999). Positive relationships between parent school involvement and public school inner-city preschoolers' development and academic performance. *School Psychology Review, 28,* 395–412.

Marcon, R. A. (2002). Moving up the grades: Relationship between preschool model and later school success. *Early Childhood Research & Practice, 4*(1). [WWW document]. http://ericir.syr.edu.

Martin, B. (1975). Parent-child relations. In F. Horowitz (Ed.), *Review of child development research: Vol. 4,* Chicago: University of Chicago Press.

Martinez, Y. G., & Valazquez, J. A. (2000). *Involving migrant families in education.* ERIC Digest (ERIC Document Reproduction Service No. ED 448010).

Marzano, R. (2000). Optimizing teachers' use of instructional time. Mid-Continent Research for Education and Learning. [WWW document]. http://www.mcrel.org.

Mathematica Policy Research, Inc., and Center for Children and Families at Teachers College, Columbia University (2001). *Building their futures: How Early Head Start programs are enhancing the lives of infants and toddlers in low-income families.* Washington, DC: Department of Health and Human Services.

Matthews, L. L. , May, D. C., & Kundert, D. K. (1999). Adjustment outcomes of developmenal placement: A longitudinal study. *Psychology in the Schools, 36*(6), 495–504.

May, D. C., & Kundert, D. K. (1993). Pre-first placements: How common and how informed? *Psychology in the Schools, 30*(2), 161–167.

McLoyd, V. C. (1990). The impact of economic hardship on Black families and children: Psychological distress, parenting, and socioemotional development. *Child Development, 61,* 311–346.

Meisels, S. J. (1992). Doing harm by doing good: Iatrogenic effects of early childhood enrollment and promotion policies. *Early Childhood Research Quarterly, 7,* 155–164.

Meisels, S. J. (1995a). *Performance assessment in early childhood education: The work sampling system.* ERIC Digest (ERIC Document Reproduction Service No. ED382407).

Meisels, S. J. (1995b, April/May). Out of the readiness maze. *Momentum,* 18–22.

Mensinger, J. (2000). *Conflicting gender role prescriptions and disordered eating in single sex and coeducational school environments.* Paper presented at the Annual Conference of the American Psychological Association, New York.

Miedel, W. T., & Reynolds, A. J. (1999). Parent involvement in early intervention for disadvantaged children: Does it matter? *Journal of School Psychology, 37*(4), 379–399.

Moore, D. (1998). What makes these schools stand out: Chicago elementary schools with a seven-year trend of improved reading achievement. *Designs for change.* [WWW document]. http://www.designsforchange.org.

Morrison, F. J., Griffith, E. M., & Alberts, D. M. (1997). Nature-nurture in the classroom: Entrance age, school readiness, and learning in children. *Developmental Psychology, 33*(2), 254–262.

Morrow, L. M., Strickland, D. S., & Woo, D. G. (1998). *Literacy instruction in half- and whole-day kindergarten.* Newark, DE: International Reading Association.

Moyer, J. (2001, Spring). The child-centered kindergarten: A position paper. Association for Childhood Education International. *Childhood Education,* 161–166.

Narahara, M. (1998). *Kindergarten entrance age and academic achievement.* ERIC Digest (ERIC Document Reproduction Service No. ED 421218).

National Association of Early Childhood Specialists in State Departments of Education. (NAECS/SDE, 2000). *Still unacceptable trends in kindergarten entry and placement.* Washington, DC: National Association for the Education of Young Children.

National Association for the Education of Young Children (NAEYC). (1987). *Standardized testing of young children 3 through 8 years of age.* Washington, DC: NAEYC.

National Association for the Education of Young Children (NAEYC). (1990). *NAEYC position statement on school readiness.* Washington, DC: NAEYC.

National Association for the Education of Young Children (NAEYC). (1995). *NAEYC position statement on school readiness.* Washington, DC: NAEYC.

National Association for the Education of Young Children (NAEYC). (1997). *Developmentally appropriate practice in early childhood programs serving children from birth through age 8.* Washington, DC: NAEYC.

National Association for the Education of Young Children & National Association of Early Childhood Specialists in State Departments of Education. (1990). *Guidelines for appropriate curriculum and assessment in programs serving young children ages 3 through 8.* Washington, DC: National Association for the Education of Young Children.

National Association of School Psychologists. (2002). *Position statement on student grade retention and social promotion.* Bethesda, MD: National Association of School Psychologists.

National Center for Early Development and Learning (NCEDL). (1998). Kindergarten transitions. *NCEDL Spotlights.* [WWW document]. http://www.fpg.unc.edu.

National Center for Education Statistics. (1997). *Fathers' involvement in their children's schools.* [WWW document]. http://www.nces.ed.gov.

National Center for Education Statistics. (1998). *Parent involvement in children's education: Efforts by public elementary schools.* Washington, DC: U.S. Department of Education.

National Center for Education Statistics. (2002). *The Condition of Education.* [WWW document]. http://nces.ed.gov.

National Center for Education Statistics (NCES). (2003). *Early childhood longitudinal study, kindergarten class of 1998–99.* [WWW document]. http://www.nces.ed.gov.

National Education Commission on Time and Learning. (1994). *Prisoners of time.* Washington, DC: National Education Commission on Time and Learning. [WWW document]. http://www.ed.gov.

Newman, P. R., & Newman, B. M. (1997). *Childhood and adolescence.* Pacific Grove, CA: Brooks/Cole Publishing Company.

NICHD Early Child Care Research Network. (1997, September). *Results from the NICHD study.* Paper presented at the Workshop on Longitudinal Research on Children, Washington, DC.

NICHD Early Child Care Research Network. (2001, April). *Quality of child care and child outcomes.* Paper presented at the biennial meeting of the Society for Research in Child Development, Minneapolis, MN.

Nichols, J. D., & Nichols, G. W. (2002). The impact of looping classroom environments on parental attitudes. *Preventing School Failure, 47*(1), 18–25.

Nielsen, J., & Cooper-Martin, E. (2002). *Evaluation of the Montgomery County public schools assessment program: Kindergarten and grade 1 reading report.* Rockville, MD: Montgomery Public Schools, Office of Shared Accountability. [WWW document.] http://www.mcps.k12mdus.

Oden, S., Schweinhart, L. J., & Weikart, D. P. (2000). *Into adulthood: A study of the effects of Head Start.* Ypsilanti, MI: High/Scope Press. ED 444730.

Ojure, L., & Sherman, T. (2001, November 28). Learning styles. *Education Week, 21*(13), 33.

Olson, L. (2000a). High poverty among young makes schools' job harder. *Education Week, 20*(4), 40, 41.

Olson, L. (2000b). Minority groups to emerge as a majority in U.S. schools. *Education Week, 20*(4), 34, 35.

Ostrowski, P. M. (1994). Effects on curriculum and instruction in the surrounding grades. *ERS Spectrum, 12*(3), 3–12.

Peisner-Feinberg, E. S., Burchinal, M. R., Clifford, R. M., Culkin, M. L., Howes, C., Kagan, S. L., & Yazejian, N. (2001). The relation of preschool child-care quality to children's cognitive and social developmental trajectories through second grade. *Child Development, 72*(5), 1534–1553.

Pellegrini, A. D., & Davis, P. L. (1993). Relations between children's playground and classroom behaviour. *British Journal of Educational Psychology, 63*(1), 88–95.

Pellegrini, A. D., Huberty, P. D., & Jones, I. (1995). The effects of recess timing on children's playground and classroom behaviors. *American Educational Research Journal, 32*(4), 845–864.

Peng, S. S., & Wright, D. (1994). Explanation of academic achievement of Asian-American students. *The Journal of Educational Research, 87,* 346-352.

Phillips, D. A., McCartney, K., & Scarr, S. (1987). Child care quality and children's social development. *Developmental Psychology, 23,* 537–544.

Pile, J. (1997). *Color in interior design.* New York: McGraw-Hill Professional Publishing.

Pouliot, L. (1999). *A double method approach or a double need: To describe teachers' beliefs about grade retention, and to explain the persistence of these beliefs.* Paper presented at the Annual Meeting of the American Educational Research Association, Montreal, Quebec, Canada, April 19–23.

Prakash, N., West, J., & Denton, K. (2003). *Schools' use of assessments for kindergarten entrance and placement: 1998–99.* Washington, DC: National Center for Education Statistics.

Prince, D. L., Hare, R. D., & Howard, E. M. (2001). Longitudinal effects of kindergarten. *Journal of Research in Childhood Education, 16*(10), 15–27.

Ramey, C. T., Campbell, F. A., & Blair, C. (1998). Enhancing the life course for high-risk children: Results from the Abecedarian project. In J. Crane (Ed.), *Social Programs that Work* (pp. 163–183). New York: Russell Sage Foundation.

Raspberry, W. (2002, May 16). Single-sex education deserves experimentation. *Washington Post.*

Readdick, C. A., & Chapman, P. L. (2000). Young children's perceptions of time out. *Journal of Research in Childhood Education, 15*(1), 81–87.

Redfield, D., & Rousseau, E. (1981). A meta-analysis of experimental research on teacher questioning behavior. *Review of Educational Research, 51,* 237–245.

Reid, K. S. (2003). Fla., Texas retain 3rd graders with poor reading scores. *Education Week, 23*(1), 25.

Reynolds, A. J., & Temple, J. A. (1998). Extended early childhood intervention and school achievement: Age thirteen findings from the Chicago longitudinal study. *Child Development, 69*(1), 231–246.

Reynolds, A. J., Temple, J. A., Robertson, D. L., & Mann, E. A. (2001). Long-term effects of an early childhood intervention on educational achievement and juvenile arrest: A 15-year follow-up of low-income children in public schools. *JAMA, 285*(18), 2339–2346.

Riley, J. (1980). *The effects of teachers' wait-time and cognitive questioning level on pupil science achievement.* Paper presented at the annual meeting of the National Association for Research in Science Teaching, Boston, MA.

Ritter, P. L., Mont-Reynaud, R., & Dornbusch, S. M. (1993). Minority parents and their youth: Concern, encouragement and support for school achievement. In N. Chavkin (Ed.), *Families and schools in a pluralistic society* (pp. 107–119), Albany, NY: State University of New York Press.

Rogers, K. B. (1998). Using current research to make "good" decisions about grouping. *NASSP Bulletin, 82,* 38–46.

Rose, M. (2003). Sizing up reform. *American Teacher,* February, 12–13.

Rothkopf, E. Z., & Billington, M. J. (1974). Indirect review and priming through questions. *Journal of Educational Psychology, 66*(5), 669–679.

Rowe, M. (1974). Wait time and rewards as instructional variables, their influence on language, logic, and fate control. Part I—Wait time. *Journal of Research in Science Teaching, 11,* 81–94.

Rowe, M. (1986). Wait time: Slowing down may be a way of speeding up! *Journal of Teacher Education, 37*, 43–50.

Rymer, R. (1994). *Genie: A scientific tragedy.* New York: Penguin.

Saluja, G., Scott-Little, C., & Clifford, R. M. (2000). Readiness for school: A survey of state policies and definitions. *Early Childhood Research and Practice, 2*(1), 1.

Samson, G., Strykowski, B., Weinstein, T., & Walberg, H. (1987). The effects of teacher questioning levels on student achievement: A quantitative synthesis. *Journal of Educational Research, 80*, 290–295.

Schneider, M. (2002). *Do school facilities affect academic outcomes?* Washington, DC: National Clearinghouse for Educational Facilities.

Schreiber, M. E. (1999). Time-outs for toddlers: Is our goal punishment or education? *Young Children, 54*(4), 22–25.

Schweinhart, L. J. (1997). *Child-initiated learning activities for young children living in poverty.* ERIC Digest (ERIC Document Reproduction Service No. ED 413105).

Schweinhart, L. J. (2001). *Recent evidence on preschool programs.* ERIC Digest (ERIC Clearinghouse on Elementary and Early Childhood Education). Champaign, IL: University of Illinois.

Schweinhart, L. J., Barnes, H. V., Weikart, D. P., Barnett, W. S., & Epstein, A. S. (1993). *Significant benefits: The High/Scope Perry preschool study through age twenty-seven.* Monograph 10 of the High/Scope Educational Research Foundation. Ypsilanti, MI: High/Scope Press.

Schweinhart, L. J., & Weikart, D. P. (1998, March). Why curriculum matters in early childhood education. *Educational Leadership,* 57–60.

Shaver, A. V., & Walls, R. T. (1998). Effect of Title I parent involvement on student reading and mathematics achievement. *Journal of Research and Development in Education, 31*(2), 90–97.

Shepard, L. A. (1997). Children not ready to learn? The invalidity of school readiness testing. *Psychology in the Schools, 34*(2), 85–97.

Shepard, L., Kagan, S. L., & Wurtz, E. (Eds.). (1998). *Principles and Recommendations for Early Childhood Assessments.* Washington, DC: National Education Goals Panel.

Shepard, L., & Smith, M. L. (1989). *Escalating Kindergarten Curriculum.* ERIC Digest (ERIC Document Reproduction Service No. ED 308989).

Sheppard, S. & Kanevsky, L. S. (1999). Nurturing gifted students' metacognitive awareness: Effects of training in homogeneous and heterogeneous classes. *Roper Review, 21*(4), 266–272.

Silvis, H. (2002). Take-home lessons: Is homework the key to raising student achievement or a drag on family time? *Northwest Education, 7*(4), 20–23.

Slavin, R. E., Karweit, N. L., & Wasik, B. A. (1993). Preventing early school failure: What works? *Educational Leadership, 50*(4), 10–18.

Southard, N. A., & May, D. C. (1996). The effects of pre-first-grade programs on student reading and mathematics achievement. *Psychology in the Schools, 33,* 132–141.

Spielhofer, T., O'Donnell, L., Benton, T., Schagen, S., & Schagen, I. (2002). *The impact of school size and single-sex education on performance.* [WWW document]. http://www.nfer.ac.uk.

Spitzer, S., Cupp, R., & Ross, P. (1995). School entrance age, social acceptance, and self-perceptions in kindergarten and 1st grade. *Early Childhood Research Quarterly, 10,* 433–450.

Springer, D. A. (1997). *The relationship between chronological age at kindergarten entrance and social skills development.* Unpublished doctoral dissertation, The Pennsylvania State University, University Park.

Stahl, R. J. (1994). *Using "think-time" and "wait-time" skillfully in the classroom.* ERIC Digest (ERIC Document Reproduction Service No. ED 370885).

Starkey, P., & Klein, A. (2000). Fostering parental support for children's mathematical development: An intervention with Head Start families. *Early Education and Development, 11,* 659–680.

Stecher, B., Bohrnstedt, G., Kirst, M., McRobbie, J., & Williams, T. (2001, May). Class-size reduction in California. *Phi Delta Kappan,* 670–674.

Stipek, D., Feiler, R., Daniels, D., & Milburn, S. (1995). Effects of different instructional approaches on young children's achievement and motivation. *Child Development, 66*(1), 209–223.

Stofflet, F. P. (1998). *Anchorage School District full-day kindergarten study: A follow-up of the kindergarten class of 1987–88, 1988–89, and 1989–90.* Anchorage, AK: Anchorage School District. ERIC Digest (ERIC Document Reproduction Service No. ED 426790).

Strassberg, Z., Dodge, K., Pettit, G. S., & Bates, J. E. (1994). Spanking in the home and children's subsequent aggression against kindergarten peers. *Development and Psychopathology, 6,* 445–461.

Sydoriak, D. E. (1987). Light and color research finalized. *CEFP Journal, 25*(3).

Tanner, C. K. (2000). *Minimum classroom size and number of students per classroom.* University of Georgia. [WWW document]. http://www.coe.uga.edu.

Terman, L., & Oden, M. H. (1959). *Genetic studies in genius: Vol. 4. The gifted group at midlife.* Stanford, CA: Stanford University Press.

Thomas, A., & Chess, S. (1977). *Temperament and development.* New York: Brunner/Mazel.

Thompson, C. L., & Cunningham, E. K. (2000). *Retention and social promotion: Research and implications for policy.* ERIC Digest (ERIC Document Reproduction Service No. ED 449241).

Toppino, T. C., Kasserman, J. E., & Mracek, W. A. (1991). The effect of spacing repetitions on the recognition memory of young children and adults. *Journal of Experimental Child Psychology, 51*(1), 123–138.

Turbiville, V. P., Umbarger, G. T., & Guthrie, A. C. (2000, July). Fathers' involvement in programs for young children. *Young Children, 55*(4), 74–79.

Turner, H. S., & Watson, T. S. (1999). Consultant's guide for the use of time-out in the preschool and elementary classroom. *Psychology in the Schools, 36*(2), 135–148.

U.S. Department of Education. (1993). *Percent of public school kindergarten teachers indicating the importance of various factors for kindergarten readiness: Spring 1993.* Washington, DC: U.S. Department of Education.

Uphoff, J., & Gilmore, J. (1984, July 26). Local research ties suicides to early school entry stress. *Dayton Daily News,* 34.

Uphoff, J., & Gilmore, J. (1986). Pupil age at school entrance—how many are ready for success? *Young Children, 41*(2), 11–16.

Vail, K. (2001). How much is too much? Homework problems. *American School Board Journal, 188*(4), 24–29.

Viadero, D. (1997, November 19). Fathers play unique role in schooling, study finds. *Education Week.*

Viadero, D. (2000, March 15). Ending social promotion. *Education Week, 19*(27), 40–42.

Viadero, D. (2002, February 20). Research: Researching the researchers. *Education Week, 21*(23), 26, 29.

Vuchinich, S., Bank, L., & Patterson, G. R. (1992). Parenting, peers, and the stability of antisocial behavior in preadolescent boys. *Developmental Psychology, 28,* 510–521.

Walker, M. (1991). *The power of color.* New York: Avery Publishing Group, 50–52.

Warash, B. G. (1991). The effects of preschool experiences on advantaged children. (Doctoral dissertation, West Virginia University, 1991). *Dissertation Abstracts International.* 53-02A, 0399.

Weiss, A. M. D. G., & Offenberg, R. J. (2002, April). *Enhancing urban children's early success in school: The power of full-day kindergarten.* Paper presented at the annual meeting of the American Educational Research Association, New Orleans, LA.

Welsh, J. (2002, November 13). Full-day kindergarten a plus. Pioneer Press. Minneapolis Public Schools (2002). All-day kindergarten narrows the gap in early literacy. [News release]. [WWW document]. http://www.mplsk12mn.us.

West, J., Denton, K., & Reaney, L. M. (2002). *The kindergarten year: Findings from the early childhood longitudinal study, kindergarten class of 1998–99.* Washington, DC: National Center for Education Statistics.

West, J., Denton, K., Germino-Hausken, E. G. (2000). *America's kindergartners.* Washington, DC: National Center for Education Statistics (NCES 2000-070).

Westat and Policy Studies Associates. (2001). *The longitudinal evaluation of school change and performance in Title 1 schools.* Washington, DC: U.S. Department of Education.

Wilen, W. (Ed.). (1990). *Teaching and learning through discussion.* Springfield, IL: Charles C. Thomas.

Winner, E. (1996). *Gifted children: Myths and realities.* New York: Basic Books.

Wohlers, A. (1995). *Gross square feet per student.* [WWW document]. http://www.cefpi.org.

Yamamoto, K. (1979). Children's ratings of the stressfulness of experiences. *Developmental Psychology, 15*(5), 581–582.

Young, B. A. (2003). *Public school student, staff, and graduate counts by state: School year 2001–02.* Washington, DC: National Center for Education Statistics.

Zahn-Waxler, C., Radke-Yarrow, M., & King, R. (1979). Child rearing and children's prosocial initiations toward victims of distress. *Child Development, 50,* 319-330.

Zakaluk, B. L., & Straw, S. B. (2002). *The efficacy of an extended-day kindergarten program: A report for the St. James School Division (1999–2000, 2000–2001).* St. James-Assiniboia School Division: Manitoba, Canada.

Zill, N. (1995). Approaching kindergarten: A look at preschoolers in the United States. *Young Children, 51*(1), 35–38.

Zill, N., Spencer-Loomis, L., & West, J. (1997). *The elementary school performance and adjustment of children who enter kindergarten late or repeat kindergarten: Findings from national surveys.* Washington, DC: National Center for Education Statistics (NCES 98-097).

Zimmerman, J. (2001). How much does time effect learning? *Principal, 80*(3), 6–11.

Zurcher, J. (2001, October 4). Sportspeak. *Ace Weekly.* [WWW document]. http://www.aceweekly.com.

Index